ONE WAY

_____

ONE TRUTH

_____

ONE LIFE

ONE

A Daily Devotional

ONE WAY

ONE TRUTH

ONE LIFE

ONE

A Daily Devotional

BARBOUR BOOKS
An Imprint of Barbour Publishing, Inc.

What would happen if we chose to live each and every day of our lives purposefully and completely focused on the One—the One who is the Way, the Truth, and the Life? Would you choose to do things a little differently? In this devotional you'll find the inspiration and encouragement needed to live each day focused completely on the One. So go ahead, dive in!

Always giving thanks for all things in the name of our Lord Jesus Christ.
EPHESIANS 5:20 NASB

I n Jesus' name, amen." Many Christians close their prayers with this phrase because the Bible says to pray in Jesus' name. The Bible also tells us to believe in His name, gather in Jesus' name, call on His name, receive children and serve in His name, suffer shame for His name, etc. What significance does the name Lord Jesus Christ have for us?

Lord implies a master-servant relationship. Jesus said those who call Him "Lord, Lord" should do what He says (Luke 6:46). The Greek name *Jesus* is Joshua in Hebrew, meaning Savior. Mary's baby would be named Jesus, "for He will save His people from their sins" (Matthew 1:21 NASB). *Christ* is Greek for the Hebrew word *Messiah*, meaning "anointed for a purpose." Both priests and kings were anointed. The Jews of Jesus' day expected the Messiah to deliver them from Roman bondage and establish His kingdom on earth. His disciples eventually understood that the Messiah was anointed first as a priest, to deliver people from the bondage of sin. At His second coming, He will be acknowledged as King.

Jesus has other names and purposes in scripture, but these three—Lord (Master), Jesus (Savior), Christ (Deliverer/King)—assure us that He can meet our needs. He is our loving Leader, sufficient Savior, and daily Deliverer when we make Him the King of our lives.

Jesus, thank You for saving me. Please, Lord, rule my life.
Messiah-Christ, deliver me from temptation, wrong choices,
and self-centeredness. In Your powerful name, amen.

GIFTED FOR BLESSING

And Jesus increased in wisdom and stature,
and in favor with God and men.
LUKE 2:52 NKJV

If there had been a "gifted" class when He was a child, Jesus would have been in it. We're really not sure how it all played out with His 100-percent divine/100-percent human nature, but He was definitely different from the other kids in the neighborhood. Yet, He was enough like them that the town elders erroneously thought of Him as "the carpenter's son" when He came back as an adult and performed miracles! We don't know the details about Jesus' childhood, whether He experienced development and maturity in the same manner as we do. Yet we do know that He never sinned, never rebelled against what was right.

Scripture tells us that He "learned"—increased in wisdom—so we can assume He was "taught" in some manner. He was way ahead of the other kids in so many ways. Talk about gifted! He was God in the flesh; He could heal disease, correct deformities, multiply meals, and resurrect the dead. He always used His divine abilities to bless others; He did not seek to gain earthly glory or get even with His enemies or curry favor with the ruling powers. He brought honor to His Father and help to others.

Lord, I want to be like You. I want to use the abilities You've given me to bless those You bring into my life. Give me the wisdom and grace to manage my gifts so that others may be helped. In Jesus' name, amen.

"She will give birth to a son, and you are to give him the name Jesus, because he will save his people from their sins."
MATTHEW 1:21 NIV

God knew, from the start, that giving humans a free will could lead to trouble, so the sinful state of humanity never took Him by surprise. Even before Eve succumbed to temptation and took a bite of the forbidden fruit, God's redemptive plan was in the works. Prophetic messengers through the ages prepared the people to watch for the Messiah who would save them from their sins.

Every generation hoped to usher in the coming Savior, but no one saw anything special about Joseph and Mary. They were betrothed, which was a legally binding premarriage agreement. Before their wedding, Joseph realized Mary was pregnant—and he knew the baby wasn't his. He wanted to quietly sever their commitment, but an angel appeared to him with the amazing announcement that the child Mary was expecting was the promised Messiah.

We can't comprehend all that went through Joseph's mind—imagine realizing you're the man chosen to raise this holy Child. We know Joseph didn't argue or waver in his determination to please God. There was no rule book, so he had to depend on the Lord to direct every step.

Sometimes we're all given responsibilities we feel unqualified to fulfill, or we face daunting challenges. Like Joseph, we must rely on God to guide us through every situation

Lord, I want to always depend on Your wisdom and strength when I face overwhelming responsibilities. Thank You for never leaving me on my own.

ABIDE IN CHRIST

If you abide in Me, and My words abide in you,
ask whatever you wish, and it will be done for you.
JOHN 15:7 NASB

At first glance, this verse could be construed to mean that Jesus is your "genie." You ask whatever you wish, and He'll do it. Sounds pretty good, right? That's not quite the point.

Do you really abide in Christ? Surrender your false sense of independence so that you can fully understand your reliance on Christ for every aspect of your life—then you can rest in His grace, love, and plan for you.

Do His words abide in you? Read, memorize, and meditate on His Word on a regular basis so that your thoughts and words are more like His.

Imagine how different your wishes would be if you truly abided in Christ and His words abided in you. Gone would be the wishes that everything would go your way and that God would remove those things or people that make life difficult for you. Instead, you would wish for God to make you and those around you more like Him every day. You would desire justice, lasting peace, and the spread of the Gospel. You would ask that God be glorified, no matter the circumstances.

Lord, help me abide in You every day. Make Your
words alive in my thoughts and what I say today.
Conform my wishes to Your perfect will.

*But He answered and said, "It is written, 'Man shall
not live by bread alone, but by every word that
proceeds from the mouth of God.'"*
MATTHEW 4:4 NKJV

After Jesus was baptized and before He began His public ministry, Jesus was led by the Spirit into the wilderness. There He met with Satan, who sought to make Jesus succumb to temptation. The devil used the scriptures, the very words of God, in trying to tempt Jesus. Yet Jesus knew the Word. He is the Word. When the devil told Him to turn stones into bread to satiate His hunger, Jesus replied with the verse from Deuteronomy 8:3—people's hearts are only truly filled with the truth that comes from the Creator. Every one of Jesus' replies was also from the Word of God.

The devil knew God's law, but Jesus' knowledge was deeper and complete, and He was not drawn away by scriptural references taken out of context. He had both mind- and heart-knowledge of the Old Testament, which provided spiritual nutrients that spurred Him to act in total conformity to God's will. God wants the same for His children today. He wants them to feast on the goodness of His words, to study the scriptures, and to know His promises. If people were to live by God's every word, to let that be their spiritual sustenance and their vigor, they could discern the deceptions of the devil and share in the victory that is Christ.

---

*Bread of Life, let me spend time daily feasting on your Word
so I can remain steadfast against Satan's attacks.*

JESUS COMFORTS THE BROKENHEARTED

The Lᴏʀᴅ is close to the brokenhearted and
saves those who are crushed in spirit.
Pꜱᴀʟᴍ 34:18 ɴɪᴠ

On September 15, 1999, Shaela Manross attended her youth group's midweek meeting at Wedgwood Baptist Church in Fort Worth, Texas. A few songs into the worship service, she heard what sounded like popping balloons in the back of the sanctuary. "But when I turned around, I saw fire shooting out the barrel of a small, handheld gun," she says.

Though the gunman killed himself later, several people were killed in the attack, including a boy who had been standing near Shaela. For years, she struggled with panic attacks, survivor's guilt, and hopelessness. Today, however, after support from her family and friends and intensive counseling to deal with the shooting, she radiates peace, joy, and selflessness. It is evident that Jesus is her all in all and that He has done a miraculous work in her life. Though she has been through other dark times, she continues to trust her Savior.

She says, "Jeremiah 29:11 says that He knows the plans He has for His children; plans to give us a hope and a future. Even now, when my circumstances seem to crush me, He brings this truth to my mind, and I am filled with joy. I am trusting that He is faithfully shaping me into the woman He desires me to be."

Lord, even when tragedies strike, help me know that
You are near. Give me peace in the midst of grief and grace
to help others who are struggling with doubt and fear.
Thank You for being close to the brokenhearted.

GOD OF THE "AHA" MOMENT

In him was life, and that life was the light of all
mankind. The light shines in the darkness,
and the darkness has not overcome it.
JOHN 1:4-5 NIV

In John's Gospel we find Jesus described as the light-bearing Word of Life. For those who would really listen, there's an illumination of truth. This is important because the Gospels are filled with so many examples of those who refused to hear what Jesus said, and He called those individuals "whitewashed tombs" (Matthew 23:27 NIV). There was no light and no real life in them because they refused the Word.

While this may seem confusing, the idea of Jesus being the "Word" may be understood as the One who brings understanding (light) and fulfillment for eternity (life).

If you knew someone had this ability, wouldn't you pay attention to what He had to say? The good news is that you can. The "aha moments" of wisdom are discovered in what Jesus said, what He did, and in who He is.

Look closely at the above verse. Do you see yourself there? Jesus is described as the light of ALL mankind. No one is ever outside the life change available in God's love, light, and life. Shrinking away from that light is as much a personal choice as accepting the truth about Jesus, and everyone gets to choose.

You have the wisdom I need. More than a story or fable, Your life
brought understanding to humans who always try to do things
their own way. May I be drawn to Your story, identify with Your
life, and choose Your leadership for my future. Amen.

Jesus took the blind man by the hand and led him out of the village.
Then, spitting on the man's eyes, he laid his hands on him and asked,
"Can you see anything now?"
MARK 8:23 NLT

Not once in my thirty-some years on earth have I had the thought to spit in someone's eye. Even if I had, I can't imagine acting on it, because spitting in someone else's eye is quite frowned upon by society.

Jesus, on the other hand, did just that. Not only did He spit in the eyes of the blind man in Mark chapter 8, but He also used spit to heal a man born blind in John chapter 9. That time, He spit on the ground, made mud, and put it on the blind man's eyes.

Mud on someone else's eyes? Now that takes direction from the heavenly Father.

In John 5:19, Jesus said that He only did what He saw His Father do. That means He had specific direction given to His heart from heaven to use spit in these healings. Jesus could have easily said, "That's too strange for me, so I'll pray for his healing my way." Instead, He obeyed the Father's instructions.

God's ways are unique and beyond our comprehension. Just as Jesus imitated His Father, we are to imitate our Lord. When He directs—even when we don't understand—we are to trust and follow His lead.

Father, teach me to trust Your leading, even when it is out of my comfort zone. I want to trust and obey You every time. In Jesus' name, amen.

HE IS OUR PEACE

For he himself is our peace, who has made us both one
and has broken down in his flesh the dividing wall of hostility.
EPHESIANS 2:14 ESV

What a hope-filled verse this is. Jesus Christ is our peace, and He has broken down every barrier. Perhaps that's why He's called the Prince of Peace. We all want peace in our lives, but sometimes that kind of harmony seems elusive.

We can't control others' attitudes or actions; only God can do that. We can't make the people around us be nice, or speak kindly, or act in love. However, we can make sure that our own lives are so filled with the Prince of Peace that we're not adding to the discord around us. When our first goal is to reflect His love in our thoughts, our words, and our actions, peace is often a natural consequence.

We need to be peace-bearers to those around us. Even when our circumstances don't carry the serenity we long for, we can keep His peace in our spirits. Our lives should be a reflection of the One who brings peace, because He is peace.

Dear Father, I want my life to be a beacon of peace to those around me.
Teach me to be an embodiment of Christ, the Prince of Peace,
to a world that so desperately needs Him. Remind me each moment
that peace isn't determined by others' actions or my circumstances.
Your peace is already mine because of Christ. Amen.

*He called out to them, "Friends, haven't you any fish?" "No,"
they answered. He said, "Throw your net on the right side of the boat
and you will find some." When they did, they were unable
to haul the net in because of the large number of fish.*
JOHN 21:5–6 NIV

Jesus' disciples knew what it was like to fish for hours and catch nothing. It could have been like the men and boys today returning from fishing. The fish-finder, bass boats, top-brand rods, and fancy reels didn't help. When John's wife rushed forward to meet him, he told her, "The fishing was great, but the catching wasn't."

The disciples might have said the same thing—until Jesus called from the shore. Much had happened. They felt discouraged. Jesus had been killed. Peter had grieved over denying Jesus three times before His death.

A number of events came together in this account: the miracle of the catch, the gift of forgiveness for Peter, the eyewitness account of the risen Jesus still working miracles, the miracle of provision as the huge catch provided fish for food and selling. Jesus proved his power as the Son of God, not dead but alive.

Think how encouraging these events are! From this, we know that Jesus lives, loves, forgives, and provides for us. From this, we know He is always with us—even beyond life on earth.

*Thank you, God, for your love that spans all my days. I bow in awe
that You forgive and see the best in me—even when I fall.*

*Then Jesus said, "Come to me, all of you who are weary
and carry heavy burdens, and I will give you rest."*
MATTHEW 11:28 NLT

Have you ever stopped to think about how difficult it must have been to live in the time of Christ? We think our lives are hard today—traffic jams, bills, pressure to succeed—but to folks who lived two thousand years ago, our problems would seem insignificant. The people Jesus taught were oppressed by politics and poverty. The elements were harsh, and survival depended on a combination of hard work and sheer luck. Life was—and still is—hard. Jesus certainly understands our weariness and the heavy burdens we carry. Yes, He has an eternal perspective on our suffering, but this verse in Matthew illustrates that He also cares deeply for us in the here and now. This verse is an invitation. We can come to Christ as we are, weary and burdened, and He promises to give us rest. What a gift!

Jesus, I do get so weary, and my burdens feel so heavy. Thank You for understanding this about me, and thank You for the promise of rest. Help me come to You as I am, and help me receive Your gift of rest. Amen.

The Spirit you received does not make you slaves, so that you live in fear again; rather, the Spirit you received brought about your adoption to sonship. And by him we cry, "Abba, Father." The Spirit himself testifies with our spirit that we are God's children.
ROMANS 8:15-16 NIV

The third of the Ten Commandments warns us not to misuse the Lord's name (Exodus 20:7). To keep the commandment well, members of the Jewish community neither speak nor read God's name Yahweh ("I AM") aloud, substituting Adonai or other names out of reverence.

The holiness of God does demand reverence and humility, but everything about how we speak to God changed when Christ went to the cross. The Holy One sent His dearest Son to earth to draw His wayward people back to Him, to make a way for His enemies to become His children. By His death and resurrection, Christ brings those who believe in Him into the family of God. No longer separated by our sins, we can now address the Almighty as tenderly as Jesus did the night before the crucifixion, when He called the Father by the familiar Aramaic name *Abba* or "Daddy" (Mark 14:36).

Through Jesus, we can pray with both intimacy and humility to the Creator of the whole universe: *our Father, who art in heaven, hallowed be Thy Name. . . .*

Abba Father, help me revere Your name in my words and my prayers. I am so grateful that I can be close to You because of Jesus. Amen.

"He must increase, but I must decrease."
JOHN 3:30 NKJV

Jesus was the One for whom everyone waited. John, the son of Zechariah and Elizabeth, dedicated his life to preparing people for the arrival of the Messiah. Years of proclaiming God's Word kindled an unquenchable flame in the heart of John to see God bring about His restoration plan. John was the voice crying in the wilderness about whom Isaiah (40:3) had prophesied, and though vitally important, he knew his message and repentance-baptism would only be fulfilled with the coming of the Rescuer. The Rescuer finally came.

John boldly proclaimed Jesus as the Lamb of God who takes away the sins of the world, the Lamb by which creation receives grace and truth. John baptized Jesus as a sign for us, but John knew he was not worthy to even tie Jesus' sandal strap. He acknowledged that his baptism was with water, but Jesus baptizes with the Holy Spirit to change hearts. John looked to Jesus as the center of his existence. Even when imprisoned and when doubts crept into his heart, John still sought his answer and refuge in Jesus. John called himself the friend of the Bridegroom (Jesus) who rejoices at the Bridegroom's voice. Jesus was truly Lord of his life, and those who claim to be followers of Jesus today must also testify that Jesus is the Son of God and seek to humble themselves under Jesus' leadership. Christians need to point away from themselves and to Christ. Then their joy, like John's, will be fulfilled.

*El Elyon (Most High God), help my prideful self decrease
so that Jesus may increase.*

RECOGNIZED AND RECEIVED

The next day John saw Jesus coming toward him and said,
"Look, the Lamb of God, who takes away the sin of the world!"
JOHN 1:29 NIV

John the baptizer accepted his role as the individual who would be very vocal about telling others the Messiah was coming. He lived in the wilderness, ate locusts and honey, and seemed a wild man, yet people still came to hear him speak, and he always had the same message:"I am the voice of one calling in the wilderness, 'Make straight the way for the Lord' " (John 1:23 NIV).

John's task was to simply set the stage for the entrance of the Messiah, but John wasn't the One to change the world.

The kind of attention he received could have left him wanting more. It could have left him thinking that Jesus would need to carve out His own followers, but because he knew who Jesus was, John intentionally shrank in significance.

Once John recognized that Jesus was the Messiah, he turned from preacher to follower. John is a great example of what it looks like to always place Jesus above everything: personal interests, possessions, ambitions, and opinions.

Let my life be an example of one who simply sets the stage for One greater
than me. Let me willingly take a back seat to an incredible message that
alters eternity for others. I want to love You more deeply, more willingly,
and more intentionally. Do Your work in me, and let me be wise enough
to know when I need to step up, and when to step aside. Amen.

Then Jesus said to his disciples: If any of you want to be my followers,
you must forget about yourself. You must take up your cross and follow me.
MATTHEW 16:24 CEV

They were a rag-tag bunch, the disciples, but in the midst of tax-collecting and fishing and surviving, they no doubt dreamed about what their future might hold. Brothers Peter and Andrew, James and John, Philip, Bartholomew, Thomas, Matthew, James, Simon, Thaddaeus, and Judas—each of these twelve men, in all their humanity, must have had deep and unexpressed longings in their souls. For one day Jesus came along and said simply, "Follow me." Then they did. They forgot about themselves, their families, and their dreams. Their friends must have thought they'd gone mad, to drop everything to follow this Teacher across the countryside. Surely they couldn't have known what they were signing up for, or even why, but something (or Someone) compelled them to risk everything and follow Him. Maybe they were desperate—longing for a change, longing for more, looking for something to fill the aching yearning in their hearts.

The life we choose to leave behind, forgetting about ourselves—is nothing compared to the reward and joy of following Jesus. Risky, yes. Worth it? A thousand times over.

Lord, like Your disciples, I too have a longing deep in my soul for something more than this world has to offer. Earthly pleasure is so temporary—I long for something eternal, something worthwhile, something worth dying for! You offer me that gift. Help me forget about me and follow You. Amen.

EYES OF COMPASSION

When He saw the multitudes,
He was moved with compassion for them.
MATTHEW 9:36 NKJV

Think of a Red Cross relief worker in a third world country; imagine a nurse in a leper colony; remember the outpouring of labor, money, and blood donations after the tragedy of 9/11 —reflections of compassion.

Think of Jesus interacting with the multitudes in Palestine—this is compassion personified. Jesus not only had compassion; He was compassion. He exuded it everywhere He went—for the blind, the maimed, the demon-possessed, the oppressed, the weary, and the sinful. He did not see merely broken humanity; He saw humans who needed Him. He could see beyond the dirt and squalor and wrong choices. He looked at them with eyes that were motivated by His divine love.

You and I can choose to do the same. In our damaged world, each of us has ample opportunity to dispense compassion in some way. The difference is that we may have to go looking for a way to serve. Crowds came to Jesus because He was known as a healer. We may need to search out the ones in need: at a ministry for the homeless, in urban youth outreach, or simply on the streets of our towns and cities. There is no decrease in the need of humanity, and so, like Jesus, we will choose to "see" it and follow His pattern of compassion.

Dear God, give me eyes of compassion, a heart that wants to help,
and hands that reach out. Amen.

AGAINST OUR NATURE

"You have heard that it was said, 'You shall love your neighbor and hate your enemy.' But I say to you, Love your enemies and pray for those who persecute you, so that you may be sons of your Father who is in heaven."
MATTHEW 5:43-45 ESV

B oy. Jesus didn't believe in doing things the easy way, did He? Loving the people who wish us harm, the people who curse us and shame us and make our lives miserable. . .that goes against every natural instinct we have.

Yet that's the point, isn't it? We are sinful by nature. When we live for Christ, He calls us to die to our natural instincts and develop a new nature. If He called us to do what comes naturally, everyone would follow Christ. However, everyone would also be self-centered and greedy, because that's who we are.

No, Christ calls us to turn against what *feels* right and do what *is* right. He tells us that if we want to be great, we must be servants, and if we want to be rich, we must give up all our stuff. Perhaps the hardest thing He requires of us is the mandate He lays out in this verse: Love those who hate us. Pray good things for those who persecute us. Then we will develop the family resemblance He longs for us to have, so everyone will know we are children of God.

Dear Father, help me truly love those who don't love me. Amen.

I can do all things through Him who strengthens me.
PHILIPPIANS 4:13 NASB

The Lord Jesus, who was raised from the dead, exalted by God, and now sits at the Father's right hand with all power and dominion, strengthens you. If you genuinely grasped this concept, how would it change your life?

Next time you feel overwhelmed, tired, and unable to face what the day has to hold—think about this: the One who defeated death strengthens you; the One who cured chronic and life-threatening illnesses with a touch of His hand or word from His mouth strengthens you; the One who raised Lazarus from the dead strengthens you; the One who withstood direct temptation from Satan strengthens you; the One who endured unjust mocking and abuse without fighting back strengthens you; the One who was willing to come to earth to be horribly mistreated and killed in order to free you from sin and death strengthens you.

Is it any wonder that in this verse Paul says that he can do all things? Paul understood who it was that gave him strength every day. You serve the same Lord as Paul. Christ offers His strength to you today and every day. Stop relying on your own strength. Rely on the abundant, everlasting, never-tiring strength of Christ.

Lord, forgive me for attempting to rely on my own strength when Your infinitely more abundant strength is available to me. Thank You for giving me the strength I need for today.

*Not that I speak from want, for I have learned to be content
in whatever circumstance I am.*
PHILIPPIANS 4:11 NASB

God created four stages in the metamorphosis from caterpillar to butterfly: egg, larva, pupa, and adult. Like the stages of our own physical growth or the four seasons, each has a specific goal. During each stage we go through spiritually, God has a goal for us as well.

The second stage is the larva or "feeding" stage. After female butterflies have laid their eggs on the backs of leaves, you can actually see the tiny caterpillar inside the egg. The larva, or caterpillar, eats the leaf that it hatches on, and each type of caterpillar will only eat a certain kind of plant. Therefore, every mama butterfly has to know exactly which kind of leaf to land on.

God's creation is full of lessons for us. What if we decided to trust that the place God has planted us is good, instead of wishing He had planted us somewhere else? A caterpillar can starve if it doesn't like the leaf it's on, and we can starve spiritually if we continue to fret and fight God's plan.

Ask yourself: Am I worrying and complaining because God has me in a place I don't like? Or am I praying for contentment? In Christ, we can find peace, joy, and spiritual food to sustain us, wherever we are.

*Lord, help me be content whatever my circumstances. I know that
Your ways and timing are perfect, and You have a reason—
and a season—for the place where You've planted me.*

GROWING LITTLE BY LITTLE

*"The kingdom of heaven is like a mustard seed, which a man took
and planted in his field. Though it is the smallest of all seeds,
yet when it grows, it is the largest of garden plants and becomes a tree,
so that the birds of the air come and perch in its branches."*
MATTHEW 13:31–32 NIV

Jesus uses a parable about growing plants to give us a glimpse of spiritual growth. From an unimpressive and fragile beginning, our commitment to grow will produce great results! Others will be able to enjoy us even more as they realize what God has done in our lives.

Rachel found every season with her tomato plants was a life and death struggle—even with those she purchased from a greenhouse. This time, she decided to start from scratch. Yet she read from the seed packet, "Start indoors 8 weeks before time to set in open ground. . . ." After another one hundred words of instructions, Rachel realized that raising tomatoes from seed might be as difficult as managing a new baby.

For the seeds to sprout, she needed the right soil, fertilizer, water, close attention, and constant care. In the end, the plants would produce a bountiful crop. It would be worth the effort.

That is God's attitude toward our growth. We are worth it. Our spiritual growth happens in small steps over time. God is patient. Have patience with yourself.

You're a mighty tree in the making.

---

*Jesus, thank You for the glimpse of the person I am to You.
Show me the paths that will lead me to growth.*

*For if he who comes preaches another Jesus whom
we have not preached. . .or a different gospel
which you have not accepted—you may well put up with it!*
2 CORINTHIANS 11:4 NKJV

Is Jesus merely the greatest teacher who ever lived? Is He a prophet of God who did His part, followed by other prophets who completed God's plan? Is He our example of how to live a perfect, sinless life and attain godhood? Various religions teach these false ideas about Christ. They fail to understand that the Jesus of the Bible is God in the flesh. He came to planet Earth for a distinct purpose—to communicate His love for us. A simple illustration may help us understand why.

Suppose you have a fish tank. Every day you feed your fish and meet all their needs for properly heated and oxygenated water, a clean tank, and protection from predators. You enjoy your fish and even love them. Yet to them, you are the scary thing that taps on the glass and makes them swim away. How could you communicate to your fish that you love them and will take care of them? You would have to become a fish.

That is what God did. He got into the fish tank for about thirty-three years, communicating love. Then He sacrificed Himself to meet our greatest need, having our sins forgiven so we could live eternally with Him. Do you know the real Jesus?

*Dear Lord Jesus, thank You for providing everything I need. I can trust You
to take care of me in this life and the next. Amen.*

For an answer Jesus called over a child, whom he stood in the middle of the room, and said, "I'm telling you, once and for all, that unless you return to square one and start over like children, you're not even going to get a look at the kingdom, let alone get in. Whoever becomes simple and elemental again, like this child, will rank high in God's kingdom. What's more, when you receive the childlike on my account, it's the same as receiving me.
MATTHEW 18:2–5 MSG

My two-year-old son's life revolves around playing, eating, and sleeping. He never wonders if we have food for lunch, and he certainly doesn't have a clue about bills, much less if we have enough money to pay them. My son lives in the moment, loves life, and instinctively trusts my husband and me. He is the definition of carefree—and a picture of what our faith should look like.

Jesus said in Matthew 6:25–26 (MSG): "If you decide for God, living a life of God-worship, it follows that you don't fuss about what's on the table at mealtimes or whether the clothes in your closet are in fashion. . . . Look at the birds, free and unfettered, not tied down to a job description, careless in the care of God. And you count far more to him than birds."

God cares for you deeply. Let that truth sink into your heart and erase worries for today and the fear of tomorrow.

Father, help me remember that You are my provider.
I don't need to worry about what I face today, for You care for me.

*For if you forgive other people when they sin against you,
your heavenly Father will also forgive you. But if you do not forgive
others their sins, your Father will not forgive your sins.*
MATTHEW 6:14-15 NIV

It's a high call, to forgive others, and this verse tells us the stakes are high. Throughout His time on earth, Jesus taught and modeled forgiveness, over and over again. From the woman at the well, to Nicodemus, to the woman caught in adultery, to those who tortured Him in the last hours of His life, Jesus consistently, obediently, and faithfully forgave everyone who sinned against Him. Just like the unforgiving servant in Matthew 18, we are essentially tortured when we refuse to forgive. It has been said that refusing to forgive another person is like swallowing poison and hoping they will die. Unforgiveness curdles in our heart like sour milk, its stench consuming everything around it. Soon we become bitter, brittle, unmanageable, and unusable as we wither away. Forgiveness washes us clean. It brings freedom, washes our hearts fresh, and revives us anew. Who would the Lord have you forgive today?

---

*Our Father in heaven, hallowed be Your name, Your kingdom come,
Your will be done, on earth as it is in heaven. Give us today our daily bread.
And forgive us our debts, as we also have forgiven our debtors.
And lead us not into temptation, but deliver us from the evil one.
For thine is the kingdom and the honor and the power
and the glory forever, amen.*

There are many who say, "Who will show us some good? Lift up the light
of your face upon us, O Lord!" You have put more joy in my heart
than they have when their grain and wine abound.
PSALM 4:6-7 ESV

When Jesus performed His miracles to display the power of the kingdom of God, some of His Jewish audience believed He was an earthly Messiah rather than a heavenly one—the victor who would topple the Roman Empire and restore Israel's glory. After the feeding of the five thousand, the excited people had intended to make Jesus king by force (John 6:15). Later, when they were looking for Him, Jesus revealed that they did not seek Him because of faith but for the promise of another free meal (John 6:26–27). They saw the immediate good Jesus could give them and missed His eternal message.

Centuries earlier, the psalmist understood the heart of God's kingdom better than Jesus' listeners. The psalmist affirmed that even when his neighbors were rolling in plenty, his joy was still greater than theirs. He drew his peace and joy from his close relationship with his God, not the things he had.

Jesus didn't promise that we'd have an easy life if we believe in Him; instead, He promised Himself—His presence, His provision, His power, His peace. He promises complete restoration, starting with our hearts. What are you looking for from Jesus?

Lord Jesus, forgive me for when I've found my satisfaction
in earthly joys instead of seeking You and Your kingdom first.
Please help me find my joy in You. Amen.

For Christ also suffered once for sins, the righteous for the unrighteous,
to bring you to God. He was put to death in the body
but made alive in the Spirit.
1 PETER 3:18 NIV

Jesus Christ did everything necessary to bring us to God. To say He suffered for our sins is such a tame statement that we can read it and not let it break our hearts. Picture that suffering. Before His crucifixion, Roman soldiers flogged Him, using a whip with sharp metal pieces attached to leather strips, until the flesh on His back was shredded. They draped a purple robe around His bloodied shoulders and taunted: "Hail, King of the Jews!" They hit Him, spit in His face, and twisted thorny twigs into a crown that pierced His scalp when they jammed it on His head. He experienced excruciating torture even before they pounded the spikes into His hands and feet to nail Him to the cross.

Why did He endure such torture? Because He loves us—you and me. He knew it was impossible for us to attain eternal life on our own, so the righteous One died for the unrighteous. When we consider His physical agony, we can't forget the spiritual battle He fought. Jesus took all our sins upon Himself. We know how our conscience troubles us when we do wrong. Multiply that by billions of sinners through the ages. That was all dumped on Him so we can live in the Spirit, forever.

Precious Jesus, Your amazing love totally humbles me. I am unworthy,
but You make me righteous. Praise Your holy name!

As often as possible Jesus withdrew to out-of-the-way places for prayer.
LUKE 5:16 MSG

Many times Jesus interacted with people—sometimes one-on-one or sometimes in crowds of thousands—who were hungry, overly zealous, tired, or angry. He dealt with people all day long who didn't know how to handle their emotions and their problems. Just imagine how exhausting that would be.

It's one reason why Jesus often took time away from people to strengthen His relationship with God. He knew that although His heavenly Father had an endless supply of resources available for Him to use, it was only when Jesus took time to connect with His Father that those resources became a reality.

In taking time away from the busyness of life to pray and praise God, Jesus refreshed Himself mentally, physically, and spiritually. Those moments were opportunities to remember that although He couldn't see His heavenly Father, God was right beside Him directing His steps.

This is also important for us to remember. The best way we can love others is by investing time in our relationship with the Lord. As we refresh ourselves in the Lord, we refocus on the One who is the most important. When we take time to focus on what we can't see, we can better serve who we can see.

Remind me, Lord, that my time with You is the most important.
When I keep that first, other things will fall into place.
In Jesus' name, amen.

CHOOSE PEACE

"Do not let your hearts be troubled. You believe in God; believe also in me."
JOHN 14:1 NIV

It's hard to imagine a life without troubles. When we get to heaven, we'll know what that feels like. Yet here, Christ told us we'd have many trials. He also said not to feel overwhelmed by those difficult circumstances. When there's stress on the outside, our hearts can have peace. We don't have to let the cares of this world permeate our spirits.

God is so big, so powerful, so almighty that He can overcome any predicament we face. He is the mountain, and our worries are like little anthills. That's why, when the disciples freaked out on their stormy boat ride, Jesus slept. He was at peace. His heart wasn't troubled, because He trusted the One who could calm the wind and sea.

If we could only lay hold of that kind of quietude, our lives would be so much better. There's no reason we can't have that peace. Total trust and tranquility of heart isn't a once-and-for-all decision, but rather a minute-by-minute choice we make. Time and again, with each new dilemma, we can choose to be anxious and troubled, or we can choose to believe in the One who has the power to see us through those troubles. When faced with the opportunity to select stress or serenity, let's choose serenity.

Dear Father, I'm sorry for becoming anxious over things instead of trusting You. When my heart is troubled, remind me who You are, and help me choose peace. Amen.

"I tell you, all those who stand before others and say they believe in me, I, the Son of Man, will say before the angels of God that they belong to me."
LUKE 12:8 NCV

L isten to what Jesus tells the angels: "See that person? He (or she) is Mine." When the Lord says that, He may be talking about you.

When we're enthusiastic about something, we talk about it. It might be a pet project, movie, book, sport, diet, job—you name it. What about Jesus? We may feel passionate about what He's done for us and our relationship with Him, but when we try to tell others about Him, our tongues feel tied.

If we've turned our lives over to Jesus, asked Him to forgive us and be our Lord, we also need to ask for the boldness to tell others about Him. Why is it so difficult to speak up about our faith? Maybe it's a battle with the devil. Yes, that may sound like an easy excuse, but he is real and he definitely doesn't want us to brag about Jesus. Ask the Lord to put us in touch with the people we should talk to, and depend on Him to help you speak up.

Maybe you're concerned about questions someone might ask. You don't need all the answers. It's okay to admit you don't know everything, but no one can argue against your experiences. Give it a try.

---

*Lord, help me never be afraid to stand before others and tell them
I believe in You. Thank You for claiming me as Your own.*

CHRIST AS RULER

He raised Him from the dead and seated Him at His right hand
in the heavenly places, far above all rule and authority
and power and dominion, and every name that is named,
not only in this age but also in the one to come.
EPHESIANS 1:20-21 NASB

How often do you think about Jesus in this light? Focus is more often placed on Jesus as the wise and gentle teacher, or the weak and dying man on the cross. Yet Jesus was not just a wise man who taught the world great things to live by—He is Lord and Ruler. He is on your side. With the Ruler of the universe on your side, what is there to fear or be anxious about? You can be confident that no matter what happens it is not out of your Savior's control. Nothing in the *whole universe* is out of His control. That's not about to change. He is Ruler now *and forever*. When the world seems dangerously unstable with leaders coming in and out of power, natural disasters shaking the earth, and evil seemingly spreading. . . remember that there is and always will be One Ruler over all of it. Though you can't possibly understand why some things happen, rest in the fact that one day our perfect Ruler will make all things clear.

Lord, I so often forget that You are reigning over all things. Help me put away my fearful thoughts and remember that You are on Your throne.

HE GIVES US ALL THINGS

*He who did not spare his own Son but gave him up for us all,
how will he not also with him graciously give us all things?*
ROMANS 8:32 ESV

Margaret lived in a boardinghouse during college. One Christmas, after scraping together her extra change, she purchased a scarf for a gift and placed it in a dresser drawer, along with her Bible. One day while she was at class, a fire broke out and burned the house down, destroying almost everything. However, the dresser from Margaret's room fell to the basement. Later, Margaret found the Bible and scarf, in perfect condition, where she had left them.

Because of the fire, she had lost everything except what had been on her back. Despondent but not beaten, Margaret caught a ride home for Christmas. During one leg of her trip, Margaret's driver stopped the car to avoid hitting a suitcase in the middle of the road. When the two women looked inside, they found no identification, just clothes and shoes—all exactly Margaret's size.

Margaret wore those clothes and shoes throughout college and well into her golden years. She cried when she relayed the story.

What do you need? Ask God to provide. Just as He gave His own Son as a sacrifice, to pave our way to heaven, He will meet your needs. Watch and pray, and see what God will do!

*Heavenly Father, thank You for providing Jesus to save me from my sins.
Please meet my physical needs, just as You've met my spiritual needs.
I trust You to do this, in Your own time and way.*

So we fix our eyes not on what is seen, but on what is unseen.
For what is seen is temporary, but what is unseen is eternal.
2 Corinthians 4:18 NIV

Miranda put her head on the table on top of her checkbook and sighed. She grumbled, "How can we work so hard and have so little money left after paying bills?" Her oldest needed braces and her youngest needed contacts. The cars she and her husband drove both needed repairs. Their living room carpet was threadbare and embarrassing. However, her salary as a teacher and his as a minister of a small church only went so far.

As tears slid down her cheeks, Miranda thought back to other times when she had no idea how they would be able to afford day care, doctors, or clothes. Every time they had prayed for God to provide, He had come through.

More than once, a church member had given them cash in an envelope "in Jesus' name, because God told me to." At other times, checks came in the mail at just the right moment. Once, they had received an unexpected inheritance from a distant relative just in time to pay her husband's seminary tuition.

"Lord, You have never failed us, and I know You won't start now," Miranda whispered. She resolved to remember that this world was not their real home and that material things were just that: things. Relationships, faith, and serving God were what mattered and what would last.

Jesus, thank You for reminding me that You are my inheritance,
and You're worth more than any earthly treasure.

Now while he was in Jerusalem at the Passover Festival, many people saw the signs he was performing and believed in his name. But Jesus would not entrust himself to them, for he knew all people. He did not need any testimony about mankind, for he knew what was in each person.
JOHN 2:23–25 NIV

We refer to those who've been hurt in relationships and struggle with extending trust as individuals with "trust issues." In the verse above, we see that Jesus wouldn't entrust Himself to the people in Jerusalem. Did Jesus experience trust issues, too?

Jesus has always known what's in the heart of people. Jesus didn't have to guess whether a person was worthy of trust. He knew those among His disciples who weren't especially trustworthy. Judas betrayed Him, Peter denied Him, and they all fled when He was arrested.

Jesus provided an example of how to manage trust issues from the cross. Jesus said, "Father, forgive them, for they do not know what they are doing" (Luke 23:34 NIV). His death on the cross offered us forgiveness and provided the only means we have of managing the bad end of misplaced trust—forgiveness. The only one Jesus was absolutely certain was forever trustworthy was God, and forgiveness was His idea.

I have withdrawn from people I don't trust. There are times when I could reach out, but I don't because I fear the potential pain of a poor decision made by someone else that could hurt me. Help me remember that even when I struggle with trust, I can still receive and demonstrate Your forgiveness. Amen.

*Here there is no Gentile or Jew, circumcised or uncircumcised, barbarian,
Scythian, slave or free, but Christ is all, and is in all.*
COLOSSIANS 3:11 NIV

Six-year-old Wendy loved fishing with Grandpa more than anything. She had learned to treasure the quiet lake surface in the early morning, the nibbles, and the excitement of landing fish. When they went fishing with her friend, Janey, there was trouble soon after.

Wendy landed a fish. Right after, she caught her grandpa by the legs in a hug.

"I love you, Grandpa."

Janey had never been fishing before. She was trying to do everything right. Watching Wendy, she thought the knee hug was part of fishing. So when she landed a trout, Janey gave the senior another hug around his legs, "I love you, Grandpa!"

Wendy shouted, "He's my grandpa, not yours! You can't have him!"

When Jesus walked the earth, He attracted many followers and accepted them all. For doing so, Jesus was publically criticized by church officials.

What a model of character that He accepts everyone!

Sometimes people feel possessive about Jesus—and their relationship with Him. Others feel that certain peoples or groups should not be included. Yet God's love is so big, there is room for everyone. Nothing should keep us from including all as believers—those who accept Christ.

*Thank you, God, for a love so big, it includes everyone who
believes in you. Help me share your love with all.*

"A new command I give you: Love one another. As I have loved you, so you must love one another."
JOHN 13:34 NIV

Christ had one rule: love. Love God first. Love others like you love yourself. Though it sounds simple, it's easier said than done.

Oh, it's no problem to love those who love us. It's a piece of cake to love the lovable, the kind, the compassionate, the witty, and the beautiful. However, what about those people who curse us and spit in our faces? What about those people who make it their goal to wreak havoc and create misery in our lives? We're supposed to love them, too?

Yes, we are. Jesus said to love one another the way He has loved us. It's a self-sacrificing kind of love.

Yuck.

One thing to remember, though, is that Jesus was no pushover. He stood for what was right, and even lost his temper when it was appropriate. After all, how often do we equate turning over some tables in a fit of rage with love?

Yet that was love. It was Christ putting God first. Notice that He didn't hurt another person when He did it. Though He called them a "brood of vipers," He did so out of tough love, to get their attention and show them a better way.

Other than that brief moment, Jesus' life was a display of gentleness, compassion, and a servant's heart. When we model our lives after Him, we'll change the dynamics of our world

---

Dear Father, teach me to love like Jesus loved. Amen.

GOD'S CHILDREN

But to as many as did receive and welcome Him, He gave the authority
(power, privilege, right) to become the children of God, that is,
to those who believe in (adhere to, trust in, and rely on) His name.
JOHN 1:12 AMP

What an awesome privilege! When we welcome Jesus into our lives, we become God's kids. We're adopted into His holy family. Don't rush past this verse; let it sink into your spirit. Picture what it means.

None of us have perfect families here on earth. They may be fun and full of love, but there are imperfections because humans are flawed. All of us have defects, not only that weird cousin who always says the wrong thing, or the troublesome uncle. Some family relationships feel scratchy and uncomfortable.

Only God is perfect, and yet He gives us the right to be His children, to live and thrive in His family. I love the way the Amplified Bible words this verse and expands the word *authority*. It makes it clear what a rich inheritance we have—a priceless legacy—from our heavenly Daddy.

Most parents experience amazing love for our children—especially when babies are brand new and we marvel at the miracle of life. Now multiply that feeling exponentially, wrap it in love beyond our comprehension, and know how much God loves each of us. When we repent and are born into God's family, all heaven rejoices (Luke 15:7). The angels have a celebration.

Thank You, dear Father, for allowing me to be part of Your family.
I am humbled and overjoyed to be called Your child.

BATTLING PERFECTIONISM

And Jesus grew in wisdom and stature, and in favor with God and man.
LUKE 2:52 NIV

This verse gives us reason to believe that Jesus, though God-in-flesh, was not born with all the knowledge that He'd had before coming to earth. Like all human babies, Jesus had a lot to learn upon arrival. The fiery, compassionate Jesus we know from scripture toddled through His first steps just like we did, His mother scooping Him up to comfort Him when He fell. Though the Gospels don't record Joseph instructing Jesus in carpentry, certainly Jesus learned from observing His earthly father's skilled hands, and then practiced to hone those techniques Himself.

For those of us who struggle with perfectionism in our lives and work, we need to turn our eyes to Jesus. It should comfort us that our Savior learned in His earthly life, and He learned without committing a single sin. We may view our mistakes as "wrong," but mistakes aren't necessarily sinful. Like a misplaced nail or uneven sanding, they are part of practicing and growing in a skill.

Jesus does not call us to live in shame, fearing criticism or failure, but to live trusting in Him for the grace and peace to work faithfully (not perfectly). When we do fail, He isn't disappointed in us, but instead keeps lavishing grace and strength on us. Do you accept yourself and your shortcomings the way that Christ accepts you?

---

*Lord Jesus, thank You that you understand what it's like
to be human and to learn new things. Please help me practice
my gifts courageously for You. Amen.*

ONE WITH THE MARGINALIZED

A woman of Samaria came to draw water.
Jesus said to her, "Give me a drink."
JOHN 4:7 NKJV

One of the most beautiful things about Jesus is His willingness to go where others won't go. After teaching in Judea, Jesus knew he had to go back to Galilee. John 4:4(NKJV) says, "But He needed to go through Samaria." Jews who lived in other regions at that time took roundabout roads to avoid passing through Samaria, where local Jews had mixed with neighboring nations and developed their own syncretistic religion. However, Jesus had to meet someone special. The Samaritan woman was of little value in the eyes of others, but Jesus, a Jewish man, spoke to her. He made Himself vulnerable by asking for water in order to give her a sense of worth. He then used His question to spark a soul-searching conversation that pointed back to Him as the Giver of Living Water that leads to eternal life. Jesus knew the woman's sins, but He also knew her heart. She was part of creation that needed redemption. When He revealed His Messiah-identity to the woman, she proclaimed this throughout the city, and many believed because of her testimony. Even more believed after hearing Jesus' words. "Now we believe. . .this is indeed. . .the Savior of the world" (John 4:42 NKJV). Where is the Samaria in my life and with which marginalized people is Jesus calling me to share his life-giving water?

Elohay Yishi (God of my Salvation), open my eyes to see and my mouth
to speak Your love to the unloved. Let me be blessed
through blessing the least and the lowly.

And Jesus answered and said unto her, Martha, Martha, thou art careful and troubled about many things: But one thing is needful: and Mary hath chosen that good part, which shall not be taken away from her.
LUKE 10:41–42 KJV

Mary of Bethany had a heart of worship. She didn't worry about the preparations for dinner that her sister, Martha, concentrated on. Instead, ignoring the social conventions of her day, she sat at Jesus' feet and listened to Him. It was very unconventional for women in Jesus' time to be interested in spiritual things to the degree Mary was. She didn't care if others didn't understand. All she cared about was Jesus' approval.

What if we were more like Mary? What if, instead of fretting over how clean our houses are, we concentrated on the state of our hearts? What if we spent more time in the Word than flirting about with the world?

Jesus desires to spend time with us, but we too often get distracted by to-do lists, bills, and the sorrows of life. We try to manage our checkbook instead of praying for provision. Or we cram one more service activity in our schedule in order to look good to our fellow believers.

Think about the ways you cater to others' approval, trying to please them. Maybe you watch movies you shouldn't watch or gossip in the name of sharing prayer requests. Perhaps you post things that are a little too perfect on social media, hoping to impress your friends.

Lord, forgive me for caring more about other's opinions than Yours. Help me seek Your approval and Yours alone.

WHEN TEMPTATION ARRIVES UNANNOUNCED

Jesus, full of the Holy Spirit, left the Jordan and was led by the Spirit into the wilderness, where for forty days he was tempted by the devil. He ate nothing during those days, and at the end of them he was hungry.
LUKE 4:1–2 NIV

Have you ever experienced the kind of hunger that leaves you with uncharitable thoughts, anger at the world, and an intense desire to fill your stomach at any cost?

Esau reached this place after missing a single meal (see Genesis 25). Sometimes it takes a day or two before a sense of desperation arrives. For Jesus, there was more than a month that passed between meals. We have no reason to believe He was less hungry than anyone else, so when the devil came to tempt Jesus, it was at a point of intense vulnerability.

The example we're given doesn't just apply to food deprivation, but to anything that leaves us exposed to the potential of abandoning that which connects us to our journey with Jesus.

Whenever we're tempted to consider something we feel is disconnected from God's plan, we should seek God's Word before we respond impulsively.

Every time Jesus was tempted by the devil He responded with scripture. The devil was persistent but ultimately left Jesus alone with an option to tempt again.

You provided the best resource for resisting temptation. Thank You for Your Word. May I hide those words, consider Your precepts, and honor Your will as I resist the adversary. Walk with me, encourage my determination, and may You be honored in my response. Amen.

*"Father, if you are willing, take this cup from me; yet not my will,
but yours be done."*
LUKE 22:42 NIV

Is obedience to God really necessary?

Jesus had prayed these words of acceptance just before He was seized and faced beatings, humiliation, and death. Death by crucifixion was a punishment primarily reserved for the worst political criminals. It was unfair. Yet Jesus had been obedient to His Father, God. The Son of God had walked into Jerusalem knowing that He would be killed.

Some people consider obedience to be negotiable. To Jesus, our Master Teacher, it's not.

As an example, a bride-to-be counseled with the minister and requested, "When you get to the part about 'love, honor, and obey,' leave off the 'obey.' I don't care for that word."

During the ceremony, with the minister facing the audience and the couple's backs to the crowd, he got to that part and asked, "Do you promise to love, honor, and. . ." he substituted another word, "submit?" As daggers shot from the bride's eyes, she hissed through clenched teeth in front of a hundred guests, "Yesssss."

Later she whispered, "I hate the word 'submit' even more! How dare you!"

Obedience is an act of respect and commitment. God's rules are boundaries to keep us safe. They make us strong in influencing our families, our communities and our world. Jesus himself said, "If you love me, you will obey my commands" (John 14:15 NCV).

*God, thank You for giving me Jesus' example of obedience.
I pledge my obedience and love to you.*

PERSPECTIVE

We do this by keeping our eyes on Jesus, the champion who initiates and perfects our faith. Because of the joy awaiting him, he endured the cross, disregarding its shame. Now he is seated in the place of honor beside God's throne.
HEBREWS 12:2 NLT

Disappointed. Betrayed. Overwrought. Dismayed. Denied. Jesus, in His humanness, would have experienced the depth of these feelings and beyond. It is impossible to imagine how Jesus could have maintained His composure throughout the long hours leading up to His death. No one would have blamed Him if He had heaped vile words of hatred and anger on His enemies. As He was perfectly One with the Holy Spirit, Christ saw far beyond the darkness and into the incomparable light of eternity. He gazed into the eyes of His Father and held that gaze, even when God momentarily turned His face, with the hope of a brilliant future. This hope, this unbreakable connection to His Father, allowed Him not only to stay silent in the face of torture but to go the distance and forgive them completely. How is it that we can forgive others as Christ forgives us? It is a supernatural feat, no doubt, but forgiveness is as essential to the Christian life as breathing. When we fix our eyes on the Lord, not on what is currently happening to us, but as Jesus did, to "the joy set before him," we have a perspective that far surpasses this moment in time. Thanks to Christ's work on the cross, we have the power to forgive as He did, and with that power lies the path to a brilliant future with Him.

Father, when I fix my eyes on the here and now, I am bitterly disappointed. People have hurt me. They let me down. I feel hopeless, afraid. Yet when I fix my eyes on You, the transformation is unimaginable. I am free—free to forgive and to live, eternally, with You. Help me forgive others as You have forgiven me. Amen.

For He [God] made Him [Jesus] who knew no sin to be sin for us,
that we might become the righteousness of God in Him.
2 CORINTHIANS 5:21 NKJV

The Bible teaches that every one of us will end up in either heaven or hell when we die. How can we qualify for a trip to heaven? What does the ticket cost?

More than anyone can pay. God requires perfect righteousness, and only Jesus meets that qualification. The Good News is that He paid for everyone's ticket when He willingly died on the cross. He took our sins and the punishment we deserve. Now He offers us His righteousness, which qualifies us for heaven.

Even though Jesus paid in full for our ticket to heaven, He doesn't force anyone to take it. He created us with the freedom to choose, and He does not violate that freedom. The sad truth is that everyone is on a train to hell, which we deserve because of our sin. (See Revelation 20:13–15.) Those who accept the ticket of Christ's righteousness get to change their destination. Philippians 3:9 (NKJV) tells us to "be found in Him, not having my own righteousness, which is from the law, but that which is through faith in Christ, the righteousness which is from God by faith." God promises everlasting life to everyone who believes in Jesus Christ for it (John 3:16). Believe and receive! Do you have your ticket?

Savior Jesus, I am righteous before God because You took my sin. Thank You for Your free gift of eternal life that guarantees my destination. Amen.

ALWAYS LIGHT

Then Jesus spoke to them again, saying, "I am the light of the world. He who follows Me shall not walk in darkness, but have the light of life."
JOHN 8:12 NKJV

If honesty were compared to light and lying were darkness, how light would our culture be? Honesty is highly prized but rarely seen today.

Think of the recent scandals in political and religious circles—all of them involved some type of dishonesty. Have you heard the jokes about used car salesmen and attorneys? Then there is the "100 Most Trusted People" poll taken by *Reader's Digest*. All of these remind us that, in today's world, honesty is a rare thing. There are threads of darkness running through the fabric of our society on every level.

Jesus, though, is all light, no darkness. He is "the way, the truth, and the life" (John 14:6 NKJV). There is no falsehood even close to Him because He embodies truth. Those who follow Him will let His light shine in their lives, and in that way, illuminate the world around them.

We are human and tempted to dishonesty. It is the thing to which we are most susceptible, like Eve in the perfect Garden who listened to a subtle serpent. Yet unlike her, we can choose to hold to God's truth and reject the darkness. Then we are truly children of Light.

Dear God, shine Your truth into my heart and life, and give me the wisdom to embrace truth and reflect the light of Jesus all around me. Amen.

DON'T BE LED BY CIRCUMSTANCE

Soon another Feast came around and Jesus was back in Jerusalem. Near the Sheep Gate in Jerusalem there was a pool, in Hebrew called Bethesda, with five alcoves. Hundreds of sick people—blind, crippled, paralyzed—were in these alcoves. One man had been an invalid there for thirty-eight years. When Jesus saw him stretched out by the pool and knew how long he had been there, he said, "Do you want to get well?"
JOHN 5:1-6 MSG

When Jesus walked through these alcoves of Bethesda, the Father directed Him to heal one man. Jesus could easily have been deterred from that simple instruction: Look at all these people who need healing. Why don't I just go down the line and heal them all? He could have let what He saw determine what He did. Clearly, though, that wasn't the case. Jesus was very purposeful in who He healed and how He healed them.

When we walk with Jesus, we too are to be purposeful. We may come across circumstances that suggest a particular action, but instead of letting circumstance dictate what we do, we should respond as Jesus did. Be responsive to God and prayerful in your actions. We may not always know why we've been asked to pray for a particular person or walk a particular direction, but we can know that when we follow God, we are helping His plan along.

Lord, I don't want circumstance to dictate the direction I take in this life. I only want to be led by You. Thank You for showing me Your way.

DEFINITION OF HOPE

Praise be to the God and Father of our Lord Jesus Christ!
In his great mercy he has given us new birth into a living hope through
the resurrection of Jesus Christ from the dead, and into an
inheritance that can never perish, spoil or fade.
1 PETER 1:3-4 NIV

It's interesting to watch how language shifts over time. Words change. Their definitions change. Sometimes, a subtle change in meaning can equal big misunderstandings.

One word that has an altered definition is the word *hope*. Today, hope often refers to a weak, unreasonable optimism. It means, "It probably won't happen, but we'll try to stay positive." Yet when Peter wrote about hope, his definition meant absolute belief in a certain, positive outcome.

In Christ, we have hope. Not just for heaven, but for this life we're currently living. No matter where we are on our journeys, He has good things in store for us.

That means we can look forward to heaven. We can also look forward to today, because He has great things in store. We have hope for tomorrow and next week and next year, because God loves us, and Christ made the way for us to have a close relationship with our adoring Father.

Next time we find ourselves thinking, *I hope today is a good day*, we can adjust the definition of the word *hope*. Then we'll know that today, and every day, will be filled with amazing reminders of God's unfailing love.

Dear Father, Thank You for giving me hope for today and for eternity. Amen.

*God loved the people of this world so much that he gave his only Son,
so that everyone who has faith in him will have eternal life
and never really die. God did not send his Son into the world
to condemn its people. He sent him to save them!*
JOHN 3:16–17 CEV

I was involved in prison ministry and met a young lady who had just been sentenced to five years. Her life, until then, was filled with horrible experiences. She'd married an abusive alcoholic when she was fifteen and soon had a baby. The man beat her repeatedly, but she never fought back. One day she saw him punch their son, and she grabbed a gun and shot her husband. As he died, he said, "But Jackie, I love you!" Even though the shooting was ruled a justifiable homicide, those words haunted her. To escape the memory, she turned to drugs, which led to robbery and prostitution.

Shortly before we met, Jackie talked to her brother, who was also in prison. Another inmate shared scriptures with him, and he trusted Jesus as his Savior. Her brother's life was totally transformed. Jackie saw amazing changes in her brother and wanted what he'd found. She had never heard the profound message of the Gospel before but accepted it as truth, and it turned her into a joy-filled, free woman. Being in prison for armed robbery couldn't restrain her happiness. It gave her a captive audience with whom to share Jesus' love.

*Thank You, Father, for sending Your Son. Thank You for incredible love,
eternal life, and for setting me free from sin!*

TO KNOW CHRIST

More than that, I count all things to be loss in view of the surpassing value of knowing Christ Jesus my Lord, for whom I have suffered the loss of all things, and count them but rubbish so that I may gain Christ.
PHILIPPIANS 3:8 NASB

These are bold words from Paul. He considered all earthly things trash in comparison to the knowleddge of Christ. Would you be willing to lose everything just to know Christ? How do you value your earthly belongings, reputation, and status in society? Are they worthless to you when compared to the passion that you have for Jesus? The Jesus that Paul was willing to lose everything for in order to know, is the exact same Jesus that you have the opportunity to know today. The value of knowing Him has not diminished since Paul's time.

There are so many distractions in life to pull your heart away from your relationship with Christ. Nothing can be more fulfilling than intimately knowing your Savior. So take time to know Him. This is a relationship that will last into eternity. In fact, in John 17:3 Jesus says that knowing God and God's Son is eternal life. So, by knowing Christ we have tasted eternal life. It's no wonder that Paul valued his relationship with Christ so highly.

Lord, give me the perspective that Paul had. May my greatest desire in this life be to know You better. Help me taste the eternal life that you have promised.

Each one must give as he has decided in his heart, not reluctantly or under compulsion, for God loves a cheerful giver. And God is able to make all grace abound to you, so that having all sufficiency in all things at all times, you may abound in every good work.
2 CORINTHIANS 9:7-9 ESV

I f the thought of giving tithe feels more akin to writing the check for your federal taxes, something is out of line. Tithing is not a "Christian tax," but rather a celebration of God's past faithfulness and His future provision.

When we give cheerfully, we reflect Jesus' nature. Our generous Savior gave up everything He had for us when we deserved nothing. He did not go to the cross begrudgingly, angrily, or out of fear. It was because of His great love for us that He gave Himself up.

2 Corinthians 9:6 also challenges us to give "bountifully." Do you give beyond the recommended 10 percent? Bountiful giving tests us, but it also gives us a chance to see how God pours out His grace on His children who seek to live as Jesus did. Prayerfully give beyond what you have before, and see how God answers. He provides for your needs so that you can continue to give bountifully. Your heart will deepen in trust and joy as you see your Provider at work.

Lord Jesus, give me a heavenly perspective on my money. Help me let go of the worries and trust You so I can give cheerfully. Help me see Your hand at work. Amen.

HIS EXTRAVAGANCE CHANGES US

We all, with unveiled faces, are looking as in a mirror at the glory
of the Lord and are being transformed into the same image
from glory to glory; this is from the Lord who is the Spirit.
2 CORINTHIANS 3:18 HCSB

At Lazarus' tomb, we again see Mary at Jesus' feet. After Jesus called for her, she poured out her anger and frustration at the loss of her brother, and at Jesus' (seeming) unwillingness to act on her brother's behalf. Then, Mary clearly saw His extravagant compassion. He wept for her loss—and His. Friends, when we grieve, He cries with us. Just because He allows us to wait, doesn't mean He doesn't care.

He then showed His immense power. After seeing Jesus resurrect Lazarus, Mary changed and became extravagant with her worship. In John 12:2–8, she anointed his feet with tears and nard, the same expensive spice used in burying someone. It seems that the time spent at his feet led Mary, and Mary alone, to understand what was about to happen to her Lord.

Instead of rebuking her—like Judas did—Jesus thanked her. There is a time for holding back, and there is a time for extravagance. Others didn't understand the "waste" of a year's worth of money, but Mary was giving her best to her dear Savior.

How can we give our best to Jesus? Today, let's spend time in humble worship at His feet, listening to His heart. There, we truly understand His power and His plans for us. There, He changes us.

Jesus, thank You for Your resurrection power. I praise You
for the ways You give extravagantly. Make me more like You.

*[Jesus said,] "In this world you will have trouble. But take heart!
I have overcome the world."*
JOHN 16:33 NIV

Would you intentionally accept a job that is hard, dangerous, and requires radical commitment? If you hesitated in answering, you should know that people make this decision every day. It's probable you've already made that choice. Some examples of those who face this choice include firemen, policemen, military personnel, and parents.

We have the example of those who willingly accept a role in life knowing this choice will bring its own share of inconvenience. There's another application to this idea when following Jesus. We're enriched beyond anything we can think by following Jesus, but our verse reminds us that trouble will be part of our lives. Why? We've been called to be different. This difference is seen in the way we talk, the places we go, and a myriad of choices we make. When noticed by those who don't like Jesus, there may be tension and trouble. We should always keep in mind that no matter how difficult things may be, the time we live on earth will be the worst of our eternity. When we die, we will spend the rest of eternity with God. Stand strong. Whatever difficulties you face won't last forever.

*You overcame the world, and You're willing to lead. Let me rest
in knowing that any trouble I face is temporary at best. Where You lead
is somewhere I can never get to on my own. Each day brings me
closer to seeing You face to face. Lead on O King Eternal. Amen.*

HYPE OR HUMILITY?

Now for some time a man named Simon had practiced sorcery in the city and amazed all the people of Samaria. He boasted that he was someone great, and all the people, both high and low, gave him their attention.
ACTS 8:9–10 NIV

Hype, buzz, and social media are imbedded in messages for products and services these days.

One slogan suggests, "It's not official until it's Facebook official."

It is said that over two hundred million people a year connect with Facebook. Any message can make it around the world on Twitter in less than thirty minutes.

Social networking plus search words embedded in website copy are essential in promoting new products and ideas, as well as building a following of readers and consumers.

Jesus didn't seek hype, buzz, and fame. He didn't sell his services. He didn't brag. Jesus modeled humility. A number of times, Jesus told the people he healed not to tell anyone. Yet when Jesus raised several from the dead, fed crowds of thousands, and healed everyone who touched him, people talked. The amazing news spread throughout His world.

Jesus' Word, the Bible, continues to be a bestseller every year at about one hundred million copies sold. It is offered in nearly 2,500 languages and covers 95 percent of the world's population.

Jesus was and is the Son of God. Who can keep such a message secret? The people of his time couldn't. Nor should we.

Thank you, Jesus, for powering Your Word in a quiet way.

The crowd was amazed and asked, "Could it be that Jesus is the Son of David, the Messiah?"
MATTHEW 12:23 NLT

The Jewish people were broken. They were oppressed by poverty and the government. For generations they waited, longed for the One who would fulfill Isaiah's promise, "The people walking in darkness have seen a great light; on those living in the land of deep darkness a light has dawned" (Isaiah 9:2 NIV). Of course, they were expecting a king, not a baby who would grow into a man and live among them. To those who had ears to hear, Jesus' identity became clear. As He taught and amazed them with His kindness and His healing, they began to realize the possibility of promise. Could this really be the Messiah? Jesus didn't need a press release or fancy ad campaigns to tell the world who He was; instead He quietly revealed His true character through His words, His actions, and His heart. The crowds were amazed and could come to no conclusion other than He was Jesus, the Son of David, the long-awaited Messiah! Like Jesus, the way we live our lives should reveal our true identity. The Bible says you are His child. Made like Him. Can others identify you by your words, your behavior, and your conduct?

Jesus, You indeed are the long-awaited Messiah, Son of David, King of kings, and Lord of lords. I am made like You. Mold my heart and my character so that everyone around me can recognize my true identity. Amen.

RESCUED

For by grace you have been saved through faith.
And this is not your own doing; it is the gift of God,
not a result of works, so that no one may boast.
EPHESIANS 2:8–9 ESV

Many people think that receiving eternal life is like trying to claw our way out of a deep ditch with slippery sides. God reaches down while we scramble up; He does His part, and we do ours. However, God does not need our help. When Jesus offered Himself as the unblemished sacrifice for our sins, He cried out, "It is finished." This was an accounting term used when a debt had been paid in full.

A better analogy for eternal life is to picture ourselves drowning in sin. We are going down for the last time and cannot save ourselves. We must be rescued (saved). The nail-pierced hand of Jesus reaches out to us. If our response is, "Lord, save me," He does! The Philippian jailer of Acts 16 felt so hopeless, he drew his sword to take his own life until Paul stopped him. "What must I do to be saved?" he asked. Paul and Silas answered, "Believe in the Lord Jesus and you will be saved" (Acts 16:31 ESV). They added no prequalifications or conditions and no payback plan. When we transfer our trust to Christ alone, he rescues us from sin and saves us forever.

Lord Jesus, Your amazing grace has saved a wretch like me from the eternal punishment I deserve. You have given my life meaning and purpose, and I know I'll be with You when I die. How I praise You. Amen.

GOOD STORIES

And he taught them many things by parables.
MARK 4:2 KJV

What kind of stories do you tell?

Some like a good joke, like my grandpa, who always had a humorous tale to share. Others prefer a narrative of personal adventure or misadventure, like my brother-in-law, who holds his listeners captive as he recounts his experiences in the woods, on the water, or elsewhere. Still others like to relay the latest news account or political saga. There is something about telling and hearing stories that speaks to us in a deep way.

Jesus, the Creator, knew this. He created this human fascination with stories, after all, and He crafted His teaching around them. All of His stories had a purpose, and they contained eternal truths. They blessed the listener and called him or her to righteousness.

Can we say the same of the stories we tell? So many of the stories shared in the workplace or at the fitness center or around the restaurant table would not fit into the pattern left to us by Jesus. They are snarky tales about coworkers or tidbits of slander that we can't really prove or off-color bits of information that no one should hear.

A parable is an earthly story with a heavenly meaning. Obviously, we can't always speak in parables, but we can make sure that the stories we do tell are ones that bless in some way, that call our listeners to higher things.

O Lord, thank You for the gift of stories; may the ones I tell bless others and bring You glory. In Jesus' name, amen.

THE MOST POWERFUL KINGDOM

And the Light shines on in the darkness, for the darkness
has never overpowered it [put it out or absorbed it
or appropriated it, and is unreceptive to it].
JOHN 1:5 AMP

When you walk into a room and flip on the light switch, what happens? Darkness leaves. Even if darkness wanted to stay, it couldn't. Light forces it to leave immediately because it is the stronger force.

When you became a Christian, you became part of God's kingdom, the kingdom of light. That kingdom is the stronger kingdom. Our enemy, the devil, rules the kingdom of darkness and is often given too much ability on this earth because Christians don't understand the power available to them through God.

James 4:7 (NLT) says, "Resist the devil, and he will flee from you." You don't have to be intimidated by what the devil puts in front of you. As evangelist Reinhard Bonnke put it, "The devil only thrives on bluster and nonsense. Let me put it this way: you, a Christian, are in a dark room all by yourself and suddenly you hear the terrible roar of a lion right behind you. You get afraid. Then you go to the light switch, turn it on, look for the lion—and all you see is a mouse with a microphone."

Jesus has conquered Satan. Because of that, you don't ever have to give in to the darkness. The enemy must bow his knee to the God-given light inside you.

Jesus, help me comprehend how powerful You truly are and how Your power
is available to help me stand against the enemy. In Jesus' name, amen.

"My soul is overwhelmed with sorrow to the point of death.
Stay here and keep watch with me."
MATTHEW 26:38 NIV

Sometimes, we need someone to sit with us. Not a Facebook friend. Not a text buddy. We need actual, in-the-flesh people to stand by our side, hold our hands, weep with us and pray with us, or tell stories and make us laugh in the face of impending disaster.

Yet the more technology gains control over our social contacts, the fewer friendships we actually build. We have hundreds, even thousands of friends from all over the world, but not a soul notices when we don't show up for church. We can't place the blame on those who don't notice when we haven't done our part to nurture actual relationships.

Christ spent countless hours with His closest friends. They traveled together, fished together, ate together, even slept under the stars together. They laughed and cried, worked and played, and through it all, relationships were built.

If Christ had sat in the same church pew or the next office cubicle but had rarely conversed with these people, He wouldn't have been able to ask them to stay and keep watch with Him. They'd have surely had other obligations. Because He invested Himself in His friends, they were willing to stay with Him in the middle of the night, in a dangerous situation. Friendship takes work, but it's always a wise investment with profitable, even priceless, returns.

Dear Father, show me how to invest in friendship. Send me real,
face-to-face people to share my life with, and help me
grow those relationships wisely. Amen.

DIVINE JUDGMENT

"I tell you the truth, whoever hears what I say and believes in the One who sent me has eternal life. That person will not be judged guilty but has already left death and entered life."
JOHN 5:24 NCV

Have you ever been in a courtroom when a jury decided a person's guilt or innocence? Whatever they declared, some people were elated and others crushed.

Can you picture standing before God, the Creator of the universe, when He judges us? He knows every thought we've ever had and all the words we've spoken. Our selfishness, pride, and nasty attitudes are openly revealed. God sees the whole picture, and we know it's not pretty. The verdict is for eternity. No one can overturn His decision. Begging for clemency won't change anything.

Satan has a gleeful smirk on his face, knowing we're finished. Yet there's a miraculous outcome of that trial. If we have trusted Jesus to forgive our sins and cleanse us from our ugly background, God looks at us through the purity of His Son. We deserve condemnation. We've earned it. Yet we're assured of His words, "I love you, My child. You are totally innocent. Enter into true life."

What a life that will be! We'll be free to worship the King forever, to dance on streets of gold, and to chat with other saints. Clocks and calendars will be out. We will enjoy every moment with no need to keep track of how long we've been there.

Heavenly Father, let me live this life in preparation for the true life to come. I stand in awe of Your mercy.

*Fixing our eyes on Jesus, the author and perfecter of faith,
who for the joy set before Him endured the cross, despising the shame,
and has sat down at the right hand of the throne of God.*
HEBREWS 12:2 NASB

Notice the example Christ sets before you in this verse. He endured the pain and shame of the cross with His eyes set on the joy that was to come. He authored and perfected faith when He had such confidence in His Father to resurrect and glorify Him that He was willing to die for a sinful people. Because of His unshakeable faith, now you too can have faith that there is immense joy set before you in eternity.

So fix your eyes on Jesus. Don't let anything in your periphery catch your eye and distract you from Him. Fixing His eyes on the joy set before Him was what enabled Christ to endure the indescribable pain and rejection that He experienced on the cross. In the same way, by keeping a sharp focus on Christ, you too can endure anything. No matter what happens here, you get to spend an eternity of unimaginable joy and glory with your Savior. Dwell on that, and it will put any present sufferings in perspective.

*Lord, Your faith in Your Father is a perfect example for me. Help me
have that same faith and that same focus. Grant me the
eternal perspective that you had while walking here on earth.*

YOU ONLY NEED GOD'S APPROVAL

"If God gives such attention to the appearance of wildflowers—most of which are never even seen—don't you think he'll attend to you, take pride in you, do his best for you? What I'm trying to do here is to get you to relax, to not be so preoccupied with getting, so you can respond to God's giving. People who don't know God and the way he works fuss over these things, but you know both God and how he works. Steep your life in God-reality, God-initiative, God-provisions. Don't worry about missing out. You'll find all your everyday human concerns will be met.
MATTHEW 6:30-33 MSG

When I was a teenager worrying about what to wear one day, my dad gave me some advice. He said, "I wouldn't worry about your clothes too much. Do you really think you're that important that people remember what you wear from day to day?"

He was right. I took a moment to think through what my school friends had worn the past few days, and with a few exceptions, I couldn't remember any of their outfits. Why would I be any different in their eyes? It reminded me that it's silly to worry about what other people think. Their thinking is often drastically different than what I imagine!

Jesus is an excellent example of this truth. He never let other people's approval dictate His decisions. He was aware of what others thought but ultimately knew that God's approval was all He needed.

Jesus, I want to follow Your example and not live by man's opinion, but only live to bring glory to God.

ROYAL ROBES

So in Christ Jesus you are all children of God through faith, for all of you who
were baptized into Christ have clothed yourselves with Christ.
GALATIANS 3:26-27 NIV

Isaiah 64:6 (NIV) tells us that without Christ, our sin makes our righteous acts like "filthy rags." We could not save ourselves by our obedience because the sin we commit undoes all the good we do (James 2:10). Before we trusted in Christ, we clutched at our filthy rags to cover our shame. When we came to Him, naked and trembling in our need, Christ clothed us. He paid for our sin with His blood and covered our shame with His worthiness. We are worthy because of His righteous works, not our own.

Yet, we often try to manufacture our own clothes again, our own worthiness. Perhaps you believe that Jesus has made a way for you to heaven, but you still feel anxious, like God is waiting for you to mess up. Anxiety lies under the surface of each day, and you work especially hard to cover the shame you still feel.

On good and bad days, we need Jesus. His worthiness covers us, regardless of "how we did" that day. Do you believe Jesus makes you worthy? Or are you trying to clothe yourself in productivity, perfectionism, or self-criticism? Stop. Look down at the royal robes you are wearing. Our King's clothes never wear out.

Dear Lord Jesus, I need to feel Your grace each day. On the hard days, please
send me reminders in Your Word that You have made me worthy. Amen.

[Jesus said,] "I am the vine; you are the branches. If you remain in me and I in you, you will bear much fruit; apart from me you can do nothing."
JOHN 15:5 NIV

If you're ever tempted to tackle life on your own, then there is a great visual of what your efforts apart from Jesus are really worth. That visual is a simple word picture Jesus used in describing how our lives are like the branches of a vine.

Jesus often spoke to an audience who understood agriculture. They had an understanding of how a branch connects to a vine, and if the branch is removed from the vine, it has limited options—death and destruction. When we remain connected to Jesus (the vine) we continue to receive all the essentials for vibrant living. We bear fruit on the vine, and that's how others can tell we are connected. Detached vines can't do that.

Jesus tells us we prove ourselves disciples when our lives are fruitful. All the fruit (spiritual life transformation) produced in our lives will always have the vine (spiritual nourishment from Jesus) as the source of fruit production.

I don't know why I try to do things on my own. Maybe it's part of human nature to try and see if I can be self-reliant. No matter why I might think this way, always remind me that I need You, not just if I want to be fruitful, but because I need to bear fruit. Keep me close. I need Your life in me. Amen.

"Whoever drinks the water I give him will never thirst. Indeed, the water I give him will become in him a spring of water welling up to eternal life."
JOHN 4:14 NIV

L et's take our water containers and fill them at Cowboy Springs," Marcie suggested to her friend, Sandy.

"Is the water good? Almost all water is contaminated these days—streams, lakes, ponds, even the oceans."

"Sure it's good! It's not mixed with the lakes. Everybody drinks that water. It's delicious! Besides, my water jugs are empty."

Cowboy Springs turned out to be a pool about the size of a washtub with a humble-looking plumbing pipe, gluey with algae and bubbling with water. Sandy thought it tasted like dirt.

Whether the spring proved tasteful or not, anyone drinking from Cowboy Springs would be thirsty again, just like any of the desert residents of Samaria.

When Jesus asked a Samaritan woman for water, He told her he possessed a spring capable of satisfying thirst forever. She puzzled over His words. He was referring to the water of salvation.

How often do we need His spiritual water? Just as we need food and water, we need Jesus. When we ache for the answers to difficult questions, when we feel lonely even around others, when we face the unknown, when we fear, when we face overwhelming odds, when we need a friend: we need Jesus.

Thank you, Jesus, for the Living Water you give us to use in our everyday lives.

THE LIVING WORD

*So the Word became human and made his home among us. He was full
of unfailing love and faithfulness. And we have seen his glory,
the glory of the Father's one and only Son.*
JOHN 1:14 NLT

Many first-time expectant mothers spend much of their pregnancies learning about childbirth. They read, take classes, and talk to other women. For nearly nine months, they immerse themselves in preparation for the moment when the long-awaited child is ready to appear. The most helpful information often comes from women who have been there. But as much as others try to share, there is nothing quite so powerful as a woman's own experience. Suddenly the words become alive. Ahhhh. . . this is what pain is. . .this is how it feels to have my heart burst in love for another human being. The words are meaningful, but it is the experience that makes it real. From the opening curtain in Genesis, telling of the dawn of creation, to the climactic events in Revelation, God reveals Himself and His plans through the stories of men and women just like us. Not only did He give us His spoken word, but He made His Word, living and alive, filled with glory. The flesh and blood experience of the Word speaks to our hearts like nothing else can.

*Father, thank You for the Word become flesh. I am in awe of You
and the way in which You chose to reveal Yourself to us. Help me to live
as one changed by the living word. Amen.*

Whoever believes in the Son has eternal life,
but whoever rejects the Son will not see life.
JOHN 3:36 NIV

D r. Walter Martin liked to remind people that there are only two ways to get to heaven: Plan A—never sin or make a mistake. When you see God, you can tell Him, "Move over; now there are two of us." Plan B— accept the sacrifice Christ made for your sins when He died on the cross. Plan A is ludicrous, so how does a person accept Christ's sacrifice? Many churches teach that it results from being baptized, confirmed receiving sacrament, or praying a certain prayer.

However, according to the Gospel of John, Jesus told individuals they needed to believe in Him. He used word pictures such as, being born again, drinking living water, coming to Him, partaking of Him, entering a door, and hearing and knowing His voice. Usually Jesus aroused curiosity and let people discover for themselves that He was the Messiah—who forgives sin. That discovery was an *epiphany*. This Greek word means "to give light, appear, become visible"—just picture the cartoon lightbulb above one's head. "But when the kindness and love of God our Savior appeared [epiphanized], he saved us, not because of righteous things we had done, but because of his mercy" (Titus 3:4–5 NIV). We are hopeless sinners, but Jesus' death and resurrection provide eternal life. Have you seen the light?

Lord Jesus, thank You that the Gospel is something to believe,
not something to do, because I could never do enough. Help me
enjoy Your love and remind me that it has no limits. Amen.

TRUST IN THE FATHER

"Father, if it is Your will, take this cup away from Me;
nevertheless not My will, but Yours, be done."
LUKE 22:42 NKJV

God has chosen to reveal Himself to us in the template of relationship. He walked and talked with the first couple in that long-ago garden. He called Abraham His friend. Through the person of Jesus, He taught us to see Him as Father.

Jesus not only taught this truth to His followers, He also modeled it for them. He often referred publicly to His Father, "I and My Father are one" (John 10:30 NKJV), and prayed to His Father, "Father, I thank You that You have heard Me" (John 11:41 NKJV). In His private moments, He spent time with His Father.

Perhaps nowhere is this wonderful bond more evident than in His agony in Gethsemane, when Jesus prayed that the Father's will be done in spite of what His humanity would desire. He realized that there was a divine plan, and He trusted the Father to do what was right.

You and I must learn that a real relationship with the Father is truly not evidenced by what we say in public, but by the amount of trust we display in the crucial moments of our lives. If we would be followers of Christ, we must embrace the same trust in the Father that He had. We must show a watching world that our God is faithful, dependable, and totally wise in whatever He chooses to do.

Dear heavenly Father, teach me to trust You as Jesus did. Amen.

*The words that I speak to you aren't mere words. I don't just make them up
on my own. The Father who resides in me crafts each word into a divine act.*
JOHN 14:10 MSG

Do you know what sets you apart from every other creature on this
earth? Your words. No other creature has the ability to think or
communicate using words as we do.

This gift of speech God has given us has power. Proverbs 18:21 (AMP)
says, "Death and life are in the power of the tongue."

What if you started every morning speaking good things to yourself?
What type of power would you activate in your life? Take a step back from
the flood of thoughts that come on a regular basis, and say something
out loud that will benefit your situation. Say, "My God provides for me
according to His riches in glory" (see Philippians 4:19). "I am more than a
conqueror in Christ Jesus" (see Romans 8:37). "By Jesus' stripes, I have
been healed" (see Isaiah 53:5).

I listed scripture behind every confession because the best words you
can say over your life are from God's Word. God's Word is truth, and as
Jesus said in John 8:32 (AMP), "You will know the Truth, and the Truth will
set you free."

I challenge you to speak good words over your life today.

---

*Jesus, You understood the power of words. May I have this
same revelation and use it for Your glory in my life.*

FINDING SOLITUDE

Very early in the morning, while it was still dark, Jesus got up, left the house and went off to a solitary place, where he prayed.
MARK 1:35 NIV

It's hard to find solitude anywhere, these days. Oh, we have plenty of alone time, at least physically. Solitude, however? That's a little tougher.

Everywhere we go, we have our phones or our tablets or our laptops. Texts or Facebook or e-mail connects us to everyone on the planet. We may be the only human being for miles, but we have access to hundreds of "friends," as well as up-to-the-minute news, at our fingertips. Our thoughts are cluttered with a jumbled mess of trivialities.

Our minds are always full, always busy. Just as we must empty out a cluttered cabinet in order to clean it, we must remove all distractions from our spirit in order to fill it back up with the peace and orderliness that only comes from God. Too often, we treat our time with God like a tweet or a text. Nothing wrong with short and sweet, but when that's all there is, the relationship will suffer.

We need to make time each day to withdraw from everyone and everything but God. We need to focus on Him alone, face-to-face, no distractions. When we do, the relationship will grow, and with it, our minds will be filled with the peace and wisdom to face everything else.

Dear Father, help me find time each day to focus only on You. Amen.

CONSIDER CHRIST

For consider Him who has endured such hostility by sinners against Himself,
so that you will not grow weary and lose heart.
HEBREWS 12:3 NASB

This verse tells you to think on Christ and the sufferings that He endured by unjust hands. Even though He was entirely blameless and holy, sinners degraded Him and treated Him as unworthy of any respect. He was rejected by the very same people that had been waiting for the Messiah for centuries. Yet, the verse tells us that He endured. He could have brought down legions of angels to fight for Him. He could have given up and decided that it wasn't worth suffering for someone else's sins. Yet He endured.

So, why does the author of this verse want you to think about these things? So that you won't grow weary and lose heart. If you are suffering unjustly or just weighted down by life, remember what Christ endured and the perfect grace with which He persevered. Because of His perseverance, the battle has been fought, and He has emerged victorious. He has secured your ending. Consider that. His endurance gives you the power to persevere no matter what because you know how this ends. So, take heart, and don't lose sight of all that your Savior has accomplished for you.

Lord, so often I just want to give up. But I'm thankful that You didn't give up,
even when Your suffering was completely unjust.
Give me the strength to persevere today.

WASH OTHERS' FEET

Having loved his own who were in the world, he loved them to the end.
JOHN 13:1 NIV

Jesus called His disciples, taught them how to heal and drive out demons, and gave them an up-close view of God the Father. Today's verse says that He showed the full extent of His love by serving them. . .by washing their feet. God calls us to wash others' feet. Let's ask ourselves: What does this look like in my own life?

Marketing geniuses spend hundreds of thousands of hours and dollars each year encouraging us to give our kids more stuff. What if, instead of buying toys for our kids (that they don't need), we surprised them by picking up their toys for them, without asking for thanks? We could describe what we're doing in light of grace.

Our upside-down world tells us that we should put ourselves first and make sure we always look our best. The culture looks down on those who can't "keep up" with the latest styles or trinkets. What if, instead of buying a new line of hair-care products (that we can't really afford), we cut off our hair and gave the extra to organizations who make wigs for cancer patients? That would show our ill brothers and sisters that we love Jesus more than our appearance. That would tell them in a tangible way that Jesus loves them, too.

Today, let's look for opportunities to wash others' feet. . .to show the full extent of our love for Jesus by serving others.

Heavenly Father, show me how to wash others' feet like You did.

HOW'S OUR PATIENT?

Therefore, as God's chosen people, holy and dearly loved, clothe yourselves with compassion, kindness, humility, gentleness and patience.
COLOSSIANS 3:12 NIV

Young man," the doctor told the eight-year-old boy on his exam table, "you're pretty sick. This medicine will make you well. But you have to take it at home, or I'll have to put you in the hospital. What will it be?"

"Home," Trevor decided.

Cross-eyed with a headache and with a scratchy sore throat nearly swelled shut, the boy went home with his mom. She settled him on the sofa and then brought him a cup of soup, water, and juice. She even offered him ice cream, but he didn't feel well enough.

Then it came time for medicine. Trevor coughed and spat it out.

"What if I read to you while you clean your spoon?"

"Okay," Trevor croaked.

But many chapters later, Mom noticed half the medicine was still on the spoon.

"Do you feel any better?"

In the book, the hero was battling his way out of an ambush. He was outnumbered six to one!

"I think after another chapter I will." Trevor feigned a cough.

Patience is a requirement in parenthood. With doses of medicine and fun fiction, Mom practiced it with Trevor while he recuperated.

Jesus characterized much patience. He explained his parables. He repeated His lessons. He accepted His disciples' doubts. He recognized the simplest faith. Jesus set the benchmark for the word *patient*.

Jesus, please give me the strength to be patient through all relationships. Thank You for your patience with me.

HEART YEARNING

They shall see His face, and His name shall be on their foreheads.
REVELATION 22:4 NKJV

In times of deep despair, we long for a redeemer we can see. Job knew that feeling when he said, "For I know that my Redeemer lives, and He shall stand at last on the earth; and after my skin is destroyed, this I know, that in my flesh I shall see God, whom I shall see for myself. . . . How my heart yearns within me!" (Job 19:25–27 NKJV). Job may not have known that his Redeemer would be God incarnate, Jesus the Messiah, but we Christians do have that knowledge. We have been redeemed with the "precious blood of Christ" (1 Peter 1:19 NKJV).

When something is redeemed, it is bought out of hock and paid for. Picture an item in a pawnshop, trapped there until someone pays its price, or redeems it. Sin has trapped us in Satan's pawnshop, so to speak, but Jesus paid in full the price demanded by our sin. By faith "we have redemption through His blood, the forgiveness of sins, according to the riches of His grace" (Ephesians 1:7 NKJV). Like Job, we long for the day when we will have the opportunity to thank Jesus in person. Until then, we can thank Him with our praise and our obedience.

Jesus, my Redeemer, You have bought me back from the penalty of sin, giving Your life for mine. I tremble with anticipation at the wonder of seeing You with my own eyes after I die. Until then, out of gratitude, I give my life back to You. Amen.

JESUS, RULE BREAKER

Indignant because Jesus had healed on the Sabbath, the synagogue leader said to the people, "There are six days for work. So come and be healed on those days, not on the Sabbath."
LUKE 13:14 NIV

Anyone who had heard Jesus preach knew He took the Law seriously (Matthew 5:17–18). Yet, according to the Pharisees, Jesus had broken one of the Ten Commandments by healing on the Sabbath—a woman with a chronically bent back (Luke 13:11–13).

The synagogue leader didn't rejoice in this miracle because Jesus didn't do it the "proper way." Through scolding the people, he chided Jesus—if He was serious about the Law, He would have barred the sick and injured from coming to Him on the Sabbath.

Sadly, the Pharisees missed both the significance of the Sabbath and of Jesus' healings. The Pharisees' complex rules for keeping the Sabbath holy made God's day of rest anything but restful for the Jews. Too focused on minutiae, the leaders also missed the heart of the Law—mercy—as demonstrated through Jesus' miracles.

We, too, can think like the Pharisees did. How often have we snubbed the work of other believers because we didn't agree with their political views or because "that's not the way our church does things"? How often have we judged others for not serving God "the right way"? Our legalism might be keeping us from seeing God's mercy at work.

Lord Jesus, forgive me for when I have loved the appearance of Law-keeping more than its heart. Please help me see where Your Spirit is working. Amen.

"This is what my Father wants: that anyone who sees the Son and trusts who he is and what he does and then aligns with him will enter real life, eternal life. My part is to put them on their feet alive and whole at the completion of time."
JOHN 6:40 MSG

What a great scripture! First, Jesus tells us the Father's desire. That leads to an explanation of our role if we want to receive eternal life. Finally, He shows us His part in the plan.

It's beautiful to realize how much our heavenly Father longs for everyone to enter real life with Him. Some people see Him as an angry God we have to please somehow, but that's a lie of the enemy. The truth is that He yearns for each person to trust in Jesus, to align ourselves with Him so we can enjoy a genuinely fulfilling life now that will segue into eternity.

He made His plan so simple. No one is excluded because they're not brave enough or smart enough or strong enough. God welcomes every single person into His eternal love, and all He asks is that we trust His Son.

Look at what Jesus will do. He will put us on our feet, alive and whole, at the end of life as we now know it. Can you see Him? He'll hold our hands to help us stand, like a loving parent who guides a child's first steps.

Precious Jesus, thank You for showing me Your way and holding me as I take each step through this life.

[Jesus said,] "I have compassion for these people; they have already been with me three days and have nothing to eat. If I send them home hungry, they will collapse on the way, because some of them have come a long distance."
MARK 8:2–3 NIV

Sizing up need and having compassion often come through tough experiences. Jesus did it quickly and often. So should we. In this passage, Jesus had enough people following Him to populate a small town. They were hungry. He knew just what to do. Feed them.

Jolene learned compassion from her own hardships. She became a single mom and a mother of twins nearly at the same time. Dropping into poverty-level existence meant she had to make a lot of changes quickly. No more diaper service. She would have to spend more on child-care while she was at work and less on food for herself. She prayed desperately for the little family's needs.

The doorbell rang and Arlene greeted her holding a box filled to the top with much-needed supplies. "We got together and had so much fun with this!"

Leader of a family church group that included Jolene, Arlene unloaded food and sundries on the table. Jolene's eyes were moist as she saw the things she passed up on her budget: shampoo, lotion, bath and dish soap, paper towels, garden vegetables, and chickens from a local farmer.

As the tough years passed, Jolene learned from her own experiences to recognize the needs of others and to act on them.

Jesus, please open my eyes to new ways to show compassion to others as you did.

PERFECT BRIDEGROOM

"All cannot accept this saying, but only those to whom it has been given."
MATTHEW 19:11 NKJV

When the disciples confronted Jesus' words on divorce in Matthew 19 with the statement that it is better for people not to marry, He replied with the verse quoted above. Jesus brings honor to the state of singleness. In His eyes, a single person is just as valuable as a married one. He knows there are few who can live an unmarried life dedicated to God in a society obsessed with finding security in a significant other. Paul was never married; that never made him any less human. Jesus was never married, and He was the only perfect human. God created man and woman to be together. However, marriage and a spouse can easily become idols. Marriage can be beautiful—it's supposed to be—but, no matter what, it will be incredibly difficult because we are sinful creatures in a fallen world. As Timothy Keller writes, we should not be obsessed with getting married nor depressed at not being so, because Jesus is the only spouse that completely satisfies. Whether married or single, be content that our great Love is Christ, and let us strive to serve Him boldly and faithfully. If God chooses to send a spouse with greater love for Him to work alongside and encourage us in our kingdom work, then we'll know that both as single and as married people we will have done our utmost through the strength of the Spirit to love God and enjoy Him forever.

Lover of my soul, let my ultimate longing be to better my relationship with Jesus.

STEADFAST HOPE

"We have this hope as an anchor for the soul, firm and secure."
HEBREWS 6:19 NIV

Have you ever been on a boat that was drifting? The feeling of rocking with the waves is hypnotic, and the boat can move much farther than you anticipated because it lulls you into complacency. In our spiritual lives, we can become complacent when things go well, not pursuing the things of God or seeking Him in prayer.

In his letter to the Hebrews, Paul describes hope as an anchor for our soul. An anchor for a ship holds it steady and in place, keeping the craft from moving too far from its set course. Without this hope, we become hypnotized by the world's allures, and we can move away from the core purpose of life: to know Jesus and make Him known.

However, when we continually seek Christ, God gives us hope that holds us steady, even when storms threaten to rock our faith. The comforting presence of the Holy Spirit also keeps us strong. If you've ever experienced devastating grief after you came to Christ, you may have experienced something supernatural and unexplainable: peace in the midst of deep sorrow. This is the hope that holds us secure: that we are not alone; our suffering is for a season; and we will see all things made right one day, in the kingdom of heaven.

Jesus, thank You for the resurrection hope You provide. It makes my mind, heart, and soul steady and strong when the winds of circumstances blow.

ANOTHER PROMISED GIFT

[Jesus said,] "I will ask the Father, and he will give you another advocate to help you and be with you forever—the Spirit of truth. The world cannot accept him, because it neither sees him nor knows him. But you know him, for he lives with you and will be in you."
JOHN 14:16–17 NIV

When we hear the term "God the Father," we might think of His work in the Old Testament, envisioning stories of Abraham, Moses, and Noah. When we hear of Jesus, we may think of the New Testament, envisioning stories of the disciples, those He healed, and Easter. How do we think of the Holy Spirit?

It shouldn't be a surprise that most people are unsure how the Holy Spirit works. They hear the name associated with God, but what/who is He? Jesus promised the arrival of the Spirit and referred to Him as an advocate. He would be "God with us" when Jesus returned to His Father. One way to think of the Holy Spirit is "One who comes alongside." He was sent to help. When you think of the Holy Spirit, think of your story. More than a conscience, the Holy Spirit speaks biblical truth and encourages us to be courageous as we walk with God.

My story always seems to merge with Your story. I am who I am because Your hand has been a part of my journey from the beginning. You give me life, hope, salvation, and a purpose for my tomorrow. Your Spirit leads even when I don't recognize His work. Thanks for the story You're still writing for me. Amen.

Even though Jesus was God's Son, he learned obedience
from the things he suffered.
HEBREWS 5:8 NLT

Imagine a toddler playing at her mother's feet in the kitchen. The stove is hot, and the mother says repeatedly not to touch it. "Ouch," Mama says. "Don't touch." The cherub looks at her face with wonder and a smile. Silly Mama, what is she saying? The gleaming white stove is a temptation. What could possibly be the harm? She reaches up tender, pink-skinned fingers, then sudden pain surges through her body. Her hand recoils in agony. From that day forward, she avoids the stove, never needing another reminder.

Pain gets our attention. The wise one learns from pain, makes corrections, and changes her ways. Our desire to avoid pain can be a powerful teacher and can protect us from suffering. Even Jesus learned obedience from the things He suffered. His hunger pangs in the wilderness sharpened His focus to His Father. Pain refined Him, and it refines us. When we learn to embrace pain and suffering, and diligently learn the lessons it has to teach us, we will become obedient, and more like Christ.

Father, it's hard for me to see pain as a gift. I hate suffering.
Yet I understand there is a purpose for it. I understand Your desire
to use it in my life to shape and refine me. Help me accept it
graciously and learn from it how to be more like You. Amen.

VOICE OF CHEER

But immediately he spoke to them and said,
"Take heart, it is I; have no fear."
MARK 6:50 RSV

There are many voices in our world. They call to us promising pleasure or wealth or prominence. Sometimes they invite us to seek revenge or inflict pain or tell us that we're worthless and urge us to destroy ourselves.

The only voice in the world that is totally "for" us is the voice of Jesus. He calls to us above the clamor of the culture and speaks truth—He loves us, He died for us, there is hope and eternal life through Him.

His is a voice of cheer. In the darkest times of life, He offers hope, peace, and redemption. The disciples' little boat was being tossed by huge waves, they were about to drown, and then they saw a vision of a figure walking on the water, a ghost they were sure. When they heard His voice, they knew everything was going to be all right.

So it is today. The addict in the crack house, the drunk in the gutter, the drug pusher in the stairwell, the porn star with her shame, the executive with his greed, the working man with his despair, the mother with her fatigue—whatever blackness surrounds us, His voice breaks through and brings us hope.

God has given us voices as well. We can reflect Jesus by being voices of cheer, pointing the way to the only Hope for us all—the Savior.

Thank You, Jesus, for being the voice of cheer. Let me reflect You
to my world. In Your name, amen.

"Be quiet!" said Jesus sternly. "Come out of him!" The evil spirit shook
the man violently and came out of him with a shriek.
MARK 1:25-26 NIV

Most children's Bible storybooks portray Jesus as a gentle, peaceful soul. That is an accurate portrayal but not a complete one. While Christ was certainly kind and compassionate, He was also a powerful force to be reckoned with. He was unyielding when He needed to stand against injustice.

It's not possible to show complete compassion if we're not able to hold ground when necessary. After all, how can we stand for what's right if we can't stand against wrong? How can we rescue others and ourselves from unfairness if we allow those who are being unfair to plow right over us?

Becoming like Christ requires us to be forceful at times. It means putting ourselves in the line of fire, and even taking a few hits, but not backing down. The key to knowing when to show softness and when to flex our spiritual muscles is love; all of Christ's actions were driven by love. God's kind of love doesn't manifest itself in a wimpy pushover, but in a disciplined soldier. When we have both gentleness and forcefulness in our arsenal, and know when to use each, we are well on our way to becoming Christlike warriors.

Dear Father, help me be stern and stand my ground when I need to.
Teach me when to be forceful, and when to be gentle.
Let all my actions be driven by love. Amen.

A CHANGE OF ADDRESS

"Do not let your hearts be troubled. You believe in God; believe also in me. My Father's house has many rooms; if that were not so, would I have told you that I am going there to prepare a place for you?"
JOHN 14:1–2 NIV

Jesus offered forgiveness and eternal life through His death, burial, and resurrection. For living life with a proper attitude, He offers the Spirit, and the fruit that comes in allowing Him to work in us (see Galatians 5:22–23). For resisting temptation, He offers the Armor of God (see Ephesians 6:10–18). In troubled times, He offers peace as an antidote to worry (see Philippians 4:6–8).

In the above verse, people would have understood that mankind was alienated from God. Jesus offered hope, but sin still separated humanity from God. The people believed in God but weren't sure how to approach Him. Jesus indicated there was a way to become part of God's family— and He was the way. As evidence of the beauty of that new relationship, Jesus indicated God desired an eternal connection, and Jesus would be responsible for eternal accommodations for those who believe. What's more? Jesus said, "If I go and prepare a place for you, I will come back and take you to be with me that you also may be where I am" (John 14:3 NIV).

I'm in awe of the many gifts You provide. I'm humbled by the sacrifice You made out of the profound choice to love me. There is hope in knowing that You are preparing a place for my eternity. You thought of everything. Amen.

HE WAS TEMPTED

For since He Himself was tempted in that which He has suffered,
He is able to come to the aid of those who are tempted.
HEBREWS 2:18 NASB

Remember that when Christ was on earth He had a human nature, just like yours. This means that sin was just as enticing to Him as it is to you. Yet He did not sin. Don't brush over the fact that Christ was tempted and yet remained sinless. This means that the temptation itself is not sin. So don't allow yourself guilt over feeling tempted. Instead, recognize that Christ was in that same place, and throw yourself onto His mercy and grace to help you resist that temptation.

It's worth noting that Christ did not come to earth in His perfect nature as God. He would not have been able to experience this world and all its heartaches and temptations as we experience it. Though He was still God, He embodied human nature. This means that He absolutely understands when you come to Him with your struggles. As the verse above states, He is able to come to your aid because He knows what it's like. So ask Him to help you and to give you the strength to resist sin as He did.

Lord, You know exactly what it feels like to be tempted. So I come to You,
not hiding my struggles, but laying them before Your feet. Please give
me the strength to stand up against temptation.

PIED BLESSING

And He said to me, "My grace is sufficient for you, for my strength is made perfect in weakness." Therefore most gladly I will rather boast in my infirmities, that the power of Christ may rest upon me.
2 CORINTHIANS 12:9 NKJV

No one likes to admit to weakness in body or spirit. Human nature strives to hide it. Yet, God has a plan in using these weaknesses. The apostle Paul had a limitation, a thorn in the flesh, which he begged the Lord to take away. Three times he pleaded to be delivered from this burden. Paul then heard the voice of Jesus and understood. Jesus was not going to take this thorn away. It existed because of humankind's fall into sin. He would, however, give Paul strength to endure.

Only when we see our own shortcomings do we realize the vastness of God's grace. We humble ourselves and recognize Jesus' strength as the only power that can help. When we focus on Jesus, we can boast in our suffering because we know it is being used to mold us. God's redemption is at work, using the results of the fall and of man's disobedience to draw creation back to Himself. The weaknesses do not have power over us. Jesus' power rests in us. The treasure is in overcoming and in having done so through complete surrender to His grace and in perfect fellowship with His power.

All-Sufficient Grace, empower me to remember that when I am weak, it is then that I am strong through Jesus.

WITH YOUR WHOLE HEART

Teach me your way, LORD, that I may rely on your faithfulness;
give me an undivided heart, that I may fear your name.
PSALM 86:11 NIV

Some days, we feel pulled in every direction by our obligations and worries. Then, when God asks us in His Word to love Him with all our hearts, minds, and strength, we're tempted to throw up our hands. "Look at me! I'm scattered all over the place! How am I supposed to keep this all together?"

During Jesus' arrest and trial, Peter's heart, usually so fervent for his Messiah, was divided by fear. Even though he had been one of Christ's closest disciples, he quickly denied any association with his Master. When he realized what he'd done, Peter wept bitter tears. Yet, after the resurrection, Christ forgave and restored Peter, even commanding Peter to continue His work once He ascended (John 21:15–19).

We may also long to love God fully but find our hearts are divided by fear or lack of trust. We might love our work, families, or goals more than we love Him. Christ's restoration of us is no less amazing than His conversation with Peter on the shore. Though we may struggle to give Him all our hearts, He continues to love us unfailingly. It is His love that transforms us.

Our Savior calls us to live in hope, trusting in His goodness and His ability to heal our divided hearts. By His mercy and grace, He makes us whole!

Father, help me pray as the Psalmist prayed, believing that Your Spirit can knit my divided heart together in love for Jesus. Amen.

GOD SMILES AT THE IMPOSSIBLE

Jesus replied, "What is impossible with men is possible with God."
LUKE 18:27 NIV

When he was still a teen, Nick Vijicic decided he would be a professional speaker and evangelist. Many might have felt the urge to laugh. Not his family. Nick had been born with no arms or legs. He required assistance in a lot of areas of his daily life. He couldn't travel alone. Yet Nick, coupled with God, achieved his goal of being a young adult who touched audiences all over the world.

One day, he smiled when responding to an interviewer's question, "No arms, no legs, no worries, mate!"

The Australian-born Christian motivational speaker includes a lot of experiences just for fun: surfing in Hawaii and skydiving. Nick sparkles with a sense of humor, such as when he asked his assistant to put him in an overhead bin in an airplane just as passengers were putting up luggage. What a surprise!

Nick is married and shares the joy with his wife of their first child, a young son. Nick has proved that God, and believing, opens the doors to opportunity and experiences.

Our great Creator can lift you with strength through any obstacle.

God loved and made an armless, legless man into a motivational speaker who inspires the world. What do you want for Him to do for you?

Lord, I submit to Your leadership and plan for me in my life.
Lift me from discouragement to making a difference.

I am the good shepherd, and the good shepherd
gives up his life for his sheep.
JOHN 10:11 CEV

HELP WANTED: Local kingdom seeks hardworking and tireless individual for caretaking job. Must never sleep or take breaks of any kind; must watch over charges twenty-four hours a day, seven days a week. No vacation, no holidays. Charges are restless, prone to wander, and are known to bellow loudly when they don't get their way. They clamor constantly for food and water, and typically their satisfaction is temporary. At times they fight loudly among themselves. They can be trained, but the process requires extreme amounts of wisdom and diligence. They are extremely vulnerable and must be protected at all times. Wolves are frequent predators, so must have the physical and mental ability to be constantly on alert. The ideal candidate will have led a perfect and blameless life, will be in constant contact with the CEO, and will possess the perfect balance of gentleness, humility, assertiveness, and self-control. No salary, housing, or transportation will be provided. Rather, the chosen individual will ultimately be asked to be tortured and then give up His life so the sheep can live forever.

My Shepherd, I am awed and amazed at Your love and compassion.
Thank You for Your goodness to me. So undeserved, yet lavished
upon me unconditionally. Teach me to listen intently for
the sound of Your sweet, soothing voice. Amen.

HOW DO WE KNOW?

*I write these things to you who believe in the name of the Son of God
that you may know that you have eternal life.*
1 John 5:13 ESV

Can we know for sure that we will go to heaven? Some Christians point to when they made a decision to trust Jesus as their Savior. Perhaps they remember what they prayed. Or they look at evidence in their lives: incidences where God has shown up, answers to prayer, or various ways they serve God. They may even help others become Christians.

Are these the best ways to show that we belong to God? People following false religions or cults can also point to their decision, their good works, and in some cases, supernatural experiences that confirm their beliefs. Instead, we need to look at what Jesus said about knowing we have eternal life. He said, "Truly, truly, I say to you, whoever hears my word and believes him who sent me has eternal life. He does not come into judgment, but has passed from death to life" (John 5:24 ESV).

So how do we know we have eternal life? Jesus said so. We are sure of heaven, not based on what we have done or are doing, but because Jesus keeps His promises. We may not feel like a Christian or act like a Christian at times, but we will never lose eternal life, because, well, it's eternal!

Jesus, my Savior, I am thankful that I will live forever with You. I can't earn it, deserve it, or pay You back. Yet I believe it because You can be trusted. Amen.

*But love your enemies, do good, and lend, hoping for nothing in return;
and your reward will be great, and you will be sons of the Most High.
For He is kind to the unthankful and evil.*
LUKE 6:35 NKJV

There are many organizations today that are built on the premise of kindness—groups that are passionate about saving animal life, flora and fauna in the rain forest, and in a larger context, the planet. The people in these groups lobby Congress, picket those whom they think oppose them, and shop with retailers who stock products in line with their views. They are active.

Jesus was active in His kindness. He recognized the areas where kindness was needed. His divine compassion prompted Him to acts of kindness—He took time to heal blind eyes and to play with little children brought to Him, and to reassure Martha that her worth wasn't based on the perfection of her home and meal. Not only that, but He was kind to His enemies, praying for them as they crucified Him.

Like Him, we must be actively kind, to our friends and to our enemies. Unseen kindness profits no one. We must be His hands and His feet, His voice and His love to others.

*O God, empower me to show kindness in my words and actions. Let me be
active in my kindness to others. In Jesus' name, amen.*

Our Father in heaven, reveal who you are. Set the world right; do what's best—as above, so below. Keep us alive with three square meals. Keep us forgiven with you and forgiving others. Keep us safe from ourselves and the Devil. You're in charge! You can do anything you want! You're ablaze in beauty! Yes. Yes. Yes.
MATTHEW 6:9-14 MSG

Did you know the Lord's Prayer can be more to you than a prayer to recite at church? What if Jesus intended it to be more of an outline of how to pray than exactly what words to use? Let me show you what I mean. (Quotes are from the King James Version.)

• *"Our Father which art in heaven, hallowed be thy name."* Worship. What a great way to start any prayer, because it reminds us who we are talking to and His position of authowrity and greatness.

• *"Thy kingdom come, Thy will be done in earth, as it is in heaven."* Put the Lord's will first in your life.

• *"Give us this day our daily bread."* Present your requests before the Lord.

• *"And forgive us our debts, as we forgive our debtors."* Confess your sins before the Father, and forgive others.

• *"And lead us not into temptation, but deliver us from evil."* Ask for God's grace and protection.

• *"For thine is the kingdom, and the power, and the glory, for ever. Amen."* End in worship.

What a beautiful way to imitate Jesus' prayer: worship, acceptance, requests, forgiveness, humility, then worship.

Lord, teach me to pray as You want me to. In Jesus' name, amen.

"Let any one of you who is without sin be the first to throw a stone at her."
JOHN 8:7 NIV

Nobody likes to be judged. Especially when those people judging us don't know the whole story or the road we've walked. That's why God is so clear in His Word. He states it time and again: we're not supposed to judge each other. That's His job.

It's easier, and a whole lot more fun, to focus on someone else's shortcomings instead of our own. It's been said that we're supposed to hate the sin and love the sinner. . .and that's true. Yet we'd be better off to hate our own sin before we focus on the sins of others. We all have plenty in our own lives that doesn't measure up to God's standards.

Since we each have our own sins to deal with, God wants us to concentrate on doing the one thing He's put us here to do: love.

Hate our own sins. Love each other. Hmmm. . .that is an interesting concept.

Next time we catch ourselves making a judgment call about another person's choices, let's take a close look at our own deficiencies. Before we point out their flaws, let's figure out a way to show them love.

Dear Father, thank You for not focusing on my sin and shortcomings. The minute I admit those sins, You forgive me. Thank You for investing so much into showing me love. Help me pour my energy into loving others, not finding their faults. Amen.

Jesus is the One whom God raised to be on his right side,
as Leader and Savior. Through him, all people could change
their hearts and lives and have their sins forgiven.
ACTS 5:31 NCV

God raised Jesus up. He demonstrated what is in store for all His children when He raised Jesus from the dead and took Him home to heaven. Other translations say God set Him on high or exalted Him to sit at the Father's right hand. The Father confirmed Jesus as our Leader, Savior, and Deliverer. He is the only One qualified to be seated beside God.

That place of honor and power is designed for the Son, but we're all invited to join them. Picture the throne of God in heaven, with throngs of angels continuously singing praises. What a magnificent image. Psalm 145:5 (NKJV) says: "I will meditate on the glorious splendor of Your majesty, and on Your wondrous works." Let your heart soar as you think about all the Lord has in store for you.

God isn't seated on the heavenly throne for an ego trip. All His works are designed to draw us to Him. He longs to forgive us and release us from the bondage of sin so we are free to spend eternity with Him. He isn't content to keep that amazing splendor just to enjoy by Himself. He prepared a special place in heaven to welcome those who love Him.

I praise You, heavenly Father, for what You have prepared for Your followers.
Thank You for counting me worthy, along with all others
who have trusted in Jesus.

"These things I have spoken to you, so that in Me you may have peace. In the world you have tribulation, but take courage; I have overcome the world."
JOHN 16:33 NASB

In this verse Jesus says that you can count on struggles and hardships in this world. It is just the way this fallen world operates. Thankfully, He doesn't leave us there. In fact, this verse is one of the most comforting verses to go to when you are in the midst of the world's tribulations. Jesus says that in Him you have peace. Everything around you might be chaotic and unstable, but resting in Him, there is perfect calm and peace. How is it that He can promise you His peace even when He guarantees that you will have struggles in this world? He has overcome the world. Could any words be more uplifting? He has overcome this world's fear, heartache, regret, violence, sorrow, and death. Run to the One who has conquered and ask Him to give you this peace that He promises. The troubles and struggles of this world may touch you for a time, but they are no match for the eternal peace of Christ that is promised to you who believe.

Lord, I am thankful that You have already conquered all the world's struggles that are surrounding me right now. Let me rest in Your peace and focus on that time when all my tears will be wiped away.

SONG OF SIMEON

*"For my eyes have seen Your salvation which You have prepared
before the face of all peoples, a light to bring revelation
to the Gentiles, and the glory of Your people Israel."*
LUKE 2:30-32 NKJV

The coming of God in the flesh requires a response. The shepherds heard the news from the glorious heavenly army. Their response: "Let us go and see what God has revealed to us." They hurried to find the truth and then made widely known what they heard and saw.

Simeon was led by the Spirit to the temple on the day Mary brought Jesus. Simeon took Jesus in his arms and blessed God. He prophesied of Jesus as the awaited "Consolation of Israel" but whose coming would also bring strife. The widow Anna joined in giving thanks to God and declared Jesus to be the redemption of Israel. The wise men from the East represented the Gentiles of whom Simeon spoke, who would receive the truth. They saw the star, "rejoiced with exceedingly great joy," (Matthew 2:10 NKJV) and traveled the farthest to worship the King.

Herod, however, was troubled at the news of this birth, and through deception and violence sought to bring about Jesus' death. There were also the chief priests and scribes, who knew the prophecies concerning a Messiah and heard the wise men's testimony of seeing the star. Despite their scripture knowledge, they could not be bothered to go, see, and be changed. What is my response?

---

*Abba, let me seek Jesus and tell others like the shepherds and the Magi.
Let me praise You and proclaim Your salvation like Simeon and Anna,
and not be rebellious or apathetic.*

HIS MASTERPIECE

For we are God's masterpiece; He has created us anew in Christ Jesus,
so we can do the good things He planned for us long ago.
EPHESIANS 2:10 NLT

When artists envision a creation, they spend time plotting, planning, and preparing. Did you know that God, as the Divine Artist, conceived of you—with your special blend of talents, personality, and intelligence—this way? He has a present and future in mind for you that far exceeds your wildest expectations. Not just in heaven, either. He wants to give you unspeakable joy, unquenchable hope, and unfathomable grace, right here, right now.

It's up to you, though, whether to receive His grace and live out His masterful plans for you. With His help, the Holy Spirit's comfort, and Jesus' compassion, you can be a world changer! In the corner of the universe where God has placed you, you can spread Jesus' love, tell others about Him, and help them find their way to the God who loves them as much as He loves you.

Will you take God's word that you are divinely inspired and uniquely equipped for the calling He has for you? Will you believe Him for the strength, endurance, and power that only He can give? Our world needs men and women who will dig deep into His Word and impart the life-changing truths of the Gospel message with fearless abandon.

Say yes to His design this very moment. You won't regret it.

Divine Creator, thank You for the way You fashioned me. Help me live the calling You envisioned for me with grace and humility.

THE BASIN

It was just before the Passover Festival. Jesus knew that the hour had come for him to leave this world and go to the Father. Having loved his own who were in the world, he loved them to the end.
JOHN 13:1 NIV

Jesus' actions seemed as absurd as the President checking coats at a restaurant, the head of the banking industry dropping by to give a personal budgeting analysis, or the owner of a car company on call to change a customer's flat tire.

It was a time that's often referred to as the "Last Supper." Jesus knew he'd be betrayed, yet He assumed the role of a servant by wrapping a towel around His waist and carrying a basin of water. He humbled Himself, and one by one He washed and dried the feet of His disciples— even those who objected.

Perhaps Jesus knew the disciples would need the memory of how He would demonstrate the need to serve, care, and love in tangible ways. The work of redemption was close, the cross waiting, and His disciples would soon spread the news of how Jesus led by serving, lived by dying, and forgave through personal sacrifice—and He never asks us to do something He was unwilling to do.

None of us are worthy of Your love. I've done nothing to earn the care You provide, but I see by Your example that I'm to serve, care, and love. The depths to which You love mankind overwhelm me. May I never view others as beyond Your love or beyond my ability to serve. Amen.

Then Jesus came to them and said, "All authority in heaven and on earth has been given to me. Therefore go and make disciples of all nations, baptizing them in the name of the Father and of the Son and of the Holy Spirit, and teaching them to obey everything I have commanded you. And surely I am with you always, to the very end of the age."
MATTHEW 28:18-20 NIV

Some Christians thrive on evangelism, stopping and asking folks in the grocery store if they know Jesus. More introverted believers may shudder at the thought. However, Jesus doesn't tell His disciples that the Great Commission is limited to fearless extroverts. His command to carry His Gospel to the world is for all who believe in Him.

The Holy Spirit has given different spiritual gifts to believers to help them obey this command (see 1 Corinthians 12). Any spiritual gift can be used to share the Gospel, whether it's teaching, showing mercy, or hospitality. Your friendships with the homeless in your community could lead to conversations about whom you serve. Inviting your neighbors into your home and life gives you opportunities to share about the One who invited you to be His friend.

In our work, our hope is always in Jesus. His authority and power is more than sufficient to bring His plan to completion, but we have the profound privilege of joining in His mighty work. In His power, go forth to share His goodness!

Holy Spirit, grant me wisdom and strength to share the Gospel through the gifts You've given. Help me recognize the opportunities when they come! Amen.

Jesus said to the people who believed in him, "You are truly my disciples if you remain faithful to my teachings. And you will know the truth, and the truth will set you free."
JOHN 8:31-32 NLT

Throughout scripture, slavery is used as a metaphor to explain our relationship to sin. Sin holds us in bondage. On our own, we are powerless to break its chains, just as the Israelites were powerless to escape from the Egyptians. The Good News of the Gospel is simple: God made a way to free us. In John 14:6 (NLT), Jesus declares that He is "the way, the truth, and the life." In Romans 5:8, Paul explains that Jesus (the Truth) died for us while we were still enslaved to sin. Romans 6:22 says that because of this, we are free from the power of sin. We are free to do the things that make us holy and allow us to spend eternity with Him. Remaining faithful to His teachings will lead to knowledge of the Truth. The Truth sets us free. Free from sin and bondage. Free from pride and selfish ambition and darkness. The Truth gives us freedom from fear, from the unknown, from anxiety and waste. The freedom Christ brings allows us to experience joy and peace beyond anything we could ever know. Have you taken hold of the freedom that is yours in Christ?

Dear Lord, I am awed and amazed by the truth of Your Word. You alone are Truth, and I confess with my mouth that You are my Lord and Savior. Without You, my end was a certain death, eternal bondage to sin and despair. Thank You for the joy and the freedom that comes from You. Help me to live, no longer as slave, but as Your child, with all the freedom You provide. Amen.

For in him all the fullness of God was pleased to dwell, and through him to reconcile to himself all things. . .making peace by the blood of his cross.
COLOSSIANS 1:19–20 ESV

C. S. Lewis said, "Fallen man is not simply an imperfect creature who needs improvement: he is a rebel who must lay down his arms." We tend to forget that without Christ we were God's enemies. Yet when we are "justified by faith, we have peace with God through our Lord Jesus Christ" (Romans 5:1 ESV). Some indigenous cultures make peace between tribes when the chiefs give one of their children to each other. That guarantees the tribes will never attack, lest their child be killed. Thus former enemies are reconciled by giving up a "Peace Child."

The Bible says that we were alienated from God by our wicked works and hostile mind. Jesus, God's Peace Child, came to our "tribe" to reconcile us to God (Colossians 1:19–22). When we trust in Christ's death as payment for our sins, we change from enemy to child of God. Romans 5:10 (ESV)goes even further. "For if while we were enemies we were reconciled to God by the death of his Son [saved from sin's penalty], much more, now that we are reconciled, shall we be saved by his life." Saved from what? From sin's power when we realize Christ lives in us to provide victory over sinning.

Lord Jesus, forgive my inflated view of self so I will appreciate my relationship with God, thanks to Your death for me. Help me enjoy fellowship as well, because of Your resurrection life. Amen.

*"The Spirit of the L*ORD *is upon Me, because He has anointed Me to preach the gospel to the poor; He has sent Me to heal the brokenhearted, to proclaim liberty to the captives and recovery of sight to the blind, to set at liberty those who are oppressed; to proclaim the acceptable year of the L*ORD*."*
LUKE 4:18-19 NKJV

D o you have a personal mission statement? Do you know what your purpose is? Do you have a plan for the way you are living your life? Many organizations today have mission statements to define their guiding principles and plot the practices they put into place.

Jesus had a mission statement. He said in John 6:38 that He came to do the will of "Him who sent Me." One day while reading the scripture in a synagogue in Nazareth, He defined that mission—heal the brokenhearted, proclaim liberty, give sight, release the oppressed, and preach God's kingdom at hand.

Jesus lived His earthly life with that focus; His earthly life was zeroed in on this mission, His Father's business.

Each of us should know our mission in life. Ultimately, it is to love God and others. Yet He has given us unique gifts and a particular setting with which to accomplish this. Today, take a little time to put into words the specific mission to which God has called you. Then, like Jesus, go and fulfill it.

Father God, thank You for calling me and gifting me for Your purpose. Clarify that mission in my mind today. In Jesus' name, amen.

LOVE LIKE JESUS DID

Observe how Christ loved us. His love was not cautious but extravagant.
He didn't love in order to get something from us but to give
everything of himself to us. Love like that.
EPHESIANS 5:2 MSG

I loved my first boyfriend selfishly. I loved how much he adored me, the time he spent with me, and the fact that the relationship was focused on me. His love was all I needed.

We highly considered marriage, but it ended up not working out. I later realized that the love I had for him would have frustrated and drained the marriage, because my love had been a love that takes.

Five years later, I met my future husband, and as we got to know each other, I began to experience the second kind of love Paul mentioned in Ephesians: the love that gives. I love my husband now in a way that I just want to give him everything I have. He's that awesome. Loving him is all I need.

Extravagant love—the Christ kind of love—truly thrives on giving to other people. When you give freely of the God kind of love, you won't be drained, because God will make sure you always receive love in return.

God wants us to love others as Christ did: extravagantly. When you love extravagantly, God will take care of you as you take care of others.

Lord, I want to love like Jesus did. Show me how to put others first
and love with an extravagant love. In Jesus' name, amen.

When Jesus saw her weeping, and the Jews who had come along with her also weeping, he was deeply moved in spirit and troubled.
JOHN 11:33 NIV

Christ is compassionate. When we are hurting, he hurts. Our tears affect him.

Yet, many of those who claim to belong to Him show little compassion. Oh, it's easy to show kindness and concern for people who live across the globe. We can write a check or drop off our old clothes at a donation center and feel we've done our part. Yet Christ offered face-to-face, in-the-flesh compassion when He saw His friend Mary was hurting. He hurt with her. Then, He did something to ease her pain: He raised her brother from the dead.

We can't all raise people from the dead, and that's not the point of this passage. The important thing is, Jesus hurt with His friend, and He did what He could to help. When people around us are hurting, we should respond as Jesus did. We should hurt with them and do what we can to ease their pain. Sometimes that means fixing a meal or sending a card. Sometimes it's just sitting with that person, holding their hand and weeping with them.

When we're hurting, it helps to know we're not isolated. We can show compassion to others by doing what we can and letting them know they're not alone.

Dear Father, thank You for showing me compassion when I'm hurting. Help me be compassionate to others. Show me practical ways to share Your love. Amen.

*"Take my yoke upon you, and learn from me, for I am gentle
and lowly in heart, and you will find rest for your souls."*
MATTHEW 11:29 ESV

Gentle and lowly in heart. . . What exactly does that mean? Some other words for gentle are calm, mild, tender, and quiet. Lowly can mean humble, modest, simple, or meek. All of these adjectives describe Christ, yet He was far from a wimpy pushover. He was—and is—all powerful, full of strength and might.

This verse holds an important key in finding peace and serenity in our lives. Too often, we go through our days in battle mode, looking for a cause to defend or a bone to pick. We want to be right, and we'll do just about anything to take our place at the top of a dispute.

Christ, on the other hand, chose His battles carefully. Actually, He only chose one battle: He fought against Satan and for us. He saved His strength and superiority for those moments of truth, when He confronted the evil that threatened to destroy the ones He loved. With us—the people He was trying to rescue—He is always gentle. He is lowly, putting our best interests in front of His own.

When we imitate Christ in this way, when we reserve our battle mode for moments of true warfare and treat the people we love with tenderness and humility, we will find peace in our relationships and rest for our souls.

---

*Dear Father, teach me to be gentle and lowly in heart.
I want to find rest. Amen.*

COURAGE UNDER FIRE

*Then the high priest said to him, "I charge you under oath by
the living God: Tell us if you are the Messiah, the Son of God."
"You have said so," Jesus replied.*
MATTHEW 26:63–64 NIV

There are times when we are forced to take a stand regardless of the consequences. It takes courage to decide how to handle a situation and stand firm.

Jackie's first love contacted her by letter years after their breakup in college. John wanted to reignite the romance. Jackie looked forward to his letters and the holidays ahead when they would be reunited.

Then Jackie learned John had renounced God and his Christianity. He bragged of living with his lover in an alternative lifestyle. She ended the relationship.

Still, John's harsh words stung her. "If you still cling to Christianity and its old-fashioned values, you're a fool." Yet Jackie stood firm. She knew she couldn't be anything but a Christian.

Jesus showed courage when he faced the priests determined to kill him. He testified again when Pilate asked if he was the king of the Jews. "You have said so," Jesus replied (Matthew 27:11 NIV). Though Jesus knew the consequences of his truthful answers, he stood firm.

Courage under fire reflects the very core of a person's values. Yet, as Christians, when we stand firm, we're not alone. Jesus has our back!

Thank you, Jesus, for showing us how to stand firm and have courage.

NO CONDEMNATION

To Him who loved us and washed us from our sins in His own blood.
REVELATION 1:5 NKJV

That's all I need to know for this life and the next. Our sin problem is solved when we trust in Jesus for eternal life. Recall the adulterous woman brought to Jesus for sentencing. According to the law, she deserved death. Jesus told those who were not sinners to go ahead and stone her. They all walked away. Even though Jesus was sinless, He said to her, "I do not condemn you, but don't do it again!" Jesus did not come to condemn the world but to save it by being "lifted up," referring to His crucifixion. Anyone who believes in Him, God's one and only Son, will never perish but will have eternal life (John 3:13–17).

Even though we still sin after we have trusted Him, Jesus will not condemn us. We belong to Him forever, but persistent sin makes us feel like avoiding Him. A child who disobeys her parents is still their daughter, but she will hide in her room, not.wanting to face what she did. When she admits she was wrong and accepts their forgiveness, the relationship is restored. So it is with Jesus. We never lose Him, but sinning makes us stop wanting to spend time with Him. It breaks our daily fellowship but not our eternal relationship.

Lord Jesus, I know my sin breaks Your heart and our fellowship.
Even though I will never be condemned by You, cause me to hate sin
so I will become more like You. Amen.

*Walking down the street, Jesus saw a man blind from birth.
His disciples asked, "Rabbi, who sinned: this man or his parents,
causing him to be born blind?" Jesus said, "You're asking the wrong
question. You're looking for someone to blame. There is no such
cause-effect here. Look instead for what God can do.*
JOHN 9:1-3 MSG

Why do bad things happen to good people? It's an ageless question that people have used as an excuse to blame God for much of the devil's doing because no one can come up with adequate answers as to why a just God would let such and such happen.

When these questions come up, I go back to what I know: God's character. He is love. He is good. He is faithful. He is just. The list could go on and on. More importantly, that list will never change (Hebrews 13:8). If you find something in the Bible or society today that causes you to question the character of God, take a step back. Is the enemy using an unanswerable question to turn you against God?

If so, remember Jesus' words in John chapter 9: "Look instead for what God can do."

Many questions we ask will never be answered, so don't sit and stew on the unknown. Instead, look for where you do see God in a situation, and discover how He will turn that situation into good (Romans 8:28).

*Lord, teach me to put aside questions that will never be adequately
answered on this earth. May I instead look for Your response
and see that as all I need to know.*

"All the prophets say it is true that all who believe in Jesus will be forgiven of their sins through Jesus' name."
ACTS 10:43 NCV

Can anything be more understandable than this scripture? It tells us all who believe will be forgiven. Not some. Not just the famous, the beautiful, or the super intelligent. Although those are welcome the same as everyone else, there is no limit to the people the Lord wants to forgive.

The only complicated part is that we have to admit we're sinners who need forgiveness, and some people have trouble with that. They may compare themselves with others, who are really messed up, so they figure they've been pretty good and don't need to be forgiven. Others might think their lives are in such a state of disaster, they are beyond God's love.

From the beginning of time, every human being has sinned except Jesus. He alone is totally pure. He pleased the Father in everything He did, and because of that, He is qualified to be the holy sacrifice who paid the price for our sins. Anyone who believes what Jesus did isn't adequate may as well say His death was worthless. It would mean His excruciating agony and death on the cross was wasted.

If salvation depends on our actions, background, or ability, we're all in trouble. Because of His sinless life, His death and resurrection, He has power to forgive our sins. No one else has done what He has.

Dear heavenly Father, how can I ever thank You for all You've done for me? I love You, and that's all You ask.

ONE WAY

*"But this I confess to you, that according to the Way which they call
a sect, so I worship the God of my fathers, believing all things
which are written in the Law and in the Prophets."*
ACTS 24:14 NKJV

In the book of Acts, the term "the Way" was used to refer to the groups of people that believed in Jesus as Messiah. Paul spoke of his mission to Damascus to imprison any who belonged to the Way (Acts 9:2). After his conversion, Paul came upon others who spoke against the Way, this time in Ephesus (Acts 19:9, 23). This term appears at least three more times in connection with Paul's testimony before Jews and gentiles (Acts 22:4; 24:14, 22). The early Church beautifully embodied Jesus' words through their identity as followers of the Way. In John 14:6 (NLT) Jesus calls himself "the way, the truth, and the life."

How is Jesus the Way? He is the way by which God came down to save creation, the only way to beat peace with God, the only way to find true freedom, the only way to overcome the brokenness in the world. He is the way to truth that brings eternal life. Paul knew these truths and dedicated his life to following Jesus. Acknowledging Jesus as the Way affects priorities, time spent daily, and interactions and conversations with others. All one's thoughts and activities come to revolve around Jesus. Though not easy, consistent time in the Bible and in prayer with a repentant heart will keep and guide people on that Way—straight and narrow.

Holy Spirit, guide my steps in the way of Christ.

WHY DO YOU SERVE?

*When he had finished washing their feet, he put on his clothes
and returned to his place. "Do you understand what I have done for you?"
he asked them. "You call me 'Teacher' and 'Lord,' and rightly so,
for that is what I am. Now that I, your Lord and Teacher, have washed
your feet, you also should wash one another's feet. I have set you
an example that you should do as I have done for you."*
JOHN 13:12-15 NIV

In Jesus' time, washing feet was a scandalously low task. It was unthinkable that a rabbi would wash anyone's feet, let alone those of his disciples. With a basin and towel, Jesus demonstrated that God's kingdom turns the world's idea of greatness upside down—servanthood is the highest calling of all (Matthew 20:25–28).

Sometimes, our motives for serving others can be mixed with the world's idea of greatness. We may not bicker about "who's the greatest" like the disciples did (Luke 9:46), but we might want to be recognized and respected for our "good citizenship." "Oh, he's such a good person. He is always involved in church and so helpful!" Compliments feel good, but earthly praise isn't the reason for our service.

Our service springs out of thankfulness to Jesus for His ultimate example of servanthood, when He sacrificed Himself for us. We model our Master when we serve and share His love through our words and actions in our communities. Are you serving for Him?

Dear Lord Jesus, sometimes pleasing You isn't my first desire. When my heart is restless, help me be content with Your pleasure in my work. Amen.

A SACRIFICIAL LIFE

*Live a life filled with love, following the example of Christ. He loved us
and offered himself as a sacrifice for us, a pleasing aroma to God.*
EPHESIANS 5:2 NLT

In the Old Testament, sacrificing was a way to show repentance and obedience to God's law. It was a messy, bloody undertaking, certainly cumbersome and time-consuming. The sacrifices of God's people were pleasing to Him and demonstrated their commitment to the Almighty. Because of Christ, we are no longer burdened by this messy task. Christ willingly gave up His position at the right hand of the Father, emptied Himself and became a man. His sacrificial death means that we can now live eternally with Him, without the rules and regulations of sacrifice.

Although we no longer are bound by this ritual, we are called to sacrifice ourselves on a daily basis. We are called to be like Christ. Yet sacrifice is hard. We often do not welcome it. We tend to focus on ourselves, what we're giving up, rather than what others may gain. While it is not natural for us to live sacrificially, it is possible, thanks to Christ's death on the cross. If He could willingly give up His life, how might you be able to sacrifice for Him?

*Jesus, thank You for living a life filled with love. Your great love
for us allowed You to willingly give Yourself as a sacrifice. I am so grateful
for Your love. Please fill me and enable me to give to others as
You have given to me. Amen.*

THE FORGOTTEN MINISTRY

But when Jesus heard it, He answered him, saying, "Do not be afraid; only believe, and she will be made well."
LUKE 8:50 NKJV

Jesus was a listener.

Nicodemus came to Him at night, bringing his questions about God; Jesus listened. Beside a well, a Samaritan woman spilled out the bitterness of her sinful life; Jesus listened. Martha unloaded to Him her frustration with her sister; Jesus listened. Parents brought their diseased and possessed children to Jesus; He listened. John the Baptist sent his followers to ask questions; He listened. The disciples questioned Him about the coming kingdom and the end of the world; He listened.

He had the answers to it all, to every question that could be asked, but He let them finish. He listened.

Listening shows that one recognizes the importance of another. It gives dignity to the one asking. The very King of kings was willing to allow others the gift of being heard. Perhaps this is a way that you and I can reflect Him to others. We live in a day of information, where there is no lack of opinion and research and knowledge. The talk shows and social media let even the untitled tell others what they should do.

Let us choose to minister to those in our sphere by listening to them. True, there is time for speaking truth. Yet we must allow others to open their hearts, to reveal their hurts and losses, to ask the questions deep within them. Then we can point them to Jesus who can help them find the answers they need.

Jesus, help me cultivate the discipline of listening so that others may find the answer in You. Amen.

THE RIGHT THING

*If you know that he is righteous, you know that everyone who does
what is right has been born of him.*
1 JOHN 2:29 NIV

Most people, if you ask them, will claim to want to do what is right. If this were really true, we'd live in a much better world. The problem lies in a shift in the definitions of right and wrong.

Many will define what is right by what feels right to them at the moment. While there are times when we should go with our gut feelings about things, we must never disregard the time-honored, God-ordained rules about what is good. His laws always have love at the roots—love for God and love for others.

When our actions are rooted in love for self, and we disregard what's best for others, we often fail to act righteously. Yet when we try to do what is right and good for as many people as possible, when we try to honor God and others with our words and deeds, we will more than likely do what is right.

Doing the right thing doesn't always make everyone happy. To the contrary, it will sometimes anger those who aren't getting their way. This may cause us to question our decisions, but we can find peace in knowing God sees our hearts. When we truly seek His wisdom and try to do the right thing, He is pleased, even when others are not.

*Dear Father, I need Your wisdom. Help me to do the right thing,
even when it's not the popular thing. Amen.*

"Therefore, my friends, I want you to know that through Jesus the forgiveness of sins is proclaimed to you. Through him everyone who believes is set free from every sin, a justification you were not able to obtain under the law of Moses."

ACTS 13:38-39 NIV

S hortly before the verses above, the Bible mentions that after Jesus was raised from the dead, He was seen by those who traveled with Him from Galilee to Jerusalem (v. 31). These people actually spent time with the resurrected Christ. They talked with Him, heard Him speak, and were so thrilled, they couldn't keep quiet about what had happened. At that time it was dangerous to be His followers, but that didn't matter to them. They were bold witnesses, though it could have meant prison or even death.

That is awesome. Most of us are too timid at times to even share with our friends what Jesus has done for us. If those early believers had kept the story to themselves, everything Jesus did might have eventually faded into forgotten history. God couldn't allow that to happen, so He empowered believers with the Holy Spirit to know exactly what to say and who to talk to.

Because of their boldness, Christianity not only survived through the centuries, but it has thrived and believers continue to multiply all over the globe. Without those early witnesses, we wouldn't know we could be set free from our sin.

Dear Lord, I praise You for the freedom You give to everyone who trusts in You. We can never truly comprehend such a magnificent gift.

CHRIST AS INTERCESSOR

Christ Jesus is He who died, yes, rather who was raised,
who is at the right hand of God, who also intercedes for us.
ROMANS 8:34 NASB

Christ lived on this earth. He dealt with temptation and suffering just as you do. He gets it. His life didn't end when He died. He was raised and sits next to the Almighty God. What does He do while sitting next to the Creator of the universe? He speaks to Him on your behalf. He intercedes for you to the Father. Your prayers are not directed to some theoretical being in the sky who you hope will listen and be able to understand enough to help you. Your prayers go to the Most Powerful God through His Son, who walked through this life and understands the heartache, joys, and temptations that you are experiencing. So pray continually. Don't hold anything back. Your words do not fall on deaf or inexperienced ears.

The phrase "in Jesus' name" that is used at the end of prayers is not just some rote words that you were taught to say in Sunday school. Jesus is the sole reason that you can offer up your prayers with such boldness to the Father. Your prayers go through Him, so pray in His name with confidence that your prayers will be heard.

Lord, thank You for living this life so that You could be
the perfect Intercessor for me.

BEGETTING ACCEPTANCE

Judah begot Perez and Zerah by Tamar. . .Salmon begot Boaz by Rahab,
Boaz begot Obed by Ruth, Obed begot Jesse, and Jesse begot David
the king. David the king begot Solomon by her who had been the wife
of Uriah. . .And Jacob begot Joseph the husband of Mary,
of whom was born Jesus who is called Christ.
MATTHEW 1:3,5–6,16 NKJV

The genealogies in the Bible are filled with unique links between, and facts about, the people of God—none more so than the genealogy of Jesus. The Old Testament mentions few women in the long lists of names, yet five women are mentioned within the first sixteen verses, which list Jesus' ancestors in Matthew's Gospel account: Tamar, Rahab, Ruth, Uriah's wife, and Mary. It makes sense that Matthew the tax collector, who had interactions with Gentile governments, calls attention to the foreigners in the line of the Messiah and that Matthew, the despised publican, presents another marginalized group (women, and mostly gentile women at that) as valuable in God's plan. Tamar, Rahab, and Ruth were not Jewish. Bathsheba was married to the gentile Uriah and Mary was a very poor young girl. Each of these women, being human, was subject to sin, but each has an amazing story of God's grace in her life. Jesus is the personification of this grace, the one who removes all barriers and brings repentant sinners back to God. Men, women, Jews, gentiles, slaves or free, all are equal in and through Jesus.

Great Sanctifier, thank You for breaking down walls. My repentant heart
comes to You, the One who sees me as valuable.

THE ONE WHO HEALS US

The Light shines in the darkness, for the darkness has not overpowered it.
JOHN 1:5 NCV

Scripture doesn't tell us much about how or where Jesus healed Mary of Magdela. It does tell us that Mary, along with several other women, provided for and supported Jesus so that He could do what God had called Him to do. She is mentioned 14 times in the Bible, and in lists her name is almost always first. She became one of his most ardent followers.

This woman, who had been tormented by Satan himself, became a walking testimony of the power of the Light to defeat darkness. Just as she waited to be healed, a few short months later, she was one of very few followers to wait at the cross.

The other disciples ran away, but not Mary. Mary stayed. She was faithful. She was faith-full. Even at the cross, she stayed by the One who had saved her from madness.

What healing do you long for? What kind of waiting is God asking you to endure? Jesus wants to comfort you; to speak your name, as He did Mary's. He wants to answer your deepest need and not just your prayers. Come to Him with all your heart, and let Him begin to shine light into your dark places.

When we experience that healing power, we are like Mary: ardent followers who testify to others about the grace and mercy of Jesus Christ.

Lord Jesus, comfort me in my afflictions, heal my hurts, and give me the strength to follow You even when everyone else abandons You.

JESUS' COMPASSION

And Jesus. . .saw a great multitude and was moved with compassion
for them, because they were like sheep not having a shepherd.
So He began to teach them many things.
MARK 6:34 NKJV

Several events moved Jesus with compassion: people who were lost like sheep, hungry people, those who needed healing, and a widow whose only son had died. Jesus was so moved with tender pity that He miraculously solved the problems of the people mentioned above. The Greek word for "compassion" denotes an emotional feeling in one's spirit. Jesus also used the word in three of His parables. He said the lord of a slave who owed him a great debt had compassion and forgave the debt. The Good Samaritan had compassion on the injured stranger, as did the Father toward his prodigal son.

These events remind us that Jesus has compassion for us as well. Will He solve all of our problems miraculously? No, even Paul said he had learned how to suffer need, but in the next verse he said Christ would strengthen him for all the things he had to do (Philippians 4:12–13). What about the promise that God would supply all the needs of the Philippians (4:19)? The context involves money. Because they had given sacrificially to others, God would supply their financial needs as well. God does meet all of our spiritual needs. When our physical or emotional needs go unmet, He gives grace and comfort when we depend on Him.

Compassionate Jesus, Your love is unlimited. I come to Your throne of grace and know You will supply mercy and help for all my needs. Amen.

[Jesus said,] "I tell you that you are Peter, and on this rock I will build my church and the gates of Hades will not overcome it."
MATTHEW 16:18 NIV

Daniel knew wood furniture. He was gifted at restoring it. When he spotted an antique wood dresser in the neighbor's yard sale, he bought it for about the price of two loaves of bread. Others passed it up because the dresser had cracks and gouges, was gummy with black shellac, and marred with permanent markers. It needed work. Yet after much time stripping, the dresser showed bare wood. Sanding, staining, and finishing, Daniel astonished the neighbors. They could not believe it was the same dresser. Daniel had the antique piece glowing with a rich soft oak finish. Its graceful beauty was showcased in the master bedroom.

God sees potential in us as Daniel sees it in wood.

Simon Peter became the leader of Christ's church despite his personality flaws: his foot-in-mouth moment at the transfiguration when he offered to put up shelters for Jesus, Moses, and Elijah; his impulsive slicing of a servant's ear when soldiers came to arrest Jesus, and three denials of Christ during the period before the crucifixion.

After our salvation, God lovingly refurbishes us into who He wants us to be. When struggling with yourself, know that you are blessed and He isn't finished with you yet.

Thank You, Jesus, for focusing on my potential instead of just my flaws.

Jesus walked on a little way. Then he knelt with his face to the ground and prayed, "My Father, if it is possible, don't make me suffer by having me drink from this cup. But do what you want, and not what I want."
MATTHEW 26:39 CEV

It is difficult to imagine the agony Jesus experienced as He anticipated His death on the cross. His pain was so great, He literally sweat drops of blood. As difficult as our suffering can be here on earth, it is hard to imagine the depth of Jesus' emotion. Jesus acknowledges, to His Father in prayer, the difficulty He was having in accepting His lot. Then He prays the words that enabled Him, and subsequently us, to do the Father's will. "Do what you want, and not what I want."

Can you imagine what God could accomplish through you if you prayed that prayer each day? We hesitate to do so, because doing what God wants sometimes involves suffering. And we humans don't like pain! Yet when we depend on the Father, and obediently do His will, even our suffering becomes a precious sacrifice to our Lord.

Father, I don't like to suffer. I spend a lot of time in my life trying to figure out how to increase my pleasure and avoid pain. Yet I willingly give myself to You. Do what You want, and not what I want. In the name of Your Son, who gave His life for me, amen.

CARNAL CHRISTIANS

Put on the Lord Jesus Christ, and make no provision for the flesh,
to fulfill its lusts.
ROMANS 13:14 NKJV

Some people believe that if we stop living like a Christian, then we aren't one. Scripture talks about a prodigal son (who was still a son), men who have turned away or strayed from the truth (2 Timothy), disciples who forsook Jesus and fled or denied knowing Him, and carnal believers (1 Corinthians 3). Not to mention the Old Testament saints who messed up for a time.

When we believe in Jesus, as John 1:18 says, we receive Him and become a child of God. A child can never undo his parentage. He may legally change his name and never contact his parents again, but that does not annul his DNA. When a Christian continues making provisions for the flesh, even living as if they did not belong to God, it displeases Him but does not cancel God's love or pluck him from God's hand. Consider 2 Timothy 2:13 (NKJV). "If we are faithless, He remains faithful; He cannot deny Himself." However, if we deny Christ, then He will deny us spiritual blessings and rewards. We lose out on fellowship with Him, sometimes for lengthy periods of carnal living, but we never lose Him. He guarantees that everyone who believes in Him has eternal life and will never perish, and He keeps His promises.

Lord Jesus, help me to put You on like a garment, surrounding myself
with Your life and power so I will deny my sinful desires
and be Your good and faithful servant. Amen.

They went to a place called Gethsemane, and Jesus said to his disciples,
"Sit here while I pray." He took Peter, James and John along with him,
and he began to be deeply distressed and troubled. "My soul is
overwhelmed with sorrow to the point of death,"
he said to them. "Stay here and keep watch."
MARK 14:32-34 NIV

P ull yourself together!" We struggle with our emotions so often! It's important to remember that our Savior experienced strong emotions throughout His earthly life, too.

The night before His crucifixion, Jesus cried out in prayer, asking for the "cup"—the crucifixion and separation from the Father—to pass from Him if possible. While Jesus was asking for another way, He also surrendered Himself to the Father—"Yet not what I will, but what you will" (Mark 14:36 NIV). Jesus remained sinless in His obedience to God even while He felt so overwhelmed that He could die from sorrow.

Jesus shows us that even the most heartrending emotions aren't sinful in themselves. It is possible to feel intense emotion but continue to trust God and act obediently (Psalm 4:4-5). Bring those feelings to Jesus freely, because He understands what it's like. In your hardest times, He won't sigh and tell you to "get it together." He invites you instead to come to Him with your burdens so He can help you carry them (1 Peter 5:7).

Lord Jesus, thank You for understanding what it's like to be human
and emotional. Help me be kind to myself when my emotions feel too
strong to bear and show me how to be obedient in the midst of it. Amen.

A BALANCING ACT

When [Jesus] got to Simon Peter, Peter said, "Master, you wash my feet?"
Jesus answered, "You don't understand now what I'm doing, but it will be
clear enough to you later." Peter persisted, "You're not going to wash my
feet—ever!" Jesus said, "If I don't wash you, you can't be part of what I'm
doing." "Master!" said Peter. "Not only my feet, then. Wash my hands!
Wash my head!" Jesus said, "If you've had a bath in the morning,
you only need your feet washed now and you're clean from head to toe.
JOHN 13:6-10 MSG

My dad once told me, "Life isn't a sprint. It's a marathon." Day after day, I realize how much this is true. Life is about learning to walk with Jesus while loving your family, loving others, and having fun.

God doesn't want us spending every moment of every day holed up in our rooms, alone, reading the Bible and never taking what we learn to the world. On the other hand, He also doesn't want us living life and never taking time to recharge our spirits by spending time with Him and reading His Word.

God's way is balanced. He loves it when you have fun playing baseball or cooking with friends or hanging out with your family. He also loves it when you spend time in the Word. He wants us to be smart in how we live: passionately, yet moderately, and most importantly, led by Him.

Jesus, You found the balance of how to love God, live life,
and love others. Help me do the same.

*This is how we know we are in him: Whoever claims to live
in him must live as Jesus did.*
1 JOHN 2:5–6 NIV

We all question our relationships with God from time to time. Am I really a believer? Am I going to heaven? If I were to stand before Christ, would He claim me as His own? John's passage tells us how we can know if our salvation is real. We must walk like Jesus walked.

What does that mean? If we look at Jesus' life, His ministry, His overall purpose for being here, we see that He was all about love and compassion. He was all about helping people understand the enormous amount of love God has for them so they would seek a closer relationship with Him.

What are we doing to show love and compassion? Not just once so we can check it off our lists. Are we living each moment to find ways to share His love? Are we seeking opportunities to point people to Him? Are we meeting needs, healing hurts, and building up people's spirits?

That's how we know we are in Christ. Oh, none of us will do the job as perfectly as He does. We'll mess up, stumble, and fall on our faces sometimes. Yet as long as we're trying, as long as we're doing our best to walk as Jesus walked, we can be confident that we are His.

---

*Dear Father, I want to live like Christ lived. Show me practical ways
to share Your love with everyone I meet today. Amen.*

ACCEPTABLE TO GOD

By faith we have been made acceptable to God. And now,
because of our Lord Jesus Christ, we live at peace with God.
ROMANS 5:1 CEV

What does it mean to be acceptable to God? Doesn't He love everyone? Didn't Jesus die for all of us?

God does love every individual ever born, on every continent, without considering their personality, ethnic background, intelligence, or financial state. He loves us all so much, Jesus gave His life to save us. That's huge! Still, it's up to each of us to come to Him in faith, accepting what He has already done.

We can't begin to imagine how much it hurts the Father when people shun His Son. Loving parents know the heartache of seeing their children treated wrongly. Yet anyone who won't trust Jesus breaks God's heart twice. Not only by rejecting His Son, but also by shutting themselves off from Him, separated for all eternity.

Jesus went all the way—did everything possible—to show us divine love. All God asks in return is for us to believe it was enough and give ourselves to Him. This request is so tiny in comparison.

There's no magic formula that makes us acceptable to God. We don't have to memorize the Bible or get a degree in theology. All He asks is for us to have faith in what Jesus accomplished when He was crucified on Calvary. Why would anyone refuse such an incredible act of love?

Dear heavenly Father, thank You for accepting me into Your kingdom,
drawing me into Your family. Nothing I do can make me
unacceptable if I have faith in Jesus.

CHRIST TASTED DEATH

Because of the suffering of death crowned with glory and honor,
so that by the grace of God He might taste death for everyone.
HEBREWS 2:9 NASB

D eath is simultaneously one of the most common and one of the most mysterious concepts. It's common because of its universality and inescapability. Yet it's mysterious because no one currently on earth has experienced it, so no one knows what to expect. Death might not seem like an incredibly uplifting devotional topic, but for you who are in Christ, it is. In death you have the greatest hope of all—the gateway into an eternity of life with your Savior.

Christ has experienced death. It could not hold Him. He tasted death for everyone. This diminishes the sting and fear of death both for you and your loved ones who are in Christ. You know Someone who has been through it and will be waiting on the other side to welcome you into glory. How incredible that the God you serve has experienced and conquered that most feared of eventualities. Even through death He will hold your hand and will not let you or any of His children walk through it alone. As Romans 8:38-39 (NASB) says nothing, not even death, can "separate us from the love of God which is in Christ Jesus."

Lord, I praise You for tasting death for me so that now, even in death,
I have the comfort of knowing that You will never leave me.

THE FACE OF JESUS

For it is the God who commanded light to shine out of darkness who has shown in our hearts to give us the light of the knowledge of the glory of God in the face of Jesus Christ. But we have this treasure in earthen vessels that excellence of the power may be of God and not of us.

2 CORINTHIANS 4:6-7 NKJV

God illuminated the hearts and minds of people and revealed his glory in the person of Jesus. Since Adam's fall, humanity has tried to fill with false treasures the holes in society and in individual hearts that can only be filled with the beauty of being with God. In Jesus that dark and pointless searching comes to an end. God shines His life-giving light so that we can know and understand that His glory is in the face of Jesus. When we follow Jesus, we are being brought back into that first perfect friendship with God. This powerful message reveals the depth of God's grace. Broken human bodies seem a poor enclosure for such life-changing knowledge and light; this, all the more, points to the power of Jesus' redemption work. What do we do with this knowledge? Do we recognize this treasure and allow Jesus to point us away from our corruptible bodies and back to God?

Father, thank You for giving me light to see Your glory in Jesus. When I am overwhelmed by the limitations of my earthen vessel body, let me keep my eyes fixed on Christ and then see your excellent power bring victory.

CHANGED IN THE WAITING

*We all, with unveiled faces, are looking as in a mirror at the glory
of the Lord and are being transformed into the same image
from glory to glory; this is from the Lord who is the Spirit.*
2 CORINTHIANS 3:18 HCSB

When a caterpillar turns into a butterfly, the chrysalis is not a resting stage. Special cells that were present in the larva grow rapidly, becoming legs, wings, eyes, and other parts of the adult butterfly. Wings are fully formed. Antennae grow, and the chewing mouthparts of the caterpillar are transformed into the sucking mouthparts of the butterfly.

While we are waiting—for a job, spouse, child, answered prayers—there are unseen activities going on spiritually. In the book of Daniel, Daniel prayed earnestly for many days without seeing a change in his circumstances. An angel arrived and told Daniel that he (Michael) had left immediately in answer to Daniel's prayer, but he got stopped along the way by Satan's demonic forces. The angel battled the demons, which made him "late" from Daniel's viewpoint.

God is always up to something. If we wait with faith in the time between a desire/prayer and its fulfillment, then like a pupa turns into a beautiful winged creature, we will be changed into a person who looks more like Christ. Such waiting is an active waiting, full of prayer, scripture-seeking, and fellowship.

Creator, thank You for creating miracles in nature, and for the greatest miracle of all—a changed life. Help me trust You in times of waiting, and know that You are at work.

A man with leprosy came to [Jesus] and begged him on his knees,
"If you are willing, you can make me clean."
MARK 1:40 NIV

Leprosy is a general name for multiple skin diseases that cause skin to decay and deform. This disease can be contagious. In the time when the Bible was written, those with leprosy had to live outside the city in less than welcoming accommodations with other lepers. These men and women had to make sure other people knew they were viewed as less than human, so they called out "Unclean!" whenever they came close to those without the disease.

Jesus was perfect, so it would make perfect sense for Him to be angry that an imperfect man with a contagious skin disease would dare approach Him. Yet, Jesus' answer to the question of healing was decisive: "I am willing" (Mark 1:41 NIV). Imagine the range of emotions this man experienced.

When others would keep a safe distance, Jesus came close and touched the man. The man left physically whole and spiritually impacted by the One who could even command health issues—the One who can take something imperfect and apply His perfection.

You can always tell me no, but I want to be as bold as the leprous man in asking. This stretches my faith, deepens my relationship, and expands my hope in You. I will ask believing You can, and will trust You if the answer fails to match my desire. May I always be bold enough to ask and courageous enough to accept Your answer. Amen.

"Love the Lord your God with all your heart and with all your soul and with all your mind and with all your strength. The second is this: 'Love your neighbor as yourself.' There is no commandment greater than these."
MARK 12:30–31 NIV

Thousands of years before teachers knew about learning styles and teaching with stories, Jesus taught about moral conduct with parables. His teaching stories still apply to our lives today.

To challenge attitudes about helping others, Jesus told the story of a wounded man—beaten, robbed, and left to die on the road to Jericho. It was a place his listeners knew well. Jesus knew his crowd and human nature as he told about the three who saw the injured man. Two were active in the synagogue: a priest and a Levite. Afraid of becoming unclean and unfit for service and worship, each walked on the other side of the road. Isn't that like some active in church today?

Who helped? Only a man who was considered a low life and from the wrong side of the tracks—a half-breed stopped to help. Due to intermarriage generations before, Samaritans were a mixture of Jew and Gentile.

Jesus' challenge about attitude stands today. Who is our neighbor? Jesus teaches that there are no walls when facing someone with a need. They may come from any race, creed, or social background. We are to love and care for them as God does for us. How will you step up to Jesus' challenge?

Thank You, Jesus, for your parables that teach us how to live and how to shine with Your light.

Jesus saw the huge crowd as he stepped from the boat, and he had compassion on them and healed their sick.
MATTHEW 14:14 NLT

Can you imagine the crowds? They were a dirty, dusty, hungry, sick, hopeless bunch. Oppressed by politics and poverty, they were like sheep without a shepherd. Wandering in search of something—anything to provide relief. Perhaps they knew nothing else about this man except that He could heal their diseases, but they were compelled to follow Him, just for the hope of sweet relief. Jesus was overwhelmed with compassion for these people. His compassion moved Him to offer a loving touch to the sick and forgotten, to offer the precious gift of sight to the blind, to reach out a hand and invite the lame to walk.

When we are in a crowd, it is easy to become discouraged and despairing at the need. We keep our gaze straight ahead, avoiding any eye contact, lest we be moved by another's suffering. After all, if we feel compassion, we may be compelled to act, and if we act. . .well, that would be risky. Ask the Lord to enlarge your heart of compassion. Dare to look into the eyes of the faces in the crowd. Wait expectantly to see what God can do through you.

Jesus, Your heart of compassion moves me. Thank You for caring so deeply about our earthly suffering, and for the gift of healing offered by You. Help me look at others through Your eyes. Give me eyes to see the suffering hearts in need of Your gracious touch. Amen.

Once again Jesus spoke to the people. This time he said,
"I am the light for the world! Follow me, and you won't be walking
in the dark. You will have the light that gives life."
JOHN 8:12 CEV

Finding your way in the dark can be quite a challenge. If you've never been down a particular path before, walking in the dark can be terrifying. There's no way to know what's in front of you, or what may be lurking in the shadows. However, with the help of a good flashlight, or even better, daylight, the same path can become a carefree walk in the sunshine.

Throughout scripture, light is used as a powerful metaphor. God used fire to lead the Israelites by night and David calls God's Word a "light unto his path." Jesus is frequently referenced as the light of the world who gives life. Shining in the darkness, light is a welcome gift of hope and assurance. Your life is illuminated by the Light of the World. Live your life as a reflection of His light.

Oh Jesus, Light of the World! You brighten my path and give me hope.
You illuminate the darkness and give me life.
I praise You for Your heavenly gift. Amen.

*"Take My yoke upon you and learn from Me, for I am gentle
and lowly in heart, and you will find rest for your souls."*
MATTHEW 11:29 NKJV

Tell someone today that he or she is meek, and it will probably not be seen as a compliment. That's because they don't understand that meekness is the protective layer around real strength.

Think about Jesus. See Him driving the thieves from the Temple, facing the palace guards in Gethsemane, and laying on the Cross while spikes were driven into His flesh? Was He weak, timid, and shrinking? Hardly. Yet, He called Himself meek or gentle in heart.

To be meek (gentle), one must keep his or her strength in check and balanced. Only the person who understands the right use of power can be truly gentle or meek.

Jesus had more power than any other person who ever walked on earth. He was God in the flesh. When Peter tried to defend Him with a sword, Jesus reminded Him that He had an army of angels at His command. He chose not to call them. He chose to give, to serve, to be led as a Lamb to the slaughter. That is real strength.

We are often tempted to display our personal power, whatever that may be, in our families, our jobs, our everyday pursuits. Christ calls us to follow Him, to choose to use our strength in meek ways, to reflect His life in our interactions with others.

*Lord, help me be meek like You. Let Your strength
keep mine in check. Amen.*

Nevertheless even among the rulers many believed in Him, but because of the Pharisees they did not confess Him, lest they should be put out of the synagogue; for they loved the praise of men more than the praise of God.
JOHN 12:42-43 NKJV

I don't want to be thrown out of the synagogue! That's like exile!" The religious rulers greatly feared what would happen if they confessed Jesus was the Messiah. Perhaps they didn't believe Jesus's promise that God would restore to believers "a hundredfold" of what they'd lost on Earth for following Him (Matthew 19:29 NKJV). Because the rulers wanted to stay on the Pharisees' good side, they remained silent about Jesus.

When we risk rejection (or worse), it's tempting to take a neutral stance on Jesus. Then, we need to ask ourselves if we truly believe Christ's promises. Jesus doesn't leave those who trust Him on their own to figure out how to live for Him. He promises His presence and His Spirit to strengthen, guide, and comfort us in anything we might face (Matthew 28:20, Romans 8:26).

Proverbs 29:25 (NKJV) tells us, "The fear of man brings a snare, but whoever trusts in the LORD shall be safe." Examine your heart. Whose acceptance or praise do you value more than Jesus? Ask Him to give you the courage you need to live wholeheartedly for Him.

Lord Jesus, forgive me for when I have not claimed You as my Savior because I've been afraid. Please help me speak and live wisely so my words and my life will show You to others. Amen.

THE TEMPTER

The tempter came to him and said, "If you are the Son of God, tell these stones to become bread." Jesus answered, "It is written: 'Man shall not live on bread alone, but on every word that comes from the mouth of God.'"
MATTHEW 4:3-4 NIV

The tempter is no respecter of persons. He tempts princes and paupers, senators and ordinary citizens. His goal is to destroy every human. He's smart; he identifies his prey's weakness and zooms in for the kill.

Jesus was a target, just like each of us. He was weak. He hadn't eaten for forty days. So of course Satan tempted the Son of God with food. He tried to trick Jesus by taunting him. "You're not really God's Son, are you? If you are, show me. I know you're hungry. Turn these stones to bread."

Turning those rocks into hot, steaming rolls would have been sin. Not because it was wrong for Christ to eat, but because He would have done it, at that moment, out of pride, to prove his identity. He'd also committed that time to God, as a time of prayer. Jesus resisted temptation with God's Word.

He didn't argue. He didn't try to be strong enough. He simply quoted God's Word, which defeats the tempter every time. The more familiar we are with God's Word, the better chance we have against the one who wants to destroy us. We may be weak, but God's Word will win every time.

Dear Father, help me keep Your Word in my heart so I can use it as a weapon against sin. Amen.

A bruised reed He will not break and a dimly burning wick He
will not extinguish; He will faithfully bring forth justice.
ISAIAH 42:3 NASB

This passage is a beautiful prophecy about the Messiah. His gentleness is so evident. He mends rather than breaks; keeps alive rather than extinguishes. If you are broken or slowly losing hope, turn to your Savior, who will never leave or forsake you. His ultimate desire for you is to bring you into closer fellowship with Him. The path to that goal may be hewn with hardships, but you serve a Lord who will gently care for you along the way.

While Christ is portrayed as gentle and kind in this passage, He is also proclaimed as One who will bring forth justice. It is overwhelming to think of all the people who are hurting others in this world. Christ does not turn a blind eye to this. In fact, it breaks His heart more than it breaks yours. Even though all is not clear in this life, you can be confident that He is a faithful Judge. In His life on earth He didn't cater to the rich and powerful. Instead He noticed the forgotten, touched the unclean, and healed the hopeless. He was, is, and always will be the Advocate for those who are hurting, lonely, and without a voice.

Lord, I ask You to mend me and give me life today. I lean on the promise
that You will judge righteously.

IN MY END IS MY BEGINNING

Then to Him was given dominion and glory and a kingdom, that all peoples,
nations, and languages should serve Him. His dominion is an
everlasting dominion, which shall not pass away,
and His kingdom the one which shall not be destroyed.
DANIEL 7:14 NKJV

Daniel served a pagan king in a foreign land. Yet he saw God protect him from the anger of prideful King Nebuchadnezzar and then deliver him from the lions' den—a miracle which led King Darius to proclaim Jehovah as the living God, steadfast forever. Daniel was afterward blessed with a look into the very heart of God, who through a night vision showed him the Son of Man coming on the clouds of heaven. In Exodus, the Cloud following the Israelites by day, symbolizing the presence of God. This Son, Jesus, was the God to whom everything was given. Jesus' authority is permanent and does not pass away. To Him belongs all praise as our Liberator. We can trust in His kingship because His kingdom will never be destroyed. Jesus gathers people of every tribe, tongue, and nation; they will recognize Him as Lord.

With such revelation, how could Daniel do anything but put his hope in God and follow Him completely? Christians today know the full revelation of Jesus as Savior, which should lead them to live each day with eternity in mind.

Ancient of Days, never let me doubt that Your power is everlasting,
as is Your love. Thank You for the hope this gives me
that I will be with Jesus in His eternal kingdom.

For I am not ashamed of this Good News about Christ. It is the power of God at work, saving everyone who believes—the Jew first and also the Gentile.
ROMANS 1:16 NLT

If Jesus was still physically on earth, and you met Him walking along a street, would you be ashamed to admit you know Him? Imagine living when He was here as a human. He had a lot of enemies—people who felt threatened by His power or who couldn't admit He was more than merely a man. Some admired Him but were afraid to be seen with Him in broad daylight, like Nicodemus, who came to talk to Jesus at night. Have you ever pictured yourself in their place?

We like to think we'd be among His friends, but even those closest to Him were frightened. Think about Peter, one of Jesus' intimate companions. He denied he even knew the Lord when the Roman soldiers whipped Jesus and eventually crucified Him.

Everything Jesus did was based on His love for you and me. He came to earth, lived a sinless life, and died a horrible death in our place. But sometimes it is hard to speak up and share the Good News of what Jesus has done.

Only those who accept the truth that Jesus is the only way will spend eternity with God in heaven. If we love Him and love our friends, how can we be ashamed to open our mouths to share the Gospel?

Dear Lord Jesus, let me never be ashamed or too timid to tell others about the awesome power of Your love.

THREE LIFE-CHANGING TRUTHS

In her deep anguish Hannah prayed to the LORD, weeping bitterly.
1 SAMUEL 1:10 NIV

Hannah was desperate for a child, crying out to God in her despair. The scriptures say she felt peace after pouring her heart out to the Lord.

Hannah didn't yet have an answer to her request, but she knew the Lord well enough to leave her problems at His feet. She didn't take revenge on her rival. Instead, she believed three life-changing truths: God had heard her prayer; God would take care of her enemies; and God was in charge of her life.

This story is the first time in the Bible God is designated by the name "the Lord Almighty" or "the Lord of hosts." The title is a reference to the sovereignty of God over all powers in the universe. Hannah knew that the God who had created the universe could be trusted with the longings of her soul.

How much richer our lives would be if we followed Hannah's example and left all our problems at the altar. After all, "God is love, and . . . as we live in God, our love grows more perfect . . . Such love has no fear, because perfect love expels all fear"(1 John 4:16-18, NLT).

I'm ready for a double portion of God's love—how about you?

Lord, forgive me for leaving my problems with You and then taking them back. Help me surrender to Your perfect will, knowing You have heard me and will take care of every area of my life.

THE BREAD OF LIFE: OUR SUSTENANCE

Jesus replied, "I am the bread of life. Whoever comes to me will never be hungry again. Whoever believes in me will never be thirsty."
JOHN 6:35 NLT

Jesus calls Himself the "bread" of life. What is bread? Bread is nourishment for our bodies. When we eat it, one of our body's needs is satisfied.

Your relationship with Jesus is like the bread you eat: it satisfies you and supplies you with what you need. As you draw on that relationship with Him, you'll find your spirit and soul satisfied in a way that nothing else can.

The interesting thing about bread is that eating it once doesn't fulfill your need for food forever. You eat over and over again to satisfy your body's hunger.

In the same way, your spirit is sustained through coming back to Jesus on a regular basis. Prayer, worship, reading the Bible, focusing your thoughts on His goodness and love—all of these things are ways you can come to the Father and discover that He is the One who completes your life. When He fills your interests, your love, and your time, you'll find that the material things of this world have no pull on you. Jesus has satisfied your soul.

Jesus, You are my satisfaction. Today, I intend to let my spirit and soul be filled with the satisfaction that comes from my relationship with You and nothing else.

Jesus said to them, "It is not the healthy who need a doctor, but the sick. I have not come to call the righteous, but sinners."
MARK 2:17 NIV

The pain is persistent and severe. You've tried over-the-counter medication, relaxing, and working through the pain, but there are persistent reminders of its presence. You decide to visit a doctor.

In the waiting room, others are experiencing health issues. You search for someone who doesn't need a doctor, but each person is there intentionally. Why? They recognize they're sick.

This is the logic Jesus expressed in today's verse. We have to first recognize we're not well—that sin wounds us—before the Great Physician can begin to heal that which we could never manage on our own.

Jesus didn't spend time with sinners to become more like them, but because they needed spiritual health benefits only He could offer. He never played a game of "How close can I get to sin without sinning" either. He maintained His integrity, never allowing a verbal alteration of the core health benefits of His message based on how it might impact the listener.

His spiritual health plan is comprehensive, available 24/7, offers personalized care, and supplies ongoing treatment. There's no application, and no waiting period. Premiums have already been paid. Call now. His office never closes.

It's so easy to coexist with life-damaging sin. I try to fix things on my own, and it's never good enough. Heal me from the inside out. Help me get out of Your way. Thanks for compassionately reminding me I can't do this on my own. Amen.

LOVE YOUR ENEMIES

"But I tell you; love your enemies and pray for those who persecute you,
that you may be sons of your Father in heaven. . . . If you love those
who love you, what reward will you get?"
MATTHEW 5:44–46 NIV

Fire trucks! Police! "Surely it's not my home!" Claudia panicked.
Yet it was! Returning from an evening church service, she learned
that a fire had been set along her fence in the most dangerous season
for wildfires. She knew who did it. Despite continuous efforts with the
perpetrator and the police to stop the vandalism, it had continued and
escalated. A caring neighbor kept the fire to a small area. It did not burn
both houses and all the sheds. Still, Claudia's repairs would cost money
she didn't have—up to four figures this time.

Would the perpetrator get the house next time? With anger boiling
within her, Claudia called her close friend, and then went to her house.

Dorie reminded her, "We know where our family and friends are with
God, but what about our enemies? Doesn't Jesus himself tell us to pray
for them? Remember on the cross, he prayed, "Father, forgive them for
they know not what they do (Luke 23:34 ESV)."

Claudia sighed and prayed with her friend. She put in place legal
documents for her protection. She knew that in the months ahead, she
was commanded by Jesus to continue to pray for the perpetrator.

Who knows where his heart for God would be then?

Father God, help me forgive and pray for my enemies,
for you see their future as well as mine.

PLEASE DON'T INTERRUPT ME!

*While He was still speaking, someone came from the ruler
of the synagogue's house, saying to him, "Your daughter is dead.
Do not trouble the Teacher."*
LUKE 8:49 NKJV

D on't you dislike being interrupted? If you're a sequential person like me, you just hate having to jump from one task to another.

Welcome to Jesus' sphere of ministry. He was continually being interrupted and called to go to another place, to touch another sick person, to minister to another need. In fact, in the story above, Jesus had been deterred from His journey to the house of Jairus by an anemic woman who reached out to touch the hem of His robe. While He talked to her, a runner came and interrupted the conversation, bringing the news that Jarius' daughter had died; there was no need for Jesus to come now, they thought.

Would you have been upset if you had been Jairus? What kind of thoughts were running through his mind? Was he tempted to lash out at the woman who detained Jesus?

Jesus had time for them both. He did not work on the schedule of others. He continued to Jairus' home and brought the little girl back to life.

In our lives there will be interruptions, but Jesus showed us that people are more important than a schedule. Taking time to minister to our toddlers or coworkers or neighbors is a way that we can follow Him in the commonplace details of living.

---

*Lord, teach me to accept interruptions and see them as opportunities
to identify with You. In Jesus' name, amen.*

Do not merely listen to the word, and so deceive yourselves. Do what it says.
JAMES 1:22 NIV

Sometimes we can be the hard-hearted soil Jesus talked about in His first parable, which He called the Parable of the Sower. He illustrated four responses people have every time the seed, the Word of God, is dispersed to them. A hard-hearted response keeps the seed from penetrating and Satan steals it. If our heart is rocky, we have no root and the seed starves and dies. A thorny heart strangles the seedling. If our heart soil is good, the seed is sustained and bears fruit.

We Christians tend to think we are the good soil Jesus described. Yet the point of the parable is doing what God says, not merely hearing it. When we practice God's Word and live by its principles, we will be fruitful and God will give more seed (truth) for us to respond to (Mark 4:24–25). However, we Christians can also have hard hearts that negate God's truth. Three times in Mark, Jesus even rebuked His disciples for having hard hearts (Mark 8:17, 6:52, 16:14).

Therefore we must be careful to practice God's truth, not merely hear it or learn it. What we believe must show up in how we behave.

Lord Jesus, help me cultivate my heart so that I have a good response to Your word and it will affect what I say and do. May I not negate, neglect, or neutralize Your truth by my careless response, but nurture it instead. I want to live it, not lose it. Amen.

CHANGE THE WAY YOU THINK

Dear friends, God is good. So I beg you to offer your bodies to him as a living sacrifice, pure and pleasing. That's the most sensible way to serve God. Don't be like the people of this world, but let God change the way you think. Then you will know how to do everything that is good and pleasing to him.
ROMANS 12:1-2 CEV

Our feelings, thoughts, and behaviors are intricately connected. Take fear, for example. We "feel" fear before we know we are afraid—our hearts begin to race, our breathing becomes shallow. The thinking follows. "There is danger." We react based on our thinking. We run or we fight. Our actions are based on the conclusions we draw. Thus, our thoughts are powerful motivators for our behaviors. In Romans, Paul challenges us to change the way we think. Instead of thinking like the people of the world, we are called to interpret our feelings differently. The world says, "take care of yourself, you're number one, the power is within you." Paul challenges us to think differently. Jesus came to be a living sacrifice, and he beckons us to do the same. We can only do this if God changes us. When we think differently, this passage says that we will behave differently. We will know "how to do everything that is good and pleasing to him." It begins with your thoughts. Turn them over to God.

Father, it is not natural for me to want to offer my body to You as a living sacrifice, but You have asked me to do so, and I want to please and serve You. Please change the way I think so that I will know how to behave in a way that honors You. Amen.

*Jesus answered, "Everyone who drinks this water will be thirsty again,
but whoever drinks the water I give them will never thirst. Indeed, the water
I give them will become in them a spring of water welling up to eternal life."*
JOHN 4:13-14 NIV

I f I could change *this* about my life, I know I'd be happy." We've all
thought this, but Jesus' interaction with the Samaritan woman at the
well suggests otherwise.

Without any explanation, Jesus knew the unhappy life the
Samaritan woman was living. She was notorious in her community
for being divorced four times and now for living with a man who
wasn't her husband. If Jesus' mission was to remove people's difficult
circumstances, He could have placed her in a happy, respectable
marriage. Instead, He gave her the best gift—acceptance, forgiveness,
and the knowledge of Himself. In response, she ran to her neighbors to
tell them about this prophet who'd told her all she'd ever done and had
treated her (of all people!) with dignity and love.

Jesus offers the same Living Water to us. He promises that He can
quench any thirst in our hearts. Our Savior puts His Holy Spirit in us to
renew us and bring life out of our parched places, regardless of what we
may have gone through.

Are there places in your life or relationships that are so dry that you
don't think anything could restore them? Let Jesus fill them with His
Living Water.

*Jesus, You know the places in my life that need Your care. Please send Your
Spirit to restore them. Thank You for Your Living Water! Amen.*

DOING MY JOB

*"Do not judge, and you will not be judged. Do not condemn,
and you will not be condemned. Forgive, and you will be forgiven."*
LUKE 6:37 NIV

This is another one of those easier-said-than-done verses. None of us likes to think of ourselves as harsh and judgmental. We may even determine to live and let live, to pray for those we disagree with and show them love and compassion. Then, something so appalling, so unbearable presents itself, and we simply can't believe it. How could a person do such a thing? How could they be so stupid or so cruel or so manipulative? Boom. We've judged another person.

God is very clear in His Word. He is the only one who is allowed to wear the judge's robe, the only one who holds the magistrate's gavel. It's His job, and His alone, to judge each human heart.

It is our job to love. Period.

When we try to take over God's job and judge another person, we actually try to push God out of His rightful place and seat ourselves on His throne. Shame on us! We need to concern ourselves with doing our jobs—loving others—and leave the judging to Him.

Oh, we should still hold strong to our convictions, but let's make sure we're attacking our own sin and not other people. Let's do battle against Satan and not against his victims. For really, isn't that what Christ did for us, when He took our punishment?

*Dear Father, forgive me for judging others. Teach me to love
and leave the judgment to You. Amen.*

THE MAIN THING

For what I received I passed on to you as of first importance:
that Christ died for our sins according to the Scriptures.
1 CORINTHIANS 15:3 NIV

I like the way the Apostle Paul referred to this message as being of "first importance"—that Christ died for our sins. Stop and think about that. Nothing is more important in the eternal scheme of things than for each of us to come to grips with that truth. It must be deeper than merely something we know in our minds. We have to let it sink in and put down roots into our hearts.

Before Paul could pass the message on, he had to receive it. The testimony of his conversion is incredible. He had been a zealous Pharisee who studied the Hebrew scriptures since his youth. He was convinced that Jesus was an imposter and everyone who believed in Him was breaking Jewish laws. Paul traveled throughout the region arresting Christians wherever he found them, until God stepped in, stopped Paul's rampage, and sent believers to teach him the truth.

Paul received the Gospel immediately when he finally listened, and from that point on, he was on fire with the message that Christ died for our sins. Not only did Paul become a powerful missionary and evangelist, his letters make up a large portion of the New Testament. His words continue to change people's lives, after two thousand years.

Heavenly Father, thank You for the Good News that Christ died for our sins.
It is of utmost importance for me to pass it on to the people in my life.

NEVER FORSAKEN

About the ninth hour Jesus cried out with a loud voice, saying, "ELI, ELI, LAMA SABACHTHANI?" that is, "My God, My God, why have You forsaken Me?"
MATTHEW 27:46 NASB

This point marks the lowest depth of Christ's suffering. At this moment, all the sin of mankind was piled on Jesus, the sacrificial Lamb. The Father turned His face away because, in His holiness, He could not bear to look on it. Jesus was completely and utterly alone. For Him, it wasn't just like someone that He loved had abandoned Him. In the Trinity, the Father and Son are One and the same. So that which happened to Christ on the cross was a mystery and a sorrow that we cannot fathom.

Think about what Christ was willing to suffer to save you. The depth of His love for the people that were responsible for His death is incomprehensible. He deserves your utmost gratitude and service. Because of what Christ went through, you will never have to utter that same agonizing cry. Those who have been covered by the sacrificial blood of Christ will never be forsaken by God. He has redeemed you and presented you blameless before the Father.

Lord, I will never understand the depth of Your suffering. But help me comprehend even the slightest bit of the depth of Your love for me. Help me recognize every day that I was bought for a price and am free only through Your sacrifice.

SPOKEN

*In the beginning was the Word, and the Word was with God
and the Word was God. He was in the beginning with God.*
JOHN 1:1-2 NKJV

St. Francis of Assisi is commonly misquoted as saying, "Preach the Gospel and, if need be, use words." However, this is not the biblical example. This godly man knew the importance of intertwining word and deed. Even a cursory look through the Gospels and the book of Acts shows the centrality of words, which were then verified by miraculous works. More importantly, Jesus is identified as the Word, which became flesh and lived among us. God chose to reveal himself through the written and spoken word. He endowed humans with this gift apart from the rest of creation. Jesus and his followers did many wonderful things, but their actions were put into context when they talked to others about God's plan. Good deeds need to be accompanied by a reason for who gives the strength and compassion for doing good. Jesus always pointed back to the Father. Christians may not always have occasion to speak, but they should always be ready, that God may get the glory and not man. Paul asks, how will others "call on him in whom they have not believed? And how are they to believe in him of whom they have never heard? And how are they to hear without someone preaching?" (Romans 10:14 ESV). Our words may often seem inadequate, but Christians have within the living breath of God.

---

*Eternal Word, guide me to speak Your truth and know the beauty
and power of words that come from You.*

THE SHIELD OF FAITH

*Above all, taking the shield of faith, wherewith ye shall be able
to quench all the fiery darts of the wicked one.*
EPHESIANS 6:16 NKJV

There is rich, life-giving treasure buried in scripture if we'll dig for it.
For example, when Paul wrote about the shield of faith, he used
the Greek word *thureos*, which refers to an oblong door that was wide in
width and long in length. The Roman soldiers in Paul's time didn't wield
dinky, small shields like we see in "Armor of God" play sets. Instead,
they used shields which were door sized. These shields covered them
completely.

What a word picture! The Holy Spirit, through Paul, was encouraging
us that our God-given faith is big and strong enough to handle any
circumstance! We don't have to worry about having too small a faith.
God's got us—and our situation—covered.

Wait: there's more! In *Sparkling Gems from the Greek*, Rick Renner
notes that the Roman soldier's shield was created with six layers of
leather. It was "extremely tough and exceptionally durable." However, "in
order to keep those shields in good shape," each soldier would oil his
shield daily to keep it "soft, supple, and pliable."

We, too, must oil our shield daily by spending time in His word and in
prayer, communing with Jesus and listening for the Holy Spirit's voice. As
we surrender our schedules and concerns to God, He gives us what we
need to serve Him and others.

*Lord, thank You for the riches of Your Word. Help me have the discipline to oil
my shield daily, so I can be prepared for all You've called me to do.*

CALM DOWN

He got up, rebuked the wind and said to the waves, "Quiet! Be still!"
Then the wind died down and it was completely calm.
MARK 4:39 NIV

It's been said that life is what happens when you're planning something else, and life is lived in a world of chaos and confusion. For Jesus' disciples, this was evident when they were in a boat during a storm. Waves pushed over and into the boat. The disciples had heard the stories. Men died in storms like this.

Somehow Jesus slept through the panic at the back of the boat. The disciples apparently didn't want to bother Jesus, so they tried to manage on their own. When they finally determined they couldn't save themselves, they woke Jesus from sleep. However, instead of asking for help, they accused, "Don't You care if we drown?" (see Mark 4:38).

Had they really been with Jesus such a short time that they hadn't observed His compassion? Why do we accuse God of not helping when we've refused, or neglected, to ask? This story ends with Jesus calming the storm in three words. These words weren't incantations or spells, they were words of authority. The One who mastered the storm also created the water, clouds, and wind, and is Master over all things.

I like to be in control. I want to prove I don't need as much help as others. Failure follows me all the days of my life. When I am struggling to hold on, remind me to accept Your helping hand. May I trust You with my past, present, and future. Thanks for always taking care of me. Amen.

A WANT AND NEED LIST FOR GOD

[Jesus said,] "This, then, is how you should pray:
'Our Father in heaven, hallowed be your name,
your kingdom come, your will be done, on earth as it is in heaven' "
MATTHEW 6:9–10 NIV

Dear God,
    Please give me eggs, milk, flour, four cans of corned beef hash, potatoes, white vinegar, pasta, toilet paper, snow boots, sixteen pairs of wool socks, ski passes for our family, a queen-sized sheet set, a discount coupon for Ace Hardware, and a metal snow shovel because the plastic is no good. Thanks for everything. P.S. You're the best!

At his disciples' request, Jesus modeled a pattern for a prayer. It was unlike anything the disciples had ever heard before.

Instead of reciting a lengthy list of needs and wants like the one above, Jesus addressed his Father, God of the universe, our Creator, Jehovah-jireh [God Who Provides], with thanks and praise. That is the way he suggested we begin. Jesus placed God's will and kingdom first. Then, he asked for daily needs and forgiveness.

"Forgive us our debts as we also have forgiven our debtors. . ." Matthew 6:12 (NIV) highlights the importance of coming to the Lord with a repentant heart. God has forgiven our debt of sin, and Jesus paid it forward.

Jesus taught that before giving an offering at the altar, "First go and be reconciled to your brother and then come and offer your gift" [Matthew 5:24 HCSB].

People always have multiple needs, but our greatest needs are God's Kingdom and Christ's love.

Jesus, we thank You for teaching us honor
and respect for You and Your Father, God.

THE THIEF HAS NO POWER

*"The thief comes only to steal and kill and destroy; I have come
that they may have life, and have it to the full."*
John 10:10 NIV

Satan's tactics are discouraging. He often seems one step ahead of us, anticipating our every move, hiding behind rocks, just waiting to trip us up. While it feels overwhelming at times, in reality, Satan only has a few tricks up his sleeve. Quite simply, he aims to steal, kill, and destroy. He's not that creative, and certainly doesn't have any power to harm a child of God. Ephesians 1:13 tells us we are sealed with the Holy Spirit, and are therefore protected from Satan's schemes. In stark contrast to Satan, Jesus boldly states that He came so that we no longer have to fear Satan's (limited) power. Jesus brings us a full and abundant life. What are some things that Satan tries to steal, kill, and destroy in you? What does it mean to live abundantly for Him? Turn your back on Satan, the liar. Turn to Jesus, the Truth. Seek Him and receive a life beyond your wildest dreams.

*Jesus, I am so grateful for Your coming and the promise of an abundant,
full life! What a joy it is to know that Satan no longer has the power
to steal from me, kill what I love, and destroy what I hold dear.
You are Life. Help me live my life, abundantly, for You. Amen.*

SLAVES TO WHAT?

For He rescued us from the domain of darkness, and transferred us
to the kingdom of His beloved Son, in whom
we have redemption, the forgiveness of sins.
Colossians 1:13–14 NASB

Many of us have read about the horrors of slavery. A person's entire existence belonged to the master, who viewed his slaves as property and determined how much each was worth. Slaves were not paid for their labor, so how could they ever get enough money to buy their freedom? They were trapped unless someone benevolent rescued them.

So when Romans 6:17 (NASB) says we used to be "slaves to sin" and that sin was master over us, we can imagine our hopeless predicament. Sin controlled our body, time, will, motives, and activities. Not that we never did anything good, but our default mode was self-absorption and independence from God. The only way to gain freedom from tyranny to self and sin was to pay for it. Yet we were utterly destitute. We needed a redeemer to pay our slave price and set us free. Jesus did that. He paid with His blood when He sacrificed Himself as the unblemished Lamb of God (1 Peter 1:18–19).

What are we doing with that spiritual freedom? Romans 6:4 (NASB) says we can live in sin if we keep yielding to it, or we can "walk in newness of life," yielding ourselves to righteousness. It depends on what masters us.

Lord Jesus, You have redeemed me from sin and Satan, but I often
feel as if they still enslave me. Help me enjoy my new life and freedom
by serving only You. Amen.

Now there was a man in Jerusalem called Simeon, who was righteous
and devout. He was waiting for the consolation of Israel.
LUKE 2:25 NIV

He had been waiting his entire life to behold the One—the Messiah. Simeon had been promised by God that he would not die until he saw the Messiah with his own eyes.

In the time of waiting, an angel appeared to Mary, and a star came to Bethlehem, shepherds were given V.I.P. invitations to come see the baby, and wise men had begun a journey from the East to honor the child. At the specified time, Mary and Joseph came to the temple to dedicate the baby Jesus. Prompted by the Holy Spirit, Simeon hurried to the temple. He had a meeting with the Messiah and all the waiting would soon end. Upon seeing Jesus, Simeon prayed, "My eyes have seen your salvation" (Luke 2:30 NIV).

Most thought the Messiah would be a political or military figure that would set Israel free, but Simeon knew Jesus was a, "Light for revelation to the Gentiles" (Luke 2:32 NIV).

Simeon understood that Jesus would one day save people from their sin and in Him there would be no discrimination.

Thanks for allowing Simeon to see Jesus. His words assure me that I can
be a child of God. The Bible makes it clear that Jesus is the Son of God,
and His love for me and my trust in Him results in a rescue from my sin.
Thanks for setting in motion all the things that lead me
to recognize You as my Savior. Amen.

FEASTING AND CELEBRATIONS

Then one of the Pharisees asked Him to eat with him.
And he went to the Pharisee's house and sat down to eat.
LUKE 7:36 NKJV

G uess what the religious leaders said about Jesus' social life? They called Him a "friend of sinners." They criticized Him for taking meals with well-known enemies of polite society. In truth, Jesus ate with the religious and the non-religious alike. He ate with his disciples in a borrowed room, fixed breakfast on the seashore, and served a meal to a crowd on a hillside. Jesus was a social person.

The Jewish culture is one of celebration. We know that Jesus participated in these customs because He went to Jerusalem for the Passover and attended a wedding in Cana. Jesus took time to celebrate the milestones of this temporal life. He enjoyed festivities with His friends and neighbors. The feasts that He participated in focused on the wonder of God-given life—honoring God's deliverance from Egypt (Passover) or the relationship of marriage (weddings) or the partaking of food together with family and friends (everyday meals).

If we would follow His example, we can embrace opportunities to make the breaking of bread a sacred thing. Maybe we can invite neighbors over for hamburgers on the deck or take a plate of cookies to a church friend who is struggling. However we do it, may we be like Jesus in all of our social affairs.

Lord, let me honor You in all my feasting, and may I use food as a way to
reach out to my neighbors and church family. In Jesus' name, amen.

In the beginning was the Word, and the Word was with God,
and the Word was God. He was with God in the beginning.
Through him all things were made; without him nothing was made
that has been made. In him was life, and that life was the light
of all mankind. The light shines in the darkness,
and the darkness has not overcome it.
JOHN 1:1–5 NIV

B efore Jesus enters our lives, we may believe we are living well, but in the end, we are stumbling along a path in the darkness if we aren't following Him. Jesus, the Light of the World, taught us to love Him by loving us first. His love is the light by which we can see all things more clearly.

Even now, we need Jesus's light. Ask your Savior to cast light on the sins you haven't been able to see in yourself. Ask Him to illuminate your community's needs and hurts so you can pray and serve the best you can. Don't be afraid, but don't rush out into darkness headlong; follow the Light, for He leads us to the work He has for us (see Ephesians 2:10). Be saturated in His brightness and glory—if we live like Jesus, wholeheartedly seeking to know and love our heavenly Father, then we will be like stars shining in the darkness (see Philippians 2:14-16).

Jesus, shed Your glorious light on all parts of my life. Help me move forward
in faith, following where You lead, my path lit by Your wisdom.
Don't let me run ahead of where You would have me. Amen.

*"Therefore, if you are offering your gift at the altar and there remember
that your brother or sister has something against you, leave your gift
there in front of the altar. First go and be reconciled to them;
then come and offer your gift."*
MATTHEW 5:23-24 NIV

C hrist was all about relationships. His very purpose in showing up here on earth was to restore the relationship between God and man. So when our relationships with each other are broken, He wants everything to stop.

When there is tension or hurt feelings or anger with another person, we should forget about all other obligations we may have to Christ or to our church. Forget about anything that isn't necessary. When a relationship is damaged, we should stop everything and do all in our power to mend it.

Then, and only then, can we continue our commitments to God in a way that will please Him. He doesn't really care about how much money we give or how many hours we volunteer organizing the church food pantry, if we can't get along with our family, friends, and acquaintances. He wants us to love each other, encourage each other, and build each other up. When we've hurt the people we're supposed to heal, when we've torn down those we're supposed to build up, Christ's words are clear. Leave everything else. Take care of the relationship. After all, our main purpose in this life is to love.

*Dear Father, help me do my part to mend broken relationships. Give me
wisdom, patience, and love, and provide opportunities for healing. Amen.*

"Therefore let all the house of Israel know assuredly that God has made this Jesus, whom you crucified, both Lord and Christ". . . . "Nor is there salvation in any other, for there is no other name under heaven given among men by which we must be saved."
ACTS 2:36; 4:12 NKJV

Peter told the devout Jews who came from afar for the Pentecost festivities that they crucified the Rescuer sent by God. They listened attentively to Peter as he explained the fulfillment of prophecies by Joel and King David which pointed to Jesus. He was the One anointed by God to sit on David's throne for eternity, and the only One who conquered death to redeem creation. Yet creation killed their Maker, King, and Lord.

The listeners were cut to the heart. "What should we do?" they asked. Peter replied that they must leave behind their sinful lives and be baptized in the name of Jesus. The religious leaders rejected this truth, as foretold in Psalm 118:22. They were, however, impressed by the boldness of Peter and John—uneducated men. The word preached, accompanied by the signs of healing, made it evident that Jesus was present among his followers through the Holy Spirit. Luke writes in Acts 4:14 that the religious leaders were dumbstruck. Tragically, their awe did not lead them to conviction. Nevertheless, God added 3000 believers to the Church that Pentecost day! Will I let my heart be sensitive to sin and come to Jesus for cleansing?

Name above all names, I repent of my sins and cling to You.
Protect me from looking for salvation in anything or anyone other than Jesus.

THE LAW AND GRACE

[Jesus said] "Do not think that I have come to abolish the Law or the Prophets; I have not come to abolish them but to fulfill them."
MATTHEW 5:17 NIV

Welcome to the age of grace, a time where every sin is covered by the sacrifice of Jesus on the cross. This is good news. However, Jesus was clear that His objective was not to offer grace as a way for sinful people to stay sinful.

Jesus warns against setting aside "the least of these commands and teach[ing] others accordingly" (Matthew 5:19 NIV). Jesus recognized the importance of the law. God sent Jesus to be the sacrifice for our sinful conduct. This would indicate God thought the law was important.

If Christians live under grace, why is the law important?

The law remains the conclusive test of our perfection. If we fail in even one area of the law, then we'll never be considered worthy of a personal relationship with God. The law always points to the need for redemption, it reminds us our best intentions will never be enough, and it encourages humility in acknowledging personal sin (see Romans 3:20).

If it were possible to keep the law perfectly, there would be no need for Jesus. Take one look at today's news and you'll understand that the law points to the many imperfections of mankind. Imperfect humanity will always need Jesus.

When I sin, may it be a reminder of the cost of grace. May my obedience allow the transformation needed to become more like You. Let me never view sin—or grace—lightly. Amen.

*My old self has been crucified with Christ. It is no longer I who live,
but Christ lives in me. So I live in this earthly body by trusting in the Son of
God, who loved me and gave himself for me.*
GALATIANS 2:20 NLT

How would it change your life if you acknowledged, every moment, the reality that Christ is *in* you? Would you speak the same? Think the same? Behave the same? When you trusted in the Son of God, you gave up your life, just like He did. The old you was crucified and left on the cross, just like Him. With Him, you have been raised up to new life. Now Christ lives and breathes and moves in you. It's a heavy responsibility, an awesome privilege, to carry our Lord within our bodies. Yet that is our call.

C.S. Lewis said, "It would seem that Our Lord finds our desires not too strong, but too weak. We are half-hearted creatures, fooling about with drink and sex and ambition when infinite joy is offered us, like an ignorant child who wants to go on making mud pies in a slum because he cannot imagine what is meant by the offer of a holiday at the sea. We are far too easily pleased." Could it be that we are settling for far less than what our Lord offers us? Let Christ live in you.

*Jesus, thank You for Your sacrifice on the cross.
Live and move and breathe in me. Amen.*

PERFECT BALANCE

And the Word became flesh.
JOHN 1:14 NKJV

We hear a lot about extremism today. Religious and political extremists are blamed for many of society's ills. It is not thought complimentary to be a radical; in fact, it is considered dangerous. Yet, on the other hand, being a "moderate" is viewed as wimpy and weak.

Jesus was the only person who ever walked the earth not given to extremes. In His personality, teaching, manner, and ministry, He was perfectly balanced.

He was merciful to those who had sinned, yet firm with the arrogant and unrepentant. He gave warnings about hell, yet provided comfort with promises of heaven. He was kind to the children, yet shrewd with the Pharisees wanting to trip Him up in His words. He ministered to the down-and-out, yet took time for the well-to-do.

Following His steps today means that you and I should seek the enabling of the Holy Spirit so that we may avoid extremes in our lives. The Holy Spirit was given for the empowerment of believers; it is impossible to be Christ-like without Him. He will give us the grace to exhibit balance in our daily lives, which is really the fruit of the Spirit: love, joy, peace, patience, gentleness, goodness, faithfulness, meekness, and self-control. These traits that Jesus had in perfect balance will grow more evident in our lives as we surrender more fully to the Spirit's leading.

---

*Dear God, help me guard against extremes in my temperament
and in my relationships and motives. I want to be balanced;
I want to be like Jesus. In His name, amen.*

UNASSUMING

But many who are first will be last, and many who are last will be first.
MATTHEW 19:30 NIV

Perhaps the most baffling, head-scratching characteristic of Christ was simply how unassuming He was. He was the Son of God. He was the Prince of Peace, the Lord of lords. He commanded the winds and seas. Yet, He never assumed the rights that came with His position. He lived the life of a simple carpenter. He chose the company of commoners over the elite. When faced with brutal, false accusations, He responded with quiet dignity instead of demanding His rights.

That quality doesn't fit well with our culture. From toddlerhood, we're trained to excel, to be the best, to make a name for ourselves. We're taught to impress others, seek leadership, and pursue privilege. When we find someone with the rare feature of being unassuming, we're impressed.

If we're to acquire this trait, we must reprogram the hard wires in our minds. We must decide that love is more important than rank and that service is more important than status. The good news is, God created us to begin with, and He can recreate us, if we allow Him to. Where we once sought to be first, He can help us be comfortable with last. Someday, with patience, we'll find our reward is greater than we ever thought possible.

Dear Father, please rewire my brain so I don't feel life is a competition. Help me be as happy with last as with first, as long as You are glorified. Amen.

LIVE FOR OTHERS

And Christ did die for all of us. He died so we would no longer live for
ourselves, but for the one who died and was raised to life for us.
2 Corinthians 5:15 cev

Jesus Christ did the unthinkable. He gave His life so we can live. When we realize the magnitude of His gift, we no longer want to live only for ourselves. We're not forced to care about others, but when our hearts are changed by the Savior, selfishness begins to crumble. We aren't satisfied to merely sit back and enjoy this new life; we want to share Jesus' love with others. We yearn to make a difference. We can't stop ourselves from reaching out!

The Lord will direct everyone who has an open heart and show us what He has planned. If we charge ahead, doing whatever pops into our minds, we may accomplish something, but we'll feel scattered and not be as effective as we should. He gives us the Holy Spirit to speak to us and to put us in contact with the people we should touch. He empowers us to say the words we should, to those He has prepared to hear.

Nothing we do earns brownie points in heaven. We don't share God's love with others because we're compelled by a stern boss. When we know we're doing what He wants, it's as though we've received a huge hug from heaven, just because the Lord loves to make His people happy.

Lord, I praise You for the marvelous gift You gave. Show me
what I can do to demonstrate Your love to others.

CHRIST THE VICTORIOUS

For He must reign until He has put all His enemies under His feet.
The last enemy that will be abolished is death.
1 CORINTHIANS 15:25-26 NASB

Anyone who has ever reigned on earth has had enemies. But no earthly ruler has ever or could ever abolish all his or her opponents. These verses tell us that Christ will do just that. Not a single enemy will remain in His eternal Kingdom. Death is the most formidable foe of all, the one that every single ruler has and will succumb to. However, Christ has already conquered death when He rose from the grave. One day in the future He will destroy it completely. One day you will dwell in a Kingdom with no fear, no threats, and no death. That is something toward which you can look forward.

When you are feeling discouraged, don't forget—you serve a victorious Lord. With a limited earthly perspective, the future may look dim. Yet you know the ending. The battle has already been fought. The victory has been secured. As you wait for the fruition of that Kingdom when Christ comes again, never lose sight of who is on the throne.

Lord, You are victorious. Help me never lose sight of that. It is so easy to become discouraged when looking around at what is happening in the world. May I always remember that these enemies are only transitory, and all, including death, will one day bow the knee to You.

PURSUE HIM, NOT PERFECTION

"Be perfect, therefore, as your heavenly Father is perfect."
MATTHEW 5:48 NIV

Every time Monica looked around her house, which was old and filled with hand-me-down furniture, she got depressed. When she looked at magazine covers at her local supermarket—calling her to "lose weight, get fit, get organized, and save money"—she felt like a failure. Surfing Pinterest or Facebook made things even worse.

Do you relate? Are you harder on yourself than you should be? God is calling us to a different standard than the one our culture sets for us. We don't need to have thin thighs, gorgeous hair, an organized walk-in pantry, or closets that make Martha Stewart jealous.

He is jealous for our time and attention. He wants us to pursue Him, not perfection. Did you know that in the verse above, the word perfect can also be translated as mature?

When Jesus said in John 10:10 (NIV), "I have come that they may have life, and have it to the full," He wasn't talking about a day planner jammed-packed with activities, or a schedule crammed with "to do's." Christ was speaking about a life of purpose, contentment, and peace. We can experience abundant life daily if we get off the hamster wheel of perfectionism, recognize our limits, and nestle close to Jesus. When we remember that He loved us enough to die for us, we can see ourselves as He does. We can accept God's mercy, and impart that mercy to the imperfect people around us.

Jesus, forgive me for pursuing the world's ideas of perfection, instead of resting in the perfection You have already imparted to me through faith.

JESUS HEALED ALL DISEASES

People brought all their sick to him and begged him to let the sick just touch
the edge of his cloak, and all who touched him were healed.
MATTHEW 14:35–36 NIV

"Your daughter's disease is incurable," the doctor told Marnie. The girl was one out of 30,000 with igA immune deficiency. The fragile three-year-old, Sarah, was at high risk for illness, including polio. With ears so blocked with infection and mucus, the toddler was nearly deaf. She didn't talk.

One Christmas, Marnie took her four children to the mall to see Santa. Andrew climbed on Santa's lap with his request, "Please fix my sister's blood. She's so sick."

Santa replied, "Andrew, I'm a Christian and I believe that God can answer your prayers." He waved Marnie and his real-life Mrs. Santa over and the three prayed together right there.

Over time, Sarah's infections began to disappear. The doctor verified the change in her blood. It was normal!

The child grew, learned, and flourished. Recently, Sarah graduated from college with honors.

Jesus healed the crippled and ill of *all* diseases, but power comes in asking and believing. To the woman who bled for twelve years, He said, "Daughter, your faith has healed you" [Mark 5:34 NIV]. To a blind man, He said, "Receive your sight; your faith has healed you" [Luke 18:42 NIV]. To the centurion whose servant was sick and Jesus healed him without being there, He said. "I tell you, I have not found such great faith, even in Israel" [Luke 7:9 NIV].

Lord, I pray believing that You can still do miracles today.

OUR WAY OF ESCAPE

*For we do not have a high priest who is unable to sympathize
with our weaknesses, but one who in every respect
has been tempted as we are, yet without sin.*
HEBREWS 4:15 ESV

Daily, the pleasures of sin tempt us to yield our body parts to evil choices. For example, we give our minds to wrong thoughts, our appetites to harmful eating, our tongues to sinful speaking and tone of voice, our eyes to overindulgence in screen time, our sex drives to immoral actions, and so on. When waves of temptation threaten us, how can we resist getting caught in the undertow? The first step is to realize the threat and acknowledge our weakness. Then ask Jesus for help. When we see the wave coming, if we call on Jesus, He will help us turn our backs and endure, usually by saying no and fleeing from the situation. No temptation exceeds our ability to escape (see 1 Corinthians 10:13).

Because Jesus experienced the same tests we do, He is our sympathetic High Priest and Helper. How did Jesus respond to temptation and trials? Hebrews 5:7–8 says He prayed (with loud cries and tears), and He let suffering teach Him to obey. Because He suffered being tempted, He is able to help us when we are tempted (see Hebrews 2:18).

*Lord Jesus, I call on You to help me resist temptation and say no to sin.
My spirit is willing, but my flesh is weak. I need conscious dependence
on You for power to overcome the sins that so easily entangle me.
All I can say is, help me, Jesus. Amen.*

PEACEMAKERS

For in him all the fullness of God was pleased to dwell,
and through him to reconcile to himself all things, whether on earth
or in heaven, making peace by the blood of his cross.
COLOSSIANS 1:19–20 ESV

Turn on the news. The world is full of strife—nations fighting nations and families breaking apart. In the midst of it all, our hope is in Jesus, the Prince of Peace. Jesus made peace between us and the Father by pouring out His own life for us. Before, we were enemies and strangers to God, but now through Jesus we are reconciled and forgiven.

As His followers, Jesus calls us to be peacemakers, to encourage and nurture peace in our families and neighborhoods, in our nation and world. We won't be able to wipe away all of humanity's problems, but we place our faith in Jesus—who promises to "make all things new" and to "reconcile to Himself all things"—and continue to follow His commands (Revelations 21:5, Colossians 1:20 ESV).

Peacemaking isn't easy. It requires asking for forgiveness and granting forgiveness. It means facing and addressing the injustices we see. We pursue peace in Jesus' strength and by His example. Even as He hung dying, the perfect Peacemaker forgave His enemies!

Pursuing peace will cost you your energy, prayers, and courage. Remember that Christ used His most precious currency to purchase the greatest peace for us, and He gave it freely.

Jesus, teach me to pursue peace. I want to seek reconciliation
and forgive as You forgive. In the face of hostility, help me
put my trust in Your eternal peacemaking. Amen.

[We] know that a person is not justified by the works of the law,
but by faith in Jesus Christ. So we, too, have put our faith in Christ Jesus
that we may be justified by faith in Christ and not by the works of the law,
because by the works of the law no one will be justified.
GALATIANS 2:16 NIV

Can the Good News that we are saved through faith in Jesus be any clearer than in this verse? No one becomes perfect by trying to obey the laws of God—it's just not possible. No matter how nice a person may be, or how hard he might try to please God with good works, it's not going to happen. Why? It only takes one mistake to keep us from perfection. There can't be any sin in heaven.

That's why it's such a privilege to depend on Jesus. He is God. He came in the shape of a human, but there was no sin in Him, so He is qualified to take on the sin of the rest of the world. That sin separates us from God, but Jesus bridged that gap and ushers us into the presence of our heavenly Father. Faith in Him erases our mistakes and imperfections.

We'd all be totally lost if the best we could do was the best we could do, because it isn't enough. We rejoice in what the Lord Jesus has done for us.

Precious Lord Jesus, there are no words to describe the amazing,
awesome love You pour out on us. All we can do is praise You.

PERMANENT SALVATION

But Jesus, on the other hand, because He continues forever,
holds His priesthood permanently. Therefore He is able also to save
forever those who draw near to God through Him,
since He always lives to make intercession for them.
HEBREWS 7:24-25 NASB

Before Christ, every priest was not able to continue in their role because eventually they would die. No one could put their faith in an earthly priest. Since death could not hold Christ, He remains a Priest and Mediator for us. He will hold this office permanently because He continues forever and will never change. When you put your faith in God through Christ, you can be fully confident that nothing can take away your salvation. Christ has saved you through His work on the cross. This salvation is permanent because He will always be the One who intercedes for you.

The responsibility for your salvation and status before God doesn't switch from person to person. It is not reliant on whether or not you have kept the law and performed the correct sacrifices. Your salvation rests solely in Christ's hands. He will not let it go. You are forever in the care of your heavenly Priest who has already made the ultimate sacrifice on your behalf.

Lord, I am thankful that my salvation is permanent because You are my Priest
and Intercessor forever. Because of this, I can continually draw
near to You in confidence, knowing that You intercede
for me like You always have and always will.

ANOINTED ONE

Then He turned to the woman and said to Simon, "Do you see this woman?
I entered your house; you gave Me no water for my feet,
but she has washed My feet with her tears and wiped them
with the hair of her head."
LUKE 7:44 NKJV

What a contrast between Simon the Pharisee and the sinful woman who wept at Jesus' feet! Simon's interest in Jesus was intellectual, but the Son of God saw the contrite heart and the deep love in the woman. God's grace through Jesus was previously revealed to her in some way. In response, she sought out Jesus, knowingly subjected herself to scorn by entering the house of a religious leader, and wept tears of repentance at the feet of Jesus. Using her hair, "a woman's crowning glory," she wiped Jesus' feet and kissed them, so submitting to His authority. Her most costly material possession, expensive oil in a jar of precious stone (alabaster), was spilled to anoint Jesus, simultaneously recognizing Him as King and foreshadowing His imminent death by preparing his body for burial. Simon did none of these acts of adoration. Instead he judged Jesus for accepting the touch of the sinful woman and for granting her forgiveness. Simon tragically did not see his own sin. He thought he needed little forgiveness, so he loved little. Yet this woman, Jesus said, loved much. How could she do otherwise with such a loving King before her?

King of kings, draw me to Your feet so I may recognize Your great forgiveness
toward me and that judgment belongs to You alone.
I love You Lord because You first loved.

*"Where you go I will go, and where you stay I will stay.
Your people will be my people and your God my God."*
RUTH 1:16 NIV

Like our Savior, Ruth was full of compassion, character, and courage. After her husband died, this Moabite woman left everything to follow her mother-in-law, Naomi, and care for her. Women in biblical times were seen as second-class citizens and property of men. Ruth knew that Naomi would be better off with someone younger to look after her. Incredibly, the covenant-making words she said to Naomi are still used in wedding ceremonies. Imagine being that devoted to your mother-in-law!

Not only was Ruth compassionate, but she had character. She gleaned in the fields, regardless of the risk to her safety and reputation. She also trusted Boaz, whom she had heard was a man of integrity. She was determined to creatively and bravely find a "kinsman-redeemer" for herself and Naomi.

Ruth also had courage. She lay at the foot of Boaz's bed as Naomi had instructed, even though she could have been sent away and disgraced for such an act. Yet she trusted Naomi and Boaz, and—more than that—she trusted God to provide for her. Little did she know that God would place her in the line of the Savior of the world!

God rewarded her faithfulness, just as He rewards us when we show courage, compassion, and character. God is pleased, and He gives us more opportunities to act like our Redeemer.

*Father, thank You for giving me the examples of Ruth—and Jesus—
in the scriptures. May I be more like them every day.*

"And when you pray, do not be like the hypocrites, for they love to pray standing in the synagogues and on the street corners to be seen by others. Truly I tell you, they have received their reward in full."
MATTHEW 6:5 NIV

The Lord's Prayer teaches us how to pray. How about some prayer attitudes to avoid?

We are never forbidden to pray in front of others, and we should never stop joining others in prayer. What exactly are we to avoid in order to gain a refined prayer life?

Jesus doesn't want "prayer hypocrites." These are individuals who want people to notice them more for praying than for remembering other instances of a life that is less God honoring. The primary reward for such prayers is the distracted attention of people listening to a conversation in which they really aren't taking part.

The second takeaway from the verse above is implied. We're confronted with the motivation for the hypocritical prayer delivery—pride. If you are really talking to God, then your prayer should be directed to Him and not used as an audible proclamation to others that you are spiritually superior. Hypocrisy and pride have no place in a prayer to the God who knows the real you. Be humble. Be authentic. Pray.

May I always work to be genuine in my prayers. Let me be concerned with really communicating my heart to You, and then willingly seeking to hear You through what You've written in the Bible. Let me be more interested in my relationship with You than what others think about my relationship with You. Amen.

*"Do not store up for yourselves treasures on earth where moth
and rust destroy and where thieves break in and steal. But store up
for yourselves treasures in heaven, where moth and rust do not destroy. . .
For where your treasure is, there you heart will be also."*
MATTHEW 6:19–21 NIV

G randma sure left a lot of stuff behind," Janie noticed as she cleaned
the pantry. When Janie opened a can of clams, black liquid oozed
out. She looked for the expiration date. "This food is decades out of date!"

"I'll say," Van commented, "She was so worried about not being
able to get groceries when the millennium came, she stocked the entire
attic with canned food. It's no good now. This could have helped so many
people!"

Later, when tackling the closets, Janie found many clothes with
price tags on them—never worn. A relative explained that Grandma had
ordered them by phone when she was too sick to get out of bed.

Grandma had invested her wealth in things, not others.

Jesus had much to say about money, collecting things, and attitude.
He himself had no earthly possessions.

When accumulating things, what is our motivation? Do we need this?
Does someone else? Jesus tells the truth: possessions on earth are
subject to wear, destruction, or theft. Consider your attitude as you invest
in possessions, time, and money.

---

*Lord, I ask that You mentor me often on how to build
the treasures of heaven on earth.*

MOVE

Go to the people of all nations and make them my disciples.
Baptize them in the name of the Father, the Son, and the Holy Spirit,
and teach them to do everything I have told you.
I will be with you always, even until the end of the world.
MATTHEW 28:19-20 CEV

Go. *Make. Baptize. Teach.* When Jesus said good-bye to His disciples, He left them with action words. Of course, He knew it would be difficult. He knew they would doubt, would question, and would have fear. He anticipates their concern and reminds them of His promise to stay with them, and us, no matter what happens. Even until the end of the world.

There is *nothing* you will face in this world without Jesus at your side. Let this knowledge propel and compel you to share the Good News with others. Allow these words to move you forward, and signify eager expectancy as you follow His charge.

Lord, thank You for the Good News of the Gospel. Thank You for the action it compels in me. Help me boldly proclaim Your name to all I meet, and thank You for Your promise that You are with me until the end. Amen.

ROCK-SOLID FAITH

*"Behold, I lay in Zion a chief cornerstone, elect, precious,
and he who believes on Him will by no means be put to shame."
Therefore, to you who believe, He is precious.*
1 PETER 2:6-7 NKJV

One thing we tend to abound in is worry. Worry reflects fear instead of faith. Yes, life is filled with fearsome things, not only involving us and our loved ones, but daily news makes us want to cocoon ourselves, if possible. However, with Jesus as our Rock, we are safe.

The land of Israel is covered with rocks. Homes and businesses and streets are built with them. Israel even exports rocks to other countries. So when 1 Corinthians 10:4 says the rock that gave the Israelites water in the wilderness was the spiritual Rock, Christ, they knew the value of a rock. Do we? If Jesus is our Cornerstone, our foundation is secure. If Jesus is precious to us, we will not worry or fear, but will lay all our problems on Him. Various psalms reveal the Lord as our Redeemer and Rock of Salvation, Fortress and Rock of Refuge, Rock of my Strength, Rock that is higher than I, and the Rock of my habitation to which I can continually come. We can sing with the English hymn writer, "Rock of Ages, cleft for me, let me hide myself in Thee."

---

*Lord Jesus, my flesh and my heart may fail, but You are the Rock
of my heart and my portion forever. You alone are my Rock
and my Salvation, my Stronghold. I shall not be shaken. Amen.*

MOTIVATED BY FORGIVENESS

Then Jesus said, "Father, forgive them."
LUKE 23:34 NKJV

When Jesus was on earth, forgiveness was more than an act of His will; it was the central theme of His life.

Each of us has a life theme—a basic motivation that energizes us and guides our decisions and actions. For some, it is an ability they possess; for others it is a long-held passion—a gift of creativity or a desire to alleviate suffering or even a longing to get revenge. For Jesus, it was the redemption of mankind: to draw sinful man and holy God together through His work on the Cross. That meant forgiving.

Jesus came to forgive. He often spoke words of forgiveness to those with whom He interacted. He spoke them to the paralyzed man lowered through a roof by four friends; He said them to a woman caught in adultery and thrown at His feet; and He said them about the soldiers who were driving spikes through His hands and feet. He forgave those who were wrong and those who wronged Him.

You and I must do the same. We cannot forgive in the same way God does, but we must pass along the gift of forgiveness to those who wrong us. It must become the core of who we are. It must become a natural response. It should motivate us. It should define us. We should be known as "forgiveness people."

Lord, thank You for forgiving me. Grant me grace to forgive others; let it be my first response to any insult or offense. I ask this in Jesus' name, amen.

JESUS USES WHAT YOU HAVE

His disciples replied, "How are we supposed to find enough food to feed them out here in the wilderness?" Jesus asked, "How much bread do you have?" "Seven loaves," they replied. So Jesus. . .took the seven loaves, thanked God for them, and broke them into pieces. He gave them to his disciples, who distributed the bread to the crowd.
MARK 8:4-6 NLT

Jesus took seven loaves of bread and fed thousands. I believe the result would have been the same if he had two loaves, ten loaves, or two hundred. Jesus didn't care about the amount; He simply used what the disciples gave Him.

You may think: *I don't have a lot to give to God.* I'd like to disagree. You have more than you think. God doesn't need a set amount. All He needs is a gift. Here are three things you can give to Him:

1.   Your time: Invest time in your relationship with God, volunteer at church, or take time to talk to people as God leads you.

2.   Your finances: Whether you have a dollar or a dime, money is a valuable resource that can be invested into God's kingdom.

3.   Your relationships: God has placed each person in your life for a reason. Allow Him to speak through you to that person, refresh you through that relationship, and let that relationship be an example of God's love to others.

What can you give to God today?

Lord, I'm glad I don't need many resources to give You, but I freely give what I do have. In Jesus' name, amen.

*"Heal the sick, raise the dead, cleanse those who have leprosy,
drive out demons. Freely you have received; freely give."*
MATTHEW 10:8 NIV

We all like free stuff, especially when it provides healing for disease, life for the dead, or really great soap. That's what Christ does for us. He offers healing for our broken, diseased, sin-scarred lives. He raises our dead spirits so we feel alive again. He drives out bad influences and gives us a clean start. He does all this at no cost to us; He paid the bill for the entire caboodle.

While His generosity doesn't hinge on our actions, He does make this request: to the best of our ability, He wants us to give to others as He's given to us.

Can we heal the sick? No. Only God can do that. However, we can certainly care for them, make them a pot of soup, visit them, send cards, or call them on the phone. Can we raise the dead? Of course we can't. Yet we can breathe new life into a person's spirit with a smile and a kind word. We can't cleanse people from sin or even from leprosy, but we can help cleanse a soul by offering forgiveness, even when it seems undeserved. None of us deserves forgiveness, yet God offers it freely.

As we imitate Christ, we must imitate His grace and generosity with the people He's placed in our lives. We'll find any sacrifice will be repaid many times over, through the blessings we'll receive in our own lives.

---

*Dear Father, help me be generous with love,
compassion, and forgiveness. Amen.*

Since therefore the children share in flesh and blood, he himself likewise partook of the same things, that through death he might destroy the one who has the power of death, that is, the devil, and deliver all those who through fear of death were subject to lifelong slavery.
HEBREWS 2:14-15 ESV

Give praise to the Resurrected Lord! Through Jesus, death is not an ending, but a door to a new life with God. Even so, death can still be frightening to believers, but our gentle Savior can sympathize with us; He understands what it feels like to die. He won't let us walk through "the valley of the shadow of death" alone.

Knowing that our eternal lives are secure in Christ puts our earthly lives into perspective. Everyone worries that they're not doing enough or experiencing enough of this life on earth. They might find themselves anxiously trying to hold back death's arrival by frantically "seizing the day." While we should cherish the time God gave us to spend in His creation, we don't have to worry about this life's experiences being "incomplete." There is still so much life to be lived with Christ in heaven! Jesus' presence and generous love will make up for anything we may have missed on earth, and He will heal the regrets in our hearts. For the present or the future, we can rest in Jesus' promise of abundant life (see John 10:10).

Lord Jesus, death and eternity still feel like unknowns. I am thankful that Your salvation gives me peace for what's to come! Please help me live fearlessly for You now. Amen.

FREED FROM FEAR

Therefore, since the children share in flesh and blood, He Himself likewise also partook of the same, that through death He might render powerless him who had the power of death, that is, the devil, and might free those who through fear of death were subject to slavery all their lives.
HEBREWS 2:14-15 NASB

C hrist became one of us in order to die, conquer the devil, and free us from fear. These verses may seem fairly straightforward, but the truths they contain cannot be taken for granted. Christ has made the devil powerless. Satan is defeated. Therefore, don't listen to the lies he tries to speak into your life and don't give into the fear that he tries to inflict. Remember that he is powerless because his ultimate weapon, death, could not hold Christ captive.

Because Christ conquered death and the devil, you no longer have to live enslaved to fear. He selflessly gave Himself up for your freedom. Live in the confidence that nothing can hold you forever, except the love of Christ. Rejoice, knowing that the battle against fear and death has been fought and has been won by your Savior.

Lord, I no longer live in fear of death or the devil because You have made both powerless. I know that only You have power over me. Since you gave Yourself up on my behalf, I am confident that in Your power You will love and care for me in this life, through death, and forever after.

"Blessed are the poor in spirit. . .Blessed are those who mourn. . .Blessed are the meek. . .Blessed are those who hunger and thirst after righteousness. . .Blessed are the merciful. . .Blessed are the pure in heart. . .Blessed are the peacemakers. . .Blessed are those who are persecuted for righteousness' sake, for theirs is the kingdom of heaven."

MATTHEW 5:1-10 NKJV

Jesus teaches the character traits that God intends for His people. The contrite and brokenhearted over sin will receive the Kingdom of God as they look to their victory in Christ. God's people must mourn over sinful hearts, after which Jesus is able to provide the comfort of redemption. Humbleness and gentleness, like Jesus, are also required. Haughtiness and pride reveal a lack of trust in God and do not bring co-inheritance of earth with Christ.

His people must desire God above all things, and Jesus will fill this hunger and thirst. They need to forgive just as Jesus did so that they may find mercy. Their hearts must be pure, cleansed by Jesus, kept from falsehood, with God as their heart's treasure; then they will see God at work. They must be ambassadors of Jesus, sharing the news that Jesus brings reconciliation with God so His people become sons of God, partaking in Christ's work. Finally, they will be persecuted because Jesus, the Master, was also hated. However, by suffering with Jesus, they will be glorified together and will share in the beautiful fellowship of God's kingdom in their hearts on earth and with resurrected bodies in heaven.

Blessed One, I am thankful that Jesus fulfills all these characteristics, and that through the Spirit's work, I can be part of the Kingdom.

NEVER ABANDONED

We are hard pressed on every side, but not crushed; perplexed,
but not in despair; persecuted, but not abandoned; struck down,
but not destroyed. We always carry around in our body the death of Jesus,
so that the life of Jesus may also be revealed in our body.
2 CORINTHIANS 4:8-10 NIV

Have you felt abandoned or ignored by God? Often, we transfer our anger and feelings of betrayal (about a person who wounded us) onto the God who hurts with us. Rest assured that God has not left you alone. He may be silent, and you may not feel His presence, but He is with you. Trust the truth of the Word, even when your emotions say something different. Emotions can't be trusted, but God can. His promises hold, whether or not we feel we can hold on.

Remember, Satan wants you to give up. He doesn't want you to be victorious, because he knows how much you can do for God—and how much God can do in you—if your wounds are healed.

Not only that—the God who loved you so much that He gave His only son to die on the cross—is FOR you. He wants your heart's restoration more than you do. Do you believe that? Whatever you've done, whatever you've been through, He is still the same: perfectly forgiving, perfectly faithful, perfectly compassionate.

Lean into that. . .let the truth soak into the driest parts of your soul. . . and be encouraged.

Reveal Your life-giving truths to me, Holy One. Though I am hard-pressed
and perplexed, I trust that You are for me and not against me.

"No one can serve two masters. Either you will hate the one and love the other, or you will be devoted to the one and despise the other. You cannot serve both God and money."
MATTHEW 6:24 NIV

Imagine President George Washington being loyal to both the United States *and* England. If that sounds ridiculous, it should. To try to envision a scenario where Washington could be loyal to both sides defies rational consideration. What about a quarterback being loyal to two different teams? These are pictures of what it's like for us to say we serve God while demonstrating a loyalty to wealth. The two don't mix well.

For clarity, it should be understood that Jesus isn't against wealth, but against the *serving* of wealth. When you *have* wealth and *serve* God, you'll use wealth as a tool to continue the work of God. When you *have* God and *serve* wealth, you'll be more interested in finding ways to enhance your relationship with wealth while taking God's love and grace for granted.

We'll always be devoted to that with which we spend the most time and attention. We'll be mastered by the promises we believe to be most true. Money promises immediacy. God promises eternity. We all must choose who we will serve.

It's easy for me to see the benefit of having all my needs and wants met right here—right now. I can develop a relationship with money that leaves my relationship with You cold. Let me grasp an eternal perspective on whom I choose to serve. May I desire to serve You well. Amen.

GRAB MY STAFF AND FOLLOW

"I am the good shepherd; I know my sheep and my sheep know me—
just as the Father knows me and I know the Father—and I lay down
my life for the sheep."
JOHN 10:14–15 NIV

When everyone headed to church for services, the Native American parents guided their toddler into the building. Though many might carry a youngster her size, the dad simply held a staff behind him. His daughter grasped it tightly and followed willingly.

Others might have used a child leash and harness. The toddler might be unwillingly led into the class.

In this case, the girl was gently guided by her father as she held onto the staff. Her father knew the way. He would keep her from danger. He was willing to do whatever had to be done to make sure she was safe.

That is the way it is with a relationship with God. He invites us to accept him, doesn't force us, and after we willingly make a decision, he leads us gently. Just as these parents kept their daughter safe, Jesus knows what it takes for us to be safe in His care.

"I am the good shepherd." Jesus described and compared the better herdsman as one who genuinely cares for his sheep, instead of being tended by a hired hand.

Where could we find such love? No other place than with Jesus, the Good Shepherd. Grab his staff and follow.

Thank You, Jesus, for Your love, care, and protection. Thanks for laying Your life down for me so that I may have an eternal one with You.

But God demonstrates his own love for us in this:
While we were still sinners, Christ died for us.
ROMANS 5:8 NIV

There's something about a baby, the purity, the sweetness, the innocence, that begs to be cuddled and loved. As they gaze into our eyes, we can't help but fall in love with them. A screaming toddler on the other hand, is not quite so loveable. God clearly did things in the right order—he allows us to fall in love with our babies while they are helpless and pure. By the time their sinful nature becomes apparent, throughout those terrible twos and dismal threes, we've already fallen hopelessly in love. This allows us to tolerate their shenanigans and discipline them in love instead of anger. Like the screaming toddler, God loves us at our worst, even our tantrum-throwing-screaming-I-want-what-I-want-and-I-want-it-now selves. He is hopelessly in love with us and allowed His Son to die for us when we were at our very worst!

Anyone can love a helpless baby. It takes the grace and the perfection of God to love us at our worst. Praise Him for His indescribable gift.

Father, what a joy and comfort it is to know that You love me
at my worst. Thank You for dying for me while I was still a sinner,
so unworthy of Your love. Amen.

*If anyone loves the world, the love of the Father is not in him. For all that
is in the world—the lust of the flesh, the lust of the eyes,
and the pride of life—is not of the Father but is of the world.*
1 JOHN 2:15–16 NKJV

How can we resist temptation? Consider what Jesus did—He quoted scripture. (See Matthew 4:1–11 and Luke 4:1–13.) Satan tried to get Jesus to yield to the lust of the flesh by performing a self-serving miracle to satisfy His hunger. "It is written. . ." Jesus answered. Satan also appealed to the lust of the eyes by offering Him all the kingdoms of the world to possess early (thus bypassing crucifixion). Again Jesus said, "It is written. . ." The pride of life was a third temptation Jesus faced. Satan even quoted scripture, twisting it to entice Jesus to misuse His power in order to promote Himself. For the third time, Jesus quoted from Deuteronomy and said, "Away with you, Satan!" (Matthew 4:10 NKJV).

We experience temptations in these same areas—*desire to do* things we shouldn't (passions), *desire to have* (possessions), and *desire to be* more important (pride). Do we have scriptures as our defense? Find verses to fight your greatest areas of weakness. Memorize them and draw them like a sword when tempted by the world, the flesh, and the devil.

*Lord Jesus, I want to love You more than anything in the world so I can resist
temptations in the areas of immorality and gluttony, love of money,
and self-promotion. Help me strengthen myself through Your word. Amen.*

EVERYDAY GRATEFULNESS

And He took the seven loaves and the fish and gave thanks.
MATTHEW 15:36 NKJV

Think of a toddler's pudgy fingers folded in prayer at the table; imagine aged, veined hands clasped over a plate—images of thankfulness. Now, picture Jesus, God in the flesh, holding up some bread and fish and giving thanks. It's amazing, isn't it? The Creator of everything was grateful for food.

It's true that Jesus was giving us a model to follow. He was teaching us to be thankful and to give thanks to God for every gift we receive, including our daily meals. It must also be that, as the perfect Man, He was personally grateful as well. Since gratefulness to God is an attribute that a perfect person would exhibit, Jesus was not only showing us how to be grateful, He was sincerely grateful Himself.

Giving thanks over one's food used to be much more common. Many families today do not pause to thank the Giver for the food they are eating. Either they are not grateful or they don't know the One to whom they owe their thanks.

As God's dear children and followers of Christ, we must express our gratefulness for every good thing we are given, commonplace or not, convenient or not. The Father gives us these things to enjoy and giving thanks to Him becomes a channel of grace in our lives as we acknowledge His provision.

---

*O God, thank You for blessing my life in great ways and in small ways.
I know You are the Source of all good things. Amen.*

Jesus responded, "Why are you afraid? You have so little faith!"
Then he got up and rebuked the wind and waves, and suddenly there
was a great calm. The disciples were amazed. "Who is this man?"
they asked. "Even the winds and waves obey him!"
MATTHEW 8:26-27 NLT

D o you know why the disciples had little faith at that moment? This wasn't the first time they had seen a miracle. They had seen Jesus do the miraculous time and again—and yet they couldn't see past the storm they faced. Their minds couldn't comprehend that Jesus' power could do anything about it—or maybe they just didn't remember.

The Sunday night after my grandpa passed away, I found myself in the disciples' position. I reflected on how God made sure everyone was able to talk to Grandpa before he passed, and the right people were at his side when he went to heaven.

Five minutes after reflecting on how perfect God's timing had been, I started to worry about the week ahead. How would I ever find time to do everything? Then I caught myself. It was as though Jesus was saying to my heart, "You have so little faith! Look at what I just did. Won't I do it again?"

As we encounter new experiences, we won't know how the Lord will provide or where He will show up, but we can always remember: if He did it for us once, He can do it again.

Lord Jesus, help me remember that every experience with You is proof
of what You can and will do for me. I trust You with my future.

THE POWER TO DO GOOD

Do not withhold good from those to whom it is due,
when it is in your power to act.
PROVERBS 3:27 NIV

Christ was generous with his time and actions. No matter what He was doing or how busy He was, when someone approached Him with a need, He met that need if He could. Since He was the Son of God, He always could.

We may not have the same instantaneous, miraculous healing powers Christ had, but we can make the choice to help people when we're able. If we're not capable of completely meeting their need, we can at least do what we can.

The above verse doesn't only refer to meeting needs. It says, "Don't withhold good from those to whom it is due." That means offering praise for a job well-done. It means doing things, big and small, to bring joy to others' hearts. It means making people smile when it's in our power to do so.

Christ came so our joy could be complete. As imitators of Christ, we should do our best to bring gladness to the people around us. In so doing, we'll also bring joy to our own hearts, as we feel the satisfaction of making our world a more pleasant, love-filled place.

Dear Father, help me recognize when I can help others by meeting a need,
offering an encouraging word, or sharing a smile. I want to bring good to the
people around me whenever it's in my power to do so. Amen.

For we do not have a high priest who cannot sympathize with our weaknesses, but One who has been tempted in all things as we are, yet without sin. Therefore let us draw near with confidence to the throne of grace, so that we may receive mercy and find grace to help in time of need.
HEBREWS 4:15-16 NASB

This verse starts out with a powerful statement—Christ can sympathize with your weaknesses. He is not some heavenly being who looks down on you with pity, unable to understand why you're struggling. Instead, He humbled Himself in order to walk in your shoes. He experienced what you experience through life on this earth. He was tempted, but did not sin. He struggled, but overcame.

How does Christ's ability to sympathize with you affect your life? It means that you can draw near with confidence to the throne of grace. No longer do God's people need to come to Him timidly and afraid of standing before His holiness. Instead, you can come boldly to the Father, knowing that Christ is the High Priest offering up your prayers for you. So go before the throne to "receive mercy and find grace to help in time of need." This mercy and grace is being offered to you freely because Christ has already paid for it. Ask for it confidently.

Lord, thank You that You understand what I'm going through. I boldly ask for the grace and mercy I need today.

JUDGMENT AND SHAME

"Do not judge, or you too will be judged. For in the same way
you judge others, you will be judged, and with the measure you use,
it will be measured to you."
MATTHEW 7:1-2 NIV

In *The Gifts of Imperfection*, shame researcher Brené Brown suggests that we judge people most harshly on issues that we feel shame about ourselves. For example, a man who feels it's shameful to be overweight might exercise constantly so he'll look better than "those other guys" at the gym. He's the resident health expert, lecturing his children on their snacks and silently judging his coworkers' lunches. Drawing attention to others' imperfections helps him process (and hide) his shame.

Jesus warns us that we will be judged by whatever standard we use to judge others. This doesn't mean we should fix our problems so we can confidently confront others about their shortcomings. Jesus calls us to approach each other with the same grace He's given us. How can we look judgmentally at our neighbors' struggles when we realize His kindness— our Savior who knows our every ugly struggle and yet looks at us lovingly?

Think about where you are hard on yourself and on others. What do you say to yourself when you feel ashamed? Would Jesus say those things, or would He accept you as you are? Practice speaking His comforting words to your heart and seeing others through His grace-filled gaze.

Jesus, forgive me for when I have judged others instead of being loving.
Thank You for Your grace toward me, and help me see people
the way You see them. Amen.

A GOD FOR GEORGE, THE TORTOISE, AND FOR YOU

Do not be anxious about anything, but in everything by prayer and petition,
with thanksgiving, present your requests to God.
PHILIPPIANS 4:6 NIV

There you are, George!" the nursery worker cried as he lifted the tortoise onto a garden cart. "It's time to go in where it is warm. Catch some Z's, watch TV, or whatever you want to do inside."

All day, the hard-shelled reptile had the run of the nursery and enjoyed a lawn created especially for his meals. Many a delighted customer found the nursery mascot—George—under the shade and foliage of plants.

When the mountain temperatures dipped low, George needed shelter or he would die. So it was the nursery staff's job to bring George inside.

Just as George needed the nursery staff, we need God. Though he doesn't need us any more than the nursery needed a tortoise, God is full of love and generosity. He meets our needs. He watches over us better than the nursery staff cares for George. How do we access God's storehouse?

Pray. Jesus taught his followers to pray, "And when you pray, do not keep on babbling like pagans, for they think they will be heard because of their many words. Do not be like them, for your Father knows what you need before you ask him" [Matthew 6:7–8 NIV].

Just pray and ask. God will always answer.

Thank You, Jesus, for Your generosity in our daily life.
It is an example to us of love in action.

*When Jesus heard this, he was amazed at him, and. . .he said, "I tell you,
I have not found such great faith even in Israel."*
LUKE 7:9 NIV

It seems that people cannot be neutral when it comes to Jesus. We
either think He couldn't possibly be the only way to God—there must be
a catch. Or we put all our faith in Him, trusting Him for this life and the
next.

These two responses had a way of astonishing Jesus. The Gospels
record two times when Jesus marveled at something. In Mark 6:6 He
marveled at the unbelief of the people in His hometown of Nazareth. They
said Jesus was an ordinary person, "the carpenter's son." Even though
He taught with wisdom and did miracles and healed, many of the people
refused to believe He was the Messiah.

The second time is Luke 7:9 when Jesus marveled at the opposite
response. A Roman centurion had sent messengers because the
centurion considered himself unworthy to see Christ in person. His
request was for Jesus to say a word and heal his servant. Jesus was
amazed at the centurion's faith. (Perhaps He also was pleased with the
centurion's concern for the life of a "mere" servant.)

This leads us to wonder how Jesus views our faith. Would He
commend us for trusting Him no matter what, or do we try to second-
guess Him and question His authority over us? The results can be pretty
amazing.

*Lord Jesus, I do not want to be guilty of distrusting You,
but at times my faith is so weak. Help me overcome my unbelief. Amen.*

GOD BLESSES PREPARATION

After that, the Word of GOD came to me: "Zerubbabel started rebuilding this Temple and he will complete it. That will be your confirmation that God-of-the-Angel-Armies sent me to you. Does anyone dare despise this day of small beginnings? They'll change their tune when they see Zerubbabel setting the last stone in place!"
ZECHARIAH 4:8-10 MSG

Jesus knew the power of preparation. He began His earthly ministry at age thirty (see Luke 3:23) and was crucified around three years later. That means only 9 percent of his life was spent actively ministering to people.

What was He doing prior to His earthly ministry? The only record of Jesus' actions prior to age thirty (excluding the story of His birth) comes in Luke 2:41–52. At the age of twelve, Jesus was conversing with religious leaders, listening, and learning. I venture to say that was what He was doing for thirty years. He spent time with His family and friends, growing spiritually just as we do. He was in a phase of preparation.

You may not feel like you're exactly where you want to be in your life, but realize that God is preparing you for your future. He is using every job you take, person you meet, and church service you attend to craft you into the person He created you to be.

Jesus, at any time, You could have propelled Yourself into full-time ministry, but You waited patiently for God's timing while preparing for the future. Help me do the same.

THE MOST MAGNIFICENT GIFT

*In Christ we are set free by the blood of his death,
and so we have forgiveness of sins. How rich is God's grace,
which he has given to us so fully and freely.*
EPHESIANS 1:7-8 NCV

Jesus set the ultimate example of giving. Most of us can't begin to understand how much He loves to give, though the joy we experience when we give may give us a hint. To me, it's more fun to watch others open gifts I've selected for them than to open my own presents at Christmas. I get weepy when I think of those who give enormous gifts—who put their lives in jeopardy for others. I think of those in the military, fire fighters, law enforcement officers, missionaries, and others who give so much. The thought of their unselfish gift leaves me feeling very humble.

The extravagant grace God pours out on us is greater than any other gift. Grace, demonstrated through the blood of Jesus, sets us free from the misery of sin and despair. Without His grace, we would all be desperately, totally lost.

We can't earn His gift of grace. We don't need a degree in theology. We can't ever be worthy of all that God so generously gives. The simple truth is that all we can do is receive. Like a child who eagerly tears into birthday presents, we should have the same eager anticipation to accept His priceless gift.

*Precious Jesus, I can't comprehend the love You have for us,
Your willingness to give Yourself, or Your eagerness for us to receive.
I thank You from the bottom of my heart.*

*"Go therefore and make disciples of all nations, baptizing them
in the name of the Father and the Son and the Holy Spirit,
teaching them to observe all that I have commanded you; and lo,
I am with you always, even to the end of the age." Amen.*
MATTHEW 28:19-20 NKJV

The Great Commission is often quoted to encourage Christian witness; however, the promise after the command holds everything together. Jesus appeared and disappeared various times between his resurrection and the time of his ascension. Dennis Johnson, in his book *The Message of Acts*, wrote that Jesus did this to accustom the disciples to the idea that Jesus is with them even if they do not always see him. On the road to Emmaus Jesus took the two disciples through all the scriptures and opened their minds to understand, just as the Spirit does today. He appeared to Peter to bring forgiveness and restoration. He appeared to Thomas to dispel his doubt. Jesus also appeared to James, Thomas's brother, to prepare James for his future role as leader of the church in Jerusalem.

The commission could not be carried out without the promise that Jesus is always with His followers even if His presence, for the time being, does not take bodily form. Through His presence, in and around them, believers are able to follow His command to go make other followers of Jesus. If we cling to the fulfillment of this promise, we have strength to do as he commanded. We have His strength, and that makes all the difference.

El Olam (God of Eternity), I am thankful that Jesus is with us to the end.

"Do not worry about tomorrow, for tomorrow will worry about itself.
Each day has enough trouble of its own."
MATTHEW 6:34 NIV

Worry is always subject to compound interest. You could borrow trouble from tomorrow and assume that it's possible to prepay the worry fee early, but you'll never effectively manage anything more than what you face in this moment. When you accept tomorrow's worry ahead of schedule, you'll pay twice; today and again tomorrow. This double payment leads to missed opportunities because of the resulting focus on uncontrollable circumstances.

God created flowers and grass. He ensures they grow to possess an incredible beauty. They never worry, yet the beauty of flowers surpasses the splendor of kings.

Jesus told His followers that God knows what each person needs. Worry prevents you from seeing His provision, following His lead, and sharing His love because anxiety rarely focuses on others and refuses to embrace faith.

The remedy for excessive worry is seeking God's righteousness. When focusing on His plans, we find that the rest of life's pursuits gain clarity.

When you think worry is the only remedy for your situation, remember, God has everything under control. Follow Him, trust His direction, and watch faith overcome worry.

When I'm tempted to worry help me look to You. When I feel oppressed
with circumstances I can't understand or control, may I look to the One
who has always existed and is acquainted with the outcome of everything
I've ever faced. Help me remember that no matter what happens,
faith guarantees I never struggle alone. Amen.

AN ANSWER FOR HOPE

Honor Christ and let him be the Lord of your life. Always be ready to give an answer when someone asks you about your hope.
1 Peter 3:15 CEV

As you think about all the things you need to bring with you for your day, do you remember to carry your hope with you? Can others see the light of Jesus in you? We are called to carry ourselves in such a way that people are compelled to ask you about our hope.

Look for ways to demonstrate hope in little and big ways. Offer a joyful perspective, take an extra moment and smile when others would frown. All of these actions quietly shine the light of Jesus. Others will be drawn to this light, and they will ask you about your hope. Be prepared to tell them! Have your answer ready.

Jesus, I honor You by living daily with You as the Lord of my life. Prepare my heart to radiate the light of Your love and draw others to that light. Help me be ready with an answer to point others to You. Amen.

Then He said to them, "Follow Me, and I will make you fishers of men."
MATTHEW 4:19 NKJV

Jesus was not a pessimist or an optimist; He was reality and hope embodied. He continually pointed the way upward, to God.

Think of the record we have of His interaction with others on earth. No one who came in faith to Him left more discouraged, more depressed, or more downtrodden. Rather, those who came to Him left healed and loved.

Human beings are prone to discourage one another; we seem very good at popping others' balloons at the party. We want to have the best story, the best Facebook status, the best children, the best home, etc, and we are not above stomping on someone else to make it happen.

Jesus didn't do that. Though He was the ultimate Person, with more to boast about than anyone, He had a humble attitude and He never put others down so He could shine brighter.

When He found some brothers in a smelly fishing boat, He didn't view them with disdain; He offered them a way up. He offered them a place in ministry, a place to shine for the Kingdom.

You and I can reflect Him as we interact with others at work, at family gatherings, and at church. In these places where everyone clamors for significance, we can find ours by giving others a chance to shine, just like He did.

Dear Lord, give me the grace to help others find a way up.
Thank You that my significance is found in You; help me
let others shine today. In Your name, amen.

GET REAL

Therefore each of you must put off falsehood and speak truthfully to your neighbor, for we are all members of one body.
EPHESIANS 4:25 NIV

W e all know it's wrong to lie. It's one of the basic truths we learn as children. Yet many of us live a lie without actually speaking it. We put only the best pictures on Facebook, we smile at church to project the image of a happy family, and we hide stuff in our closets when someone rings the doorbell. We want others to think we have it all together, so we strive to portray a perfect picture.

While it's not necessary to air our dirty laundry in public, perhaps we need to reevaluate our desires to depict ourselves in a way that's not true. After all, though we may admire those who seem perfect, most of us can't really relate to those people. We are drawn to people who have walked difficult roads, who struggle and strive just like we do. We're attracted to folks who are real.

When we put off falsehood, people are drawn to us. When we take off our masks, others will seek us out, and real relationships are forged. After all, who are we trying to impress? As Christians, we are all on the same team. Our team is stronger, the more we support each other in our weaknesses. That support can only come when we put off falsehood and speak truthfully to one another.

Dear Father, help me portray an honest picture of my walk with You. I want to reflect Your goodness in the midst of my trials. Amen.

THE GREATEST GIFT

For it is by free grace (God's unmerited favor) that you are saved (delivered from judgment and made partakers of Christ's salvation) through [your] faith. And this [salvation] is not of yourselves [of your own doing, it came not through your own striving], but it is the gift of God.
EPHESIANS 2:8 AMP

The Amplified Bible makes this verse so rich by fully developing the words to help us understand what the original Greek meant. We sometimes talk about being saved, but people may not have a clue what that means. We might not really be sure about it ourselves. This scripture tells us we're delivered from judgment and we can take part in Christ's salvation, through faith.

Then Paul, who wrote this as a letter to the church in Ephesus, made it clear that salvation wasn't anything they could accomplish on their own, no matter how hard they tried. It was God's gift two thousand years ago, and nothing has changed about that. God's offer is still the same. The corporate rat race, climbing the social ladder, and Wall Street success are all of no consequence.

The only thing that matters for eternity is a simple decision to trust in the work Christ Jesus already did for us. Just because that decision is simple doesn't mean it's insignificant. It's critical! It means the difference between eternal life with God, or total separation from Him forever. What will you choose?

Our Father in heaven, I thank You for the gift of salvation. I pray that You will pour out the Holy Spirit to show people the simplicity of turning to You.

He shall see the labor of His soul, and be satisfied. By His knowledge My righteous Servant shall justify many, for He shall bear their iniquities.
Isaiah 53:11 NKJV

Intense anguish occurred in the garden of Gethsemane as Jesus fought to obey God's plan. He asked for the cup of wrath to be taken away, for the needed sacrifice to be done some other way. In the end, Jesus' response was always, "Your will be done" (Matthew 26:42 NKJV). As Isaiah prophesied many years before, the Father was satisfied and joyous because He knew how hard the work was for the Son to remain obedient. There were so many temptations to seek an "easier" way, but Jesus knew the truth meant the cross. Through the cross, he brought believers justification before God as Jesus bore their sin once for all time.

Believers today are called to the same kind of dying-to-self obedience as that of the Master. It is never easy because human nature is fallen, and it fights against the things that are good. Jesus told the disciples to be watchful and to pray because the spirit is willing but the flesh is weak. Though seemingly impossible, obedience to God is necessary so that His children can grow in spiritual maturity and be lights in a dark world. Jesus equips his followers with the Holy Spirit to guide them into obedience, which is perfected as they grow in their love of Him.

Yahweh, Your joy is our strength. Help me always bring You joy through my obedience and know the power of your peace.

PERFECT IS AS PERFECT DOES

Therefore you are to be perfect, as your heavenly Father is perfect.
MATTHEW 5:48 NASB

Is this verse daunting to you? Including the rest of the Sermon on the Mount, it has puzzled (and infuriated) many people, including its first listeners. The Pharisees thought they kept the Law pretty well, thanks to their hyperspecific rules. Yet Jesus taught that keeping the Law required more than us fulfilling righteous actions that other people can see. We must also keep the Law in what only the Father can see—our hearts. No matter what our outward actions are, He knows our motives and hidden thoughts, and who we are in secret.

Yet the Sermon on the Mount wasn't meant to shame its hearers into working harder to keep God's Law. Fixing outward behavior doesn't change the heart. Just as a teacher may discover that when he gives his students new rules, their attitudes remain rebellious even as they obey. Jesus preached the Sermon on the Mount to help us realize just how far we are from fulfilling what God's Law requires. When we see how unholy and hopeless we are in light of its demands, Jesus's message of salvation is more than welcome—it's essential!

Where does your imperfection weigh on you? Lay your worries at Jesus' feet. It's He, not you, who accomplished your perfection before God. It is perfectly complete! He will strengthen you by His grace to grow, to love, and follow His ways.

Jesus, I trust that You have made me perfect in God's eyes. Let that peace permeate my heart as I seek to follow Your Word. Amen.

TAKE YOUR TROUBLES TO JESUS

I took my troubles to the LORD; I cried out to him,
and he answered my prayer.
PSALM 120:1 NLT

Nancy stared at the ceiling, tears streaming down her face. Her husband of twenty years had filed for divorce, and today she would meet him—and his lawyer—in a mediation hearing. She couldn't believe her life had turned out this way.

They were both believers, or so she'd thought. Bill had been a good father to their two children—Hannah, fifteen, and Jeff, twelve—up until a few months before he asked for a separation. After his lay-off at work, he turned sullen and moody. He stopped attending church and started drinking. . .and he had an affair with a college sweetheart he'd recently reconnected with online.

Nancy hadn't wanted the divorce and had asked Bill to reconsider. She told him she forgave him and wanted them to be a family again. Yet he'd wanted nothing to do with her.

"Lord, help me," Nancy prayed. "I need your strength today. I can't do this on my own."

As clearly as if someone had spoken out loud, she heard the Lord speak to her spirit: *"You don't have to."*

Nancy sat up, dried her tears, and headed for the shower. She would pray with the kids after breakfast, before dropping them off at school. He would be their Father now, and He would be Nancy's husband.

"Thank you," she prayed. "Thank you."

Jesus, thank You for Your faithfulness. When others betray or disappoint me,
draw near to me and help me avoid becoming bitter.

THE VALUE OF RESPONSE

"What do you think? There was a man who had two sons. He went to the first and said, 'Son, go and work today in the vineyard.' "'I will not,' he answered, but later he changed his mind and went.'"
MATTHEW 21:28–29 NIV

In a perfect world, children would obey the first time, and every time after that, with great enthusiasm. In a perfect world, there would be no reason to doubt, no fear of betrayal, and a firm belief that when someone gives their word, they'll follow through.

We don't live in a perfect world.

Jesus spoke of those who talk as if they follow but hold back when putting feet to their faith. He also spoke of those who indicated no interest in God but ultimately accept the gift of the One who paid the price for forgiveness and eternal life.

His illustration was simple. There were two sons. The first was told to work on the father's behalf. He said he would not, but changed his mind and went to work. The second son was told to do the same thing. He said yes, but didn't follow through.

Today this might be similar to those who have the appearance of committed followers but lack follow through versus those who say they have no interest yet decide to follow. Jesus wants more than promises, He wants committed followers.

I want to go where You lead, say what You've shown in Your word, and engage Your commands with a willing heart. Give me the courage to follow through. Give me a heart that longs to see You lead in my life. Amen.

FILLING THE HOUSE AND THE HEART WITH GOD

"When an impure spirit comes out of a person, it goes through arid places seeking rest and does not find it. Then it says, 'I will return to the house I left.' When it arrives, it finds the house unoccupied, swept clean and put in order. Then it goes and takes with it seven other spirits more wicked than itself, and they go in and live there."
MATTHEW 12:43–45 NIV

M om, listen! It echoes in here!" Robbie cried as the family was ready to shut the door for the last time as they moved to another home.

"Honey, it does! But we'll be able to fill up the next house with our things, your toys, fun, and laughter!"

"Will this house always echo?" Robbie wanted to know.

"Just while it's empty and for sale. Someday another family will fill up this house with their camping gear, kids, toys, and laughter!"

Jesus used similar words to clearly show that cleaning up one's life without filling it up with God leaves lots of room for Satan to enter. It's like a house that has been sitting vacant too long. Instead of being filled up with the happy sounds of a family, it may be vandalized by those with evil intentions.

Filling up your house and heart with God starts with devotionals like these. Fill your house, heart, mind, and soul each day with God. God's word prevents vandalism of your heart, your home, and your family.

Thank You, God, for filling me, my heart, and my home with Your Spirit.

JUDGE NOT

So we have stopped evaluating others from a human point of view. At one time we thought of Christ merely from a human point of view. How differently we know him now! This means that anyone who belongs to Christ has become a new person. The old life is gone; a new life has begun!
2 CORINTHIANS 5:16-17 NLT

Judging others comes far too easily for us. The bedraggled woman on the train—we immediately assume she's made a series of poor decisions. We don't look long enough to see the abuse in her dark past. We see the homeless man who (we assume) chooses to beg instead of working at a real job. In our haste, we fail to look into his eyes to see the quiet desperation that is bound in mental illness. The drug addict, the wanderer. . .we are so prone to judge others through the lens of a human point of view.

However, when we belong to Christ, we become a new person. We have spiritual cataract surgery. Our eyes are no longer blinded by judgment. Instead we are blessed with His corrected vision. When our old life is gone, we are no longer compelled to see others through arrogance and judgment. Ask Him for eyes to see.

*Jesus, give me Your eyes. Help me see others as You do,
rather than through my human frailty. Amen.*

For you have been called for this purpose, since Christ also suffered for you, leaving you an example for you to follow in His steps.
1 PETER 2:21 NASB

How do we put up with a difficult person, especially someone for whom we work? First Peter 2:18–23 encourages us to follow Jesus' example. We should carry out our responsibilities with "all respect" to the boss—even unreasonable ones. They may not deserve it, and we may not feel it, but we can treat them respectfully anyhow. When we suffer unfair treatment and endure it with a clear conscience before God, this pleases Him, and He gives us grace (favor) to be patient and bear it. In fact, we are "called" for the purpose of following in Christ's steps by responding to suffering His way. Jesus did not sin with His mouth. Like Him, we should make no attempt to deceive (in order to get out of a bad situation), to revile (speak evil of another), or to threaten (try to get even). Instead, we should keep entrusting ourselves and our circumstances to God like Jesus did. This does not condone putting up with abusive or criminal behavior from anyone, nor from taking legal action when called for, but it deals with submitting to our God-given authorities and being a gracious employee. When a supervisor irritates us, shows favoritism, or assigns tasks we consider unfair, we should do what Jesus would do.

Lord Jesus, when I suffer wrongfully, please help me control what I say and how I respond, so my attitudes and actions will honor You. Amen.

He humbled Himself and became obedient to the point of death,
even the death of the cross.
PHILIPPIANS 2:8 NKJV

Did you ever think about the fact that Jesus was obedient to His Father in heaven?

It is one of the great mysteries of the Godhead. Jesus, as the second Person of the Trinity, is fully God, yet in His capacity as the Son, He is obedient to the Father. Scripture tells us that the Father sent the Son—a gift of love for His fallen creation. Yet, Jesus, as the sacrificial Lamb, laid down His own life on the cross. He was not forced; He wanted to redeem mankind.

Jesus willingly followed the Father's plan for His life on earth. As He entered into His earthly ministry, He was submissive to His Father, spending time with Him in prayer and asking Him to bless food for the multitudes and thanking Him for hearing His request when He raised Lazarus from the dead.

The ultimate obedience of Jesus was His surrender to His Father's will in the Garden of Gethsemane as He prepared to face the cross. He said, "Not my will, but Yours, be done" (Luke 22:42 NKJV).

As we seek to follow His steps, may you and I willingly obey like He did, whatever the cost may be.

Jesus, thank You for going to the cross for me;
help me obey as willingly and as freely as You did. Amen.

THE MIRACULOUS CAN HAPPEN

Jesus said, "If? There are no 'ifs' among believers. Anything can happen."
MARK 9:23 MSG

When negative news comes, it's easy to assume the worst. *I'll never be able to pay all my bills. . . . They'll never love me again. . . . It's an incurable disease.* Yet, did you know we serve a God who makes the impossible a reality?

Mark 9:23 (NKJV) says, "All things are possible to him who believes." Jesus knew He didn't need to live confined to natural circumstances. For example, in Mark 6:45–52, Jesus sent His disciples across the lake, and He stayed back to pray. When He finished praying and wanted to rejoin His disciples, He didn't borrow a boat or walk around the lake. He decided to travel across the lake by defying natural law and walking on water.

We can operate in this same knowledge: What we see and naturally expect doesn't need to be the end of the road; it can simply be a pathway to the miraculous.

Jesus said in Matthew 17:20 (MSG), "The simple truth is that if you had a mere kernel of faith, a poppy seed, say, you would tell this mountain, 'Move!' and it would move. There is nothing you wouldn't be able to tackle."

The next time bad news comes your way, don't immediately think through all the potential negative outcomes. Instead, think about it from the perspective of faith. Anything can happen. . .including a miracle.

Jesus, show me how to embrace Your miracle-working power.
I want to see Your reality become true in my life.

"Until now you have not asked for anything in my name. Ask and you will receive, and your joy will be complete."
JOHN 16:24 NIV

This concept is perhaps the hardest one for us to grasp. God loves us, and He waits anxiously to give us things that will fill our hearts with joy. He didn't create us for misery and suffering. He created us for His delight and pleasure, and it delights Him to see His children smile.

Not that He spoils us. No, in order to receive His blessings, we must be "blessable." We must be obedient, honoring Him with our thoughts and words and actions. When we live our lives to please Him, He longs to please us.

We still live in a fallen, broken world where bad things happen. People get sick. Relationships fail. Bills pile up. Living for God isn't a fail-proof formula for success and wealth and nonstop laughs. Just as a good parent longs to delight his child, God longs to delight us. When we follow Christ, we can tell Him the desires of our hearts, knowing He cares about us and yearns to deluge us with His love.

Too often, we go to God when we're in crisis. He wants us to do that. Yet He also wants us to ask for things that will thrill our hearts, knowing He is the source of all good things.

Dear Father, thank You for this reminder that I can ask You for anything. You know the desires of my heart. My greatest desire is to honor You and to make You smile. Amen.

CANCELLED DEBT

Having canceled out the certificate of debt consisting of decrees against us,
which was hostile to us; and He has taken it out of the way,
having nailed it to the cross.
COLOSSIANS 2:14 NASB

The imagery in this verse is wonderful. Consider if all your sins were listed on a legal document. Each sin is a decree against you, ruining your reputation and your future prospects. In fact, this document is so hostile that it has sentenced you to death. Now imagine that this legal certificate is taken from you and nailed to the cross on which Jesus hangs. It is covered in His blood and is therefore no longer valid.

This is what Christ did for you as He died on that cross. Next time you feel overwhelmed by the length of your certificate of debt, just remember that it is gone. It is totally invalid. Don't wallow in the guilt and therefore deny the atoning work of Christ. However, don't forget that this certificate existed and was hostile to you. Only when you fully grasp the depth of your sin does the immensity of the sacrifice and grace of Christ come into perspective.

Lord, I am overwhelmed by Your sacrifice for me. Because You died, I
can now live in freedom. Let me remember that certificate of debt only to
increase my love and gratitude toward You. Forgive me of my sins,
and help me walk in newness of life.

So when the centurion, who stood opposite Him, saw that He cried out like this and breathed His last, he said, "Truly this Man was the Son of God!"
MARK 15:39 NKJV

There were different reactions to Jesus' death, just as there had been at his birth. In the last two days before the crucifixion, Jesus dealt with frightened disciples who fled, blasphemous religious leaders, a faithless king Herod, the rebellious and hateful mobs, and the fearful governor, Pilate. The centurion (along with the thief on the cross) was the only one to proclaim Jesus' identity. This foreign oppressor recognized Him. What brought him to make such a declaration? Everything: the weather, Jesus' sacrificial actions, his obvious innocence, his love in the face of jeering crowds, and most importantly the Holy Spirit working in the soldier's heart. As Pastor Andrew Rollinson from St. Andrews pointed out, the centurions in the Bible are all described as exceptional. In the story of the centurion Cornelius (Acts 10), Jesus brings Gentiles into peace with God. God changed these soldiers' hearts to see peace in the face of Jesus and to testify to His divinity.

This man of war looked upon the only Person who could bring lasting peace in the hearts of humans. Do I acknowledge Jesus with the same awe? The Bible does not reveal how he spent the rest of his life, but how will I live today with the knowledge that He died so I could live filled with His peace?

King of Peace, You have made a way back to God!
Let me walk today on this path of peace.

SHAKE, RATTLE, AND ROLL!

[Jesus said] "Whoever welcomes one of these little children in my name welcomes me; and whoever welcomes me does not welcome me but the one who sent me."
MARK 9:37 NIV

"Let's not sit there," Clyde whispered to his wife at church. "That wiggly kid is already sitting at the end. He never stops shaking the whole row of seats. I can't stand it! By the time we leave, I'm vibrating as if I've been using a belt sander for an hour!"

Teachers, who share much of their time and lives with children of all ages, may remember students who didn't just vibrate a row of seats. Maybe as kindergarteners, they ate mud, couldn't color in the lines, talked out of turn, blurted out secrets, and forgot their lunch every day, but they grew up to do great things. Even in Jesus' time, children weren't perfect. Most adults then did not consider pint-sized residents important until grown. To some, giving attention to kids seemed like a waste of time. Yet Jesus taught that children are important. He loves them and us. Those who mentor and teach children of all ages, especially about Jesus, are investing in what God deems as precious—all of his children (young and old).

Teachable, trusting, joyous, enthusiastic, and full of energy! That's what children have to offer—even while they shake, rattle, and roll.

Father, I thank You for the gift of children. Show me how to infuse their positive attitudes into my adult life.

The Son is the radiance of God's glory and the exact representation of his being, sustaining all things by his powerful word. After he had provided purification for sins, he sat down at the right hand of the Majesty in heaven.
HEBREWS 1:3 NIV

W hen Moses descended from Mount Sinai after receiving the Ten Commandments from God, the Israelites begged for Moses to cover his face, for the radiance of God's glory reflected there was too bright for them (Exodus 34:29-30). Before Jesus came to earth, the holiness and radiance of God was too much—we could not know Him personally because of our sin. God revealed Himself to His people through the prophets and the Law, but the Law could not bring us close to God. It showed us our sinfulness and inability to keep all of it. Unworthy to stand before Him, our relationship was distant and tinged with fear.

Yet God, the Three in One, is as loving as He is holy. The Father sent His Son in approachable human flesh to remove the separation between Himself and His creation. On earth, Jesus set aside His full glory to live among us—to show us the Father's mercy, love, and grace through His life and work (John 14:9). By His blood, He brought us near to the Father. Now, we can stand in His radiant presence without fear of judgment. Rejoice in being reconciled with Your Creator through your Savior!

Father God, thank You for the close relationship I have with You through Jesus! Teach me to understand Your ways through Your Word. Amen.

WALK WITH CONFIDENCE

Then they entered Capernaum. When the Sabbath arrived,
Jesus lost no time in getting to the meeting place. He spent the day
there teaching. They were surprised at his teaching—so forthright,
so confident—not quibbling and quoting like the religion scholars.
MARK 1:21-22 MSG

Read through the Gospels, and you'll see a recurring theme. Every step Jesus took, every word He spoke, and every decision He made exuded confidence. He knew who God created Him to be and understood God's power enabled Him to go far beyond what He could do on His own.

God wants us to walk with the same confidence Jesus had. Where does it come from?

First, confidence comes from what you know. You'll be the most confident in the things you know the most about. Read the Bible. Listen to messages from ministers. Study the Word. Become confident in what God's Word says and who He created you to be.

Second, confidence comes from who you know. When I go somewhere by myself, I live out of what I know. When I go somewhere with my husband, I live from what we know. My confidence increases because I have twice as much brain power, muscle, and insight into the situations we face together.

Jesus' confidence came from knowing He was backed by His heavenly Father. We, too, are backed by our heavenly Father: His knowledge, wisdom, power, and grace. We can be as confident as Jesus was that we're not in this alone. Jesus and His Father are on our side.

Remind me, Lord, that You back me up.
I can live confidently because You are on my side.

DESTINED FOR GREATNESS

For we are God's handiwork, created in Christ Jesus to do good works,
which God prepared in advance for us to do.
EPHESIANS 2:10 NIV

Many of us want to do great things. We feel it in our bones—we're destined for greatness. While this is true, our definition of greatness may differ slightly from God's definition.

We're not great because of who we are, but because of who created us. Just as any work signed by Michelangelo has great value, simply because of the signature, we have great value because of God's imprint on our lives. He created us so we could glorify Him, not ourselves.

The way we honor Him is by doing good works. Sometimes, those works are grandiose. More often, they're mundane, and go without notice. He created us to share His love by speaking to the outcast, by helping the helpless when no one else sees, by doing the laundry and cooking dinner and sweeping the porch—all with a pleasant attitude.

Just think. God prepared those little opportunities in advance, just so we'd have ways to share His love and point people to Him. Some of those actions are easy, and others are hard. Still, they are all worth it, for they help us live out our purpose and fulfill the destiny God designed. When we do good things and share His love, we become truly great in His eyes.

Dear Father, I want to do all the good things You've planned for me,
no matter how big or small they may seem. Help me stay true to Your
purpose for my life. Amen.

But we are citizens of heaven, where the Lord Jesus Christ lives. And we are eagerly waiting for him to return as our Savior. He will take our weak mortal bodies and change them into glorious bodies like his own, using the same power with which he will bring everything under his control.
PHILIPPIANS 3:20-21 NLT

Do you ever try to imagine what heaven will look like? I think the most beautiful place on this earth will pale in comparison, but even more than considering the locale, what will it *be* like? We will be surrounded by love, joy, and everything good, with no fear or disease or disaster. It stretches our minds beyond capacity because we've always been in the midst of this tainted environment.

Our bodies will be glorious. We won't compare ourselves to professional athletes or beauty pageant winners but will know we are perfectly created by our Savior. We will be infused with wisdom to understand the many things we couldn't comprehend before. We will no longer deteriorate with age but will be renewed continually.

Beyond everything else, we will see Jesus Christ. We will know Him with an intimacy we can't yet imagine. We will finally, truly understand the love that brought Him to earth and to the cross. If there was any hesitation when we were in our mortal bodies about accepting His salvation, we will probably be amazed to remember we ever doubted His ability or His love. We will be home, forever.

Lord God, though I can't picture heaven, I long to be there.
With You. I know it is perfect.

FAITH CONQUERS FEAR

[When] I am afraid, I will trust in thee.
PSALM 56:3 KJV

Experiencing fear doesn't mean you don't have faith. . .it means you are human. David didn't say, "I'm not afraid because I trust in Thee" in the psalms. He wrote, when "I am afraid, I will trust in thee." In *Jesus Lives*, Sarah Young writes, "Fear does not 'trump' trust: They can co-exist."

When we face devastating diagnoses and catastrophic circumstances, we often feel paralyzed with worry. We may have no energy to pray or study the Word. However, we can turn in faith to Jesus and simply say, "Help." We can voice His name over and over, knowing that His name has power, and He is eager to give us peace.

Authentic, vibrant faith doesn't mean we know all the answers, but we trust the One who holds them (and us). We don't see an end to our suffering or understand how to take another step, but we place our confidence in God above all else—even when Satan screams that we should figure out our own solution, or give up entirely. Fear causes us to flail about and reach for false saviors. Faith in the one true Savior is the lifeboat saving us from death (spiritual and physical). We may still get wet, but we won't drown.

What are you afraid of today? What situation is threatening to derail your faith and take over your emotions? Speak the name of Jesus. Ask Him for help. He may not give you all the answers you yearn for, but He promises to give you peace.

Jesus, help me today. I need You desperately.

[Jesus said,] "For the kingdom of heaven is like a landowner who went out early in the morning to hire workers for his vineyard."
MATTHEW 20:1 NIV

There is incredible power in storytelling. Jesus provided context for complicated concepts through parables, creating emotionally connected learning.

Jesus described a landowner who needed help harvesting a crop. He visited the market and found men who hadn't been employed that day. They accepted his offer, which included a full day's wage. At lunchtime he found more men who hadn't been hired and agreed to pay them a full day's wage if they would work. This same process took place three more times throughout the day.

Each worker was paid a full day's wage. This generosity offended those who'd been working since early morning. Why would the owner pay someone the same wage for working an hour as those who'd worked all day? The landowner questioned why generosity was an issue.

People come to Jesus at different times, yet there's no difference in the offer of salvation. One who believes early in life is not saved to a greater degree than an elderly man or woman saved today. This parable demonstrates that it's never too late to come to Jesus, and His love is not based on the date of salvation.

In a society that places emphasis on accomplishments, it can be hard to accept that You simply want us to receive the generosity of salvation. Help me never be envious of those who accept You later in life. This is proof that You never give up on any of us. With gratitude, amen.

*"My prayer is not for them alone. I pray also for those
who will believe in me through their message."*
JOHN 17:20 NIV

We are comforted and strengthened when someone says, "I'm
praying for you." How does it make you feel to know that Jesus is
praying for you? In John 17:6–9 He prayed for His apostles first—those He
was sending out into the world. He asked God to protect and keep them
unified. Grant them His complete joy as they remember His words. Keep
them from the evil one. Make them holy as they live out the truth of God's
words.

His prayer requests for "those who will believe"—that's us!—
involve fellowship, love, and future glory (John 17:21–26). That we will be
unified with each other and with God and Christ; experiencing complete
fellowship in Christ so unbelievers will know God's love through us. He
prays for us to be with Him in eternity to behold His glory. He prays that
we will know and experience God's love. The reason for these requests
is so the world will believe in Him because of us and so we will know He
loves us. Amen, anyone?

---

*Lord Jesus, thank you for interceding for me and for all believers who
comprise Your Body, the Church. May we grasp the unity and love You desire
for us, so people who know us will come to know You and experience Your
love, too. May I not do anything to sabotage Your message to the world or to
neglect Your love for me. Amen.*

ON THE DEFENSIVE

And when He came near the gate of the city, behold, a dead man was being carried out, the only son of his mother; and she was a widow. . .When the Lord saw her, He had compassion on her and said to her, "Do not weep." Then He came and touched the open coffin, and those who carried him stood still. And He said, "Young man, I say to you, arise." So he who was dead sat up and began to speak. And He presented him to his mother.
LUKE 7:12-15 NKJV

Widows and orphans are high on God's list of concerns. His heart feels for those who are alone and defenseless.

When Jesus walked the earth, He reflected the Father's love for those who could not help themselves. In that time, a woman without a husband or son had no help for her old age. There was no social security, and she would have no means of support. I can imagine Jesus smiling with joy as He "presented" this son back to His mother.

Jesus called Himself the "Good Shepherd." Not only does He give His life for the sheep, but He cares for those who are weak and defenseless.

We must do the same. If we call ourselves by His name, we must stand up for those who cannot speak, cannot defend themselves. We must be on the defensive for them.

O God, help me be strong in my defense of the unborn, the physically and mentally disabled, the elderly, and the bereft. Make me a light of Your love to those who need my strength. In Jesus' name, amen.

For he has rescued us from the dominion of darkness and brought us into the kingdom of the Son he loves, in whom we have redemption, the forgiveness of sins.
COLOSSIANS 1:13-14 NIV

H ave you ever been in a terrifying situation, with little hope of escape? Whether or not you've gone through a traumatic incident, we've all been there. Every one of us was trapped in a hopeless place, maybe without even realizing it.

Jesus is in the rescue business. Whether we trusted in Him as our Lord when we were children and never went through much ugly stuff, or were ignorant of His love until much later, we've all been in Satan's darkness. Those who accept Jesus as Lord and Savior when they are young may not have to endure horrible experiences, but the truth is that even those are constantly being rescued. A friend says, "I was saved from drugs, alcohol, promiscuity, and many other evils because I received Jesus as my savior when I was five years old." That's a beautiful testimony!

The devil does his best to keep us from knowing the One who promises eternal life. Those who believe Satan's lies find themselves in a desperate situation, heading for eternal separation from God.

Yet Jesus never ceases to pursue any of us. He reveals the Good News to everyone. If we listen and turn to Him, we are redeemed and forgiven. We become truly free.

Lord Jesus, I desire to share the Gospel with all the people in my life. Please give me the right words and make my life a living Bible for others to read.

ONE MEDIATOR

For there is one God, and one mediator also between God and men,
the man Christ Jesus, who gave Himself as a ransom for all,
the testimony given at the proper time.
1 TIMOTHY 2:5-6 NASB

This verse states that there is one God. There are not multiple options of who you want to serve or who has control of your fate. That being said, the verse goes on to tell us that there is only one Mediator between this God and men. Christ is your only way to the Father. You need a "middle man." Otherwise you could not stand before the perfect holiness of God. Christ became a man in order to mediate for the rest of mankind.

Christ was the ransom that set humanity free. Sin was holding you and all of humanity hostage. It would not let you out of your bondage until a ransom was paid. This payment required a sacrificial death. Christ stepped in so that you could be returned to your Father. If not for the mediation of Christ, your sin would put you directly in the line of God's wrath. Instead, He died, and you walk freely. What an incredible Mediator you have.

Lord, thank You for becoming the ransom when I was the one who deserved
the wrath of God. You set me free from my bondage to sin. Because of You,
I can come before the Father as a blameless child.

THE GREAT FORGIVER

And be kind to one another, tenderhearted, forgiving one another,
even as God in Christ forgave you.
EPHESIANS 4:32 NKJV

In Matthew 18:21–22 (ESV) Peter interrupted Jesus' discourse on how to settle a disagreement with a fellow believer to ask: "How often should I forgive someone who sins against me? Seven times?" Peter thought he was being generous by using the "all-inclusive" number seven. Jesus surprised Peter by saying, "seventy times seven," thus giving a sense of the infinite need to forgive. This is impossible without the prior example of Jesus.

We think how incredible that people like Sabina Wurmbrand could serve a meal to a German soldier who may have killed her Jewish family on the Eastern front, or how a Nigerian widow can forgive the Boko Haram soldier who murdered her husband and children. The first Christian martyr, Stephen, forgave his murderers as they were stoning him. People can only forgive because they know the great forgiveness of Jesus, who was killed by His own creation and yet still won the victory over death to bring them salvation. On the cross Jesus asked the Father to forgive his wayward sheep: "Father, forgive them" (Luke 23:34 NKJV). They did not know what they were doing and neither do most people today who reject the peace of forgiveness through Jesus. However, those who lift their hurt and anger to God will find that Jesus sets them free from bondage.

Jehovah Jireh, set me free to forgive. Provide me with the great love of Jesus.

STOP THE STUMBLING

"If anyone causes one of these little ones—those who believe in me—to stumble, it would be better for them to have a large millstone hung around their neck and to be drowned in the depths of the sea."
MATTHEW 18:6 NIV

The New Testament is a manual for believers, providing instructions for our personal life, but also details on how to accurately communicate when teaching His truth. From children to adults, Jesus placed a high value on both correct teaching (see 2 Timothy 2:15) as well as doing everything we can not to be a stumbling block to the growing faith of others (see 1 Corinthians 8:9).

Children offer a simple acceptance of a faith message that may not make sense to those who believe logic is the litmus test for all life decisions. Those young in the faith need to be nurtured and encouraged. Jesus knew that we're human and mistakes would be made in dealing with children in the faith. He also wanted to be clear how important this issue is to Him.

Some who share with those who believe in Jesus may be more interested in sharing *their* personal experience and perspective rather than God's truth. To avoid stumbling, or causing others to stumble, you should always check all opinions with God's Word.

I never want to cause someone to stumble. I never want to falter. Only You have the words of life. Let me embrace Your teaching with a passion that recognizes truth in the light of what You've already taught. Make me a disciple of Your will so others may be introduced to You. Amen.

BREAKING THE BARRIERS

There is neither Jew nor Gentile, neither slave nor free, nor is there male and female, for you are all one in Christ Jesus.
GALATIANS 3:28 NIV

Unfortunately, the widespread stereotype of an American Christian is a smiling person who says, "Have a nice day," but underneath is hypocritical and judgmental. That description also fits the Pharisees, the most religious of the Jews. The Pharisees accused Jesus of being a drunkard and a glutton because He was known for hanging out with people with bad reputations. Yet, for all of the Pharisees' ire, those people loved having Jesus around. He treated them with dignity and shared the Truth with them, telling them to sin no more. He reserved His harshest words for the Pharisees and their hypocrisy!

Christ tears down the structures that the world puts up between people—structures of economic inequality, racism, sexism, and other forms of oppression. Through His sacrifice, He unifies believers so that they can be one family, made equal by God's grace. However, the early church struggled against being "respecters of persons," and believers still battle with prejudice today. Whether it's conscious or not, we recoil from certain groups of people, believing stereotypes and passing judgment because of the color of their skin or the lives they've led. Who are they? Ask the Spirit to reveal to you the people toward whom you act as a "respecter of persons."

Lord Jesus, "search me. . .and know my heart; test me and know my anxious thoughts. See if there is any offensive way in me, and lead me in the way everlasting" (Psalm 139:23-24 NIV).

OVERCOMER

"I have told you all this so that you may have peace in me.
Here on earth you will have many trials and sorrows.
But take heart, because I have overcome the world."
JOHN 16:33 NLT

O ne in eight people do not have enough to eat. Every ten seconds, a child dies of starvation. Across the world, believers are persecuted; many are terrified for their lives. There are wars, sickness, and disease. When we think of all that is happening in our world, when we focus on all its trials and tribulations, our natural response is to become anxious. It is easy to lose hope.

As He was about to return to heaven, Jesus prepares his disciples for the worst. Despite the sorrows and trials promised, Jesus offers blessed news. "I have overcome the world." No longer do we have to be anxious and afraid, because Jesus has already overcome. How can you live in such a way that reflects this victorious mindset?

Jesus, You weren't kidding when You said we would have many trials and
sorrows. When I focus on my problems, my heart becomes heavy and
weary. Lighten my load. Help me find my heart and the hope that You have
overcome the world. Amen.

A NEW CREATION

So from now on we regard no one from a worldly point of view. . . .
Therefore, if anyone is in Christ, the new creation has come:
The old has gone, the new is here!
2 CORINTHIANS 5:16–17 NIV

Being "in Christ" is how the New Testament speaks of Christians. Such a relationship gives us a new perspective on life and affects how we view people. We see them in one of two ways—those who also are in Christ and those who need to be. Because Christ's love compels us to die to self and live for Him, we want to help others experience His new life, too (2 Corinthians 5:11–15). Viewing God's creation through new eyes makes us realize our responsibility to be His ambassadors, persuading people to become reconciled to God through Christ (2 Corinthians 5:18–21).

The phrase "a new creation" appears one other time in the New Testament. In Galatians 6:14–15, Paul affirmed that the physical world was as good as dead to him, and he to the world. Therefore, appearances and religious observances, whether someone was Jewish or Gentile, meant nothing to him. What mattered instead was the "cross of our Lord Jesus Christ." Like Paul, our position in Christ means our old way of looking at people and things has gone. We now realize our new responsibility to make Jesus' death and resurrection known to those who need new life "in Christ."

Lord Jesus, help me see people's needs with spiritual eyes so I will be Your ambassador to bring them the good news that You died and rose again so they can have eternal life. Amen.

A SABBATH CUSTOM

So He came to Nazareth, where He had been brought up.
And as His custom was, He went into the synagogue
on the Sabbath day, and stood up to read.
LUKE 4:16 NKJV

What is your "Sabbath" custom?

Jesus made a habit of being in worship. Numerous times in the Gospels there is reference made to the fact that Jesus was in the synagogue, sometimes teaching, sometimes healing, but present. Though He was God in the flesh, He followed the principles given to Moses long ago and kept the Sabbath day holy.

The fourth commandment, like the others, is still in effect. We are to reserve one day a week for rest and worship. Because Jesus rose from the grave on the first day of the week, Sunday, the New Testament Christians began gathering on that day instead of Saturday. This has been the Christian tradition ever since.

In recent years, Sabbath-keeping has fallen out of vogue. The "blue laws" of yesteryear are no more. Retailers score big business on Sunday, and arenas are packed for sporting events and concerts. To many, Sunday is just another work day.

The example of Jesus reminds us to be careful of "the Lord's Day." He had a custom of being in the "Father's house" on the Sabbath. If that was His custom, it should be ours as well.

Dear Lord, show me how to honor the day we keep as the Sabbath.
Guide me as I make choices about how to follow Your example
of rest and worship. In Jesus' name, amen.

PRAY FROM YOUR HEART

*"Here's what I want you to do: Find a quiet, secluded place
so you won't be tempted to role-play before God. Just be there as simply
and honestly as you can manage. The focus will shift from you to God,
and you will begin to sense his grace."*
MATTHEW 6:6 MSG

There are two kinds of prayer: rote vs. real.

Rote prayer is what you rattle off before meals or bedtime. You know exactly what to pray because you've prayed the same thing so many times. Although you are purposeful about your prayer, it's easy to slip into reciting it without much thought.

Then there is prayer from your heart. Prayer from your heart is honest. It's real. It doesn't have a script or a reason behind every word. It's you talking to your heavenly Father as though He were right next to you. You're explaining your praise, prayers, worship, fears, love, frustration, and joys. You're laying your heart before God with no pretension about what you "should" pray or "shouldn't" say.

Because you do regularly repeat certain prayers, rote prayer will always have its place and can be heartfelt in nature. On the other hand, it's important to purposefully engage in real, honest prayer, which is rarer, because it generates a heartfelt connection with God that can be created no other way.

*Lord, help me pray like Jesus did: real prayers from my heart. It's in those
prayers that my focus can shift to You and Your grace.*

COMPLETE JOY

I have told you this so that my joy may be in you
and that your joy may be complete.
JOHN 15:11 NIV

C hrist didn't have an easy life. The son of a carpenter, He undoubtedly grew up knowing what it meant to work hard. The son of parents who weren't married when they discovered His existence, He surely had to deal with hurtful gossip and rumors. When He finally left the carpentry business for full-time ministry, certain important people hated Him so much, they wanted Him dead.

Yet Jesus was joyful. In spite of it all, he carried gladness in His heart, for He found delight in doing His Father's work. How could that be? How can we infuse that kind of joy into our own lives?

First, we must understand the meaning of joy. It's not the same thing as happiness. We may not be happy about our circumstances, the way others treat us, or the current state of our relationships. Happiness has to do with our current circumstances. . .but joy has to do with our future.

No matter where we are in life or what's happening to us, we have a glorious future! Those of us who claim membership in God's family can know, without doubt, that we will come out on top. That is certainly reason to rejoice.

Dear Father, I know You want me to be joyful. Teach me to recognize joy
and to live in that joy every day. Amen.

God did not choose us to suffer his anger but to have salvation through our Lord Jesus Christ.
1 THESSALONIANS 5:9 NCV

D o you picture God as an angry judge? Do you think He's eager to knock people down and trample them in His wrath? That's not who He is.

The God of the Bible is the image of love. 1 John 4:8 (NKJV) says: "He who does not love does not know God, for God is love." Do you really get that? Not only is God loving, He *is* love. He won't do something that is ultimately unloving, because it would go against His very nature. Love is who He is.

The most incredibly loving act in the history of the world was to send His Son, Jesus, to die for us so we can live. Do you realize that if you were the only person who needed a Savior, God would have allowed Jesus to pay the price for you? He'd do anything so He could welcome you into His arms for all eternity.

Being the perfect image of love doesn't mean God never gets angry, but His anger is against evil, not us. We may not understand everything, but we know the devil rebelled against God, and since then, he has done his best to tempt everyone to turn against the Lord. It surely breaks God's heart when people believe the lies and won't receive the love He offers.

Thank You, heavenly Father, for the salvation we have through Jesus Christ. Thank You for showing us that all we must do is open our hearts to receive Your goodness.

Jesus Christ is the same yesterday and today and forever.
HEBREWS 13:8 NASB

Your life is constantly changing. This world is constantly changing. The transitory and unstable nature of earthly things means that you can't fully rely on any of it. Yet Christ is the unchanging Rock that you can always run to. He was, is, and always will be the same. What does this mean for your life? It means you can trust and rely on Him. He doesn't act on whims or cultural shifts. You won't ever try to go to Him and find that He's not there. It also means that you can claim all of the promises in the Bible. Salvation, adoption, redemption, and eternal life are all promises that you can hold on to because they have been fulfilled by the One who will not change.

His unchangeableness also means that you should beware of trying to mold Him to fit what you or your culture wants. We know who Jesus is and what He stood for through the Bible. If anyone tries to tell you that the Jesus of the Bible is outdated or antiquated, don't listen. The Jesus that we know from the Bible *has not changed*.

So even when those you love the most change, remember that the One who loves you more than anyone is the same and always will be.

*Lord, I am thankful that I can rely on You because You will remain
the same through all eternity.*

DESCENDANT LIGHT

*"I am the light of the world. He who follows Me shall not walk
in darkness, but have the light of life."*
JOHN 8:12 NKJV

B artimaeus, the blind beggar of Jericho, "saw" something others
did not in Jesus. The news that Jesus of Nazareth was walking
by prompted Bartimaeus to shout, "Jesus, Son of David, have mercy
on me!" (Mark 10:47 NKJV). He somehow knew that the carpenter from
Galilee was actually King David's heir. The title he used and the plea for
mercy showed his belief in Jesus as Messiah. When others attempted to
silence his cries, Bartimaeus shouted all the louder. Even in his physical
blindness, God was drawing him to see Jesus as the Light. Bartimaeus
threw aside his beggar's garment and came when Jesus called him.
To Jesus' question, "What do you want me to do?" he gave an obvious
answer: "Teacher, to receive my sight."

Jesus knew what Bartimaeus wanted, but he had to ask Jesus
specifically so that everyone could recognize the answer as a clear
provision of a specific need. Bartimaeus gained his sight because he
asked and Jesus mercifully listened. Jesus continues to prompt and
answer, and light the way so his followers do not walk in the darkness of
confusion and disbelief. In Hebrew, Bartimaeus means "son of filth." His
faith and God's mercy gave him a new identity that day. He "received his
sight and followed Jesus," living no more in physical darkness nor in the
spiritual darkness of shame (Mark 10:52 NIV).

*Light of Life, thank You for revealing Yourself to me. Guide me today.
Give me strength to follow faithfully.*

JESUS GIVES WISDOM AND DISCERNMENT

He will not judge by what he sees with his eyes,
or decide by what he hears with his ears.
ISAIAH 11:3 NIV

Mom, can I watch that movie? All my friends are," said Robin's oldest son, Jeremiah.

Robin glanced up from her magazine and looked at her fifteen-year-old. "What's it rated?"

"Well, it's 'R'," Jeremiah answered.

Robin smiled and patted the couch beside her. "Sit down a minute. What do *you* think you should do?"

Jeremiah sat beside her and looked down at his feet. "Well, you have to have an adult with you, and you won't go with me.

"True—and maybe you shouldn't put that stuff in your mind."

Jeremiah squirmed. "Yeah, you're probably right."

Robin hugged her son. "You're growing up, and you're going to make these kinds of decisions on your own in a couple of years. I want you to own your faith and your values, and not just ask my permission or talk me into something."

Jeremiah slumped against the couch cushions. "Okay. Thanks," he said.

In today's scripture, Isaiah writes that Christ does not judge by only what is seen. He has God-given discernment and wisdom—things we desperately need in our culture. With Jesus' help, we can make God-honoring choices. By prayerfully and humbly seeking His will in scripture and asking godly friends for input, we'll find invaluable discernment and wisdom for daily decisions.

Lord, I know You have the ability to help me discern what is true
and good. Help me rely on the Holy Spirit, scripture,
and wise mentors when I make difficult decisions.

"Go to the lake and throw out your line. Take the first fish you catch;
open its mouth and you will find a four-drachma coin.
Take it and give it to them for my tax and yours."
MATTHEW 17:27 NIV

Whether Jesus wanted to pay taxes or not is less relevant than how He went about paying the two-drachma temple tax. Jesus only touches on the principle of taxation before He sent Peter on a fishing expedition. Peter is given very specific details: 1) the lake would be the body of water he would need to fish, 2) the first fish would be enough, 3) he was to look inside the mouth of the fish and find, not just any coin, but a four-drachma coin, 4) the disciple was to take the coin to pay for the tax for Peter and Jesus, and 5) simple math tells us the need was met specifically with no excess.

How many times have you heard another Christian express that when a need was the most pressing, God supplied the need to the 'last dollar'? Perhaps this is true because when the need is greatest, and it is met so specifically, we can do little more than attribute the miracle to the One who knew where to find a fish.

Whenever I am overwhelmed and I see no way out, help me remember that You meet my actual needs. I may make less than the best choices, and I may suffer consequences, but when it comes to my needs, You can be trusted to meet them. Let me worship before, during, and after You supply. Amen.

UNCONDITIONAL LOVE—FOREVER AND ALWAYS

For I am convinced that neither death nor life, neither angels nor demons,
neither the present nor the future, nor any powers, neither height nor depth,
nor anything else in all creation, will be able to separate us from the love of
God that is in Christ Jesus our Lord.
ROMANS 8:38–39 NIV

The older of the teen brothers, Ron, stood in the high school cafeteria and announced to all who would listen, "My brother, Rick, has never been kissed, never had a date, and doesn't have a girlfriend!" Even the vice principal heard the teen's bold proclamation from a few tables away.

Rick was humiliated. He couldn't believe the brother he loved would do that. Rick reddened with anger. Later at home, his rage exploded in his very first fistfight with his sibling. Stitches followed.

The two brothers eventually forgave each other and learned to honor each other as they became adults and moved away. They stayed close with texting, calls, and e-mails. Like the love between these siblings, the love we have for each other may be bruised by words and thoughtless acts.

God's love is not like that. He doesn't come to us with conditions, to-do lists, and qualifications. We are His creations. We are one of a kind. We are Jesus' friend, and He bridges the gap for any of our shortcomings. What's left is a forever love from God that lasts beyond life on earth to heaven and back.

Lord, we thank You for Jesus Christ and Your steadfast love
that spans all experiences and lifetimes.

FAITHFUL TO THE TRUTH

Jesus answered, "I am the way and the truth and the life.
No one comes to the Father except through me."
JOHN 14:6 NIV

Does your idea of "defending the faith" mean getting involved in theological arguments on social media with friends and family? Maybe you just click away from those heated discussions, feeling relieved but also a little guilty. What does it mean to be faithful to the Truth?

Jesus declares that He is the Truth. Since all God's truth is contained in a Person, we understand the core foundations of our existence through a relationship with Him, not rote facts. Jesus lived out what He preached among the Jewish people, His life and work recorded for us in scripture. We are "faithful to the truth" when we are faithful to Jesus in how we worship and represent Him with our lives.

Every day, we need to live connected to the Truth, demonstrating what we believe from scripture with our actions and words. The vital ingredient is love (1 Corinthians 13:1-3). Without love, our claim on the Truth is hollow and comes off as self-righteousness. Just as we were given knowledge of Jesus through grace, we should be grace-filled when we share the Truth with our neighbors, spurred on by the love and compassion Christ places in our hearts. As a wise pastor used to say, "We're just beggars showing other beggars where the bread is."

Jesus, whether You'd have me speak up in a discussion about Your Word or show You through my helping hands, let my actions be animated by Your love. Thank You for showing me Truth! Amen.

WHO'S ON FIRST?

He is also head of the body, the church. . .so that He Himself will come to have first place in everything.
COLOSSIANS 1:18 NASB

We can become too possessive of our possessions. When protecting our things becomes more important than nurturing our relationships, our priorities need reexamined. Likewise, when our career goals or hobbies threaten our marriage or cause us to neglect our children, we must change our perspective. If we belong to Jesus, we should think of Him as our Owner and live for eternity, not earth, for He is our life! (Colossians 3:1–4). Jesus is Creator and Sustainer of all things, and Head of the Church. Keeping this in mind, we will try to please Him with our lifestyle, goals, decisions, and behaviors.

With Jesus as the Head of our lives, we will recognize that everything we have is a gift from Him and did not originate with us. First Corinthians 4:7 (NASB) asks, "What do you have that you did not receive?" C.S. Lewis illustrates it this way: a child who wants to purchase a gift for her dad must borrow the money from him since she has no other resource. The dad provides the money for his own gift so the child can express her love and appreciation for their relationship. I must view everything I have as a "loan" for me to oversee wisely, in dependence on God and with gratitude for His bounty.

Lord Jesus, I need the mindset that You own me and my things so I will love You over myself. Train me to give up my sense of entitlement and addiction to myself. Amen.

WELL TIMED

And when He had sent the multitudes away, He went up on the mountain by
Himself to pray. Now when evening came, He was alone there.
MATTHEW 14:23 NKJV

J esus came from eternity, where there is no time. He allowed Himself
to become subject to the constraints of time when He was born on
this earth.

Jesus knew that a human body needs rest as well as activity. As
the perfect Man, He always used His earthly time in the best way. Being
perfectly balanced and all-wise, He guarded His schedule and took time
off when He needed it. There was no frivolity in His schedule, no wasted
hours; He took time for ministry, for leisure, for others, and for private
worship/fellowship with His Father.

He was conscious of the Father's plan and fulfilled it completely. He
was able to maintain the perfect schedule of work and leisure, ministry
and rest, though there were some who did not understand His timing. The
disciples wondered why Jesus took time for a detour through the land of
Samaria one day, but Jesus knew a sinful woman by Jacob's well needed
His words of forgiveness and hope (John 4:3–42).

You and I are not able to perfectly balance our daily schedules; we
need the wisdom and power of the Holy Spirit. He will guide us as we
strive to follow Christ's example in the use of time.

Lord, may I be surrendered to Your Spirit so that He can direct me
in setting my schedule. Help me always to have time to do Your will.
In Jesus' name, amen.

WHEN HE COMES

For the Lord Himself will descend from heaven with a shout,
with the voice of the archangel and with the trumpet of God,
and the dead in Christ will rise first. Then we who are alive and remain
will be caught up together with them in the clouds to meet the Lord
in the air, and so we shall always be with the Lord.
1 THESSALONIANS 4:16-17 NASB

Christ is coming again. Let that truth affect your daily life. Be encouraged by it because He comes to gather His children to spend eternity with Him. Yet also be warned. No one knows when He will come again. Live your life prepared to meet your Savior.

It will be a glorious coming. There will be no subtlety whatsoever. Imagine how awe-inspiring, terrifying, and joyous this scene will be. All of those who are in Christ will be caught up together in the clouds to meet the Lord. You will meet your Savior face-to-face. That last phrase is one of the most beautiful of all—"we shall always be with the Lord." In fellowship with all the believers through all time, you will be in the constant presence of the Lord. Remember, as you walk through hard times in this life, Christ is coming to bring you home to spend eternity with Him.

Lord, it is so hard to keep this eternal perspective as I face the day.
Don't let me forget that You are coming.

Jesus answered, "It is written: 'Man does not live on bread alone,
but on every word that comes from the mouth of God.'"
MATTHEW 4:4 NIV

According to the nutritional food pyramid, breads and grains should make up the largest portion of our daily calories. Without them, we'd have a hard time meeting our nutritional needs. Remove the bread, and we'll stay hungry.

God's Word is our bread! No wonder so many of us go through life spiritually starved. Though we live in a time when God's Word is freely available on the Internet, when Bibles can be found for pennies at any thrift store, when many of us have multiple copies of this book. . .we often let the wisdom found within its pages sit unread, unconsumed, undigested. Our Bibles gather dust, and we starve.

Yet when we make time every day to chew on God's Word, when we think about it and meditate on it and hide it in our hearts and carry it with us to snack on through the day, we feel satisfied. Our spirits grow and flourish with the nutrition found there, and we go from malnourished to thriving and muscle-bound.

God's Word is our spiritual nutrition. Unlike actual bread, it won't cause us to become overweight. The more we take in, the healthier we become.

Dear Father, I want to be strong and healthy in spirit. Show me how to study Your Word, and help me digest it into my life. Amen.

JESUS REWARDS PERSISTENCE

From there Jesus took a trip to Tyre and Sidon. They had hardly arrived when a Canaanite woman came down from the hills and pleaded, "Mercy, Master, Son of David! My daughter is cruelly afflicted by an evil spirit." Jesus ignored her. . . . Then the woman came back to Jesus, went to her knees, and begged. "Master, help me." He said, "It's not right to take bread out of children's mouths and throw it to dogs." She was quick: "You're right, Master, but beggar dogs do get scraps from the master's table." Jesus gave in. "Oh, woman, your faith is something else. What you want is what you get!" Right then her daughter became well.
MATTHEW 15:21-23, 25-28 MSG

Not only did Jesus ignore this Canaanite woman in Matthew chapter 15, He essentially called her a dog. (Imagine the headlines that story would create in today's world!) Yet the woman didn't let those things faze her. She kept focused on the reason she was there. Her daughter needed healing, and Jesus was able to accomplish what she wanted.

All too often we get offended when God doesn't act the way we want, and as a result, we give up our pursuit of Him. This woman exemplifies not only the persistence we need, but also the humility that enables us to receive from God.

God knows how our lives fit into His greater plan. It's our job to humble ourselves and realize His ways are always worth pursuing.

Despite the fact I can't fully understand Your ways, Lord, I lay my opinion down and choose to persistently follow You.

IT'S ABOUT HEALING

But Jesus was saying, "Father, forgive them;
for they do not know what they are doing."
LUKE 23:34 NASB

Forgiveness is really about healing relationships. Our relationship with God was permanently damaged because of sin. Since the wages of sin is death, Christ paid those wages for us, and He forgave us. It's done. Over with. In the past. Now our relationship with God can be fully restored.

Every day, we're given opportunities to model forgiveness. People hurt us, and our relationships are damaged. Often, we hurt others without intending to do so. Even when we're intentionally cruel, we usually don't understand the full scope of our actions. When we consider how much God has forgiven us, and how He fully restored our relationship to Him despite all the pain we caused Him, we see our own hurts in a new light. If He forgave us for rejecting Him, why wouldn't we forgive those around us?

Just as God wanted to heal the broken relationship with us, He wants us to promote healing in our relationships with each other. That's why forgiveness is so important to Him. He forgave us, and He wants us to forgive one another. Forgiveness is the key to healing in relationships, for us and for the person we forgive.

Dear Father, thank You for forgiving me of so much. Help me forgive
those who've hurt me, even though it's hard. I want to promote healing in
those relationships, just as You made the way for healing
in my relationship with You. Amen.

THE RIGHT TIME

He gave his life to purchase freedom for everyone. This is the message God gave to the world at just the right time.
1 TIMOTHY 2:6 NLT

When Jesus lived on earth, the world was filled with turmoil. Cruel dictators kept citizens firmly controlled. There was lawlessness on every side. Not so different from today except that now, with instant communication, we all know what's going on almost immediately, even from the opposite side of the globe.

The message of salvation God gave to the world at "just the right time" is still the same. Anyone who hasn't been transformed by Jesus can allow Him to do His miraculous work any time, and that is "just the right time" for that person. The Lord knows what each individual needs. He is ready at precisely the right moment to reveal the truth, that Jesus gave His life to purchase our freedom.

When that marvelous truth penetrates our hearts and we give Him control of everything, we learn the delight of a freedom that goes beyond our understanding. We may live in a free country and have a successful life, but until we relinquish everything to Jesus, we are prisoners of sin. Once we allow the Lord to begin His work in us, we realize what we never could comprehend before.

Whenever we're willing, He is already waiting, and all of heaven rejoices. None of the heavenly beings think we've been slow; they simply welcome us home.

Thank You, Father God, for sending Jesus to each one of us at just the right time. Thank You, Jesus, for giving Your life to purchase our freedom.

And while being reviled, He did not revile in return;
while suffering, He uttered no threats, but kept entrusting Himself
to Him who judges righteously; and He Himself bore our sins in His body
on the cross, so that we might die to sin and live to righteousness;
for by His wounds you were healed.
1 PETER 2:23-24 NASB

Christ was vilified for absolutely no good reason. Yet, He didn't retaliate. He didn't let the crowds know why they were wrong and He was right. He didn't call down legions of angels to prove to everyone that He really was God. Instead He entrusted Himself to God, who judges righteously. Just like Christ, when you face wrongful accusations or encounter unjust suffering, recognize that the ultimate Judge is watching. Christ understands that in the end, it doesn't matter what those on earth think of you as long as you are blameless in the sight of God.

It is *because* God is a righteous Judge that Christ had to die. Someone had to pay for all these sins. So Christ died that we might die to sin. In doing so, He made us alive to righteousness. The suffering and wounds that were inflicted on Him were the healing poultice to your sins. What an amazing Savior you serve.

Lord, like You, help me continually entrust myself to the Father who judges righteously. Thank You for the scars on Your body that stand for my salvation.

But when Jesus saw it, He was greatly displeased and said to them,
"Let the little children come to Me, and do not forbid them;
for of such is the kingdom of God."
MARK 10:14 NKJV

The disciples were amazed at Jesus' association with yet another marginalized group in society. Jesus points his followers to the fact that children also have something to teach. They exhibit a unique sense of humility, knowing their own weakness as they trust in the strength of their parents. These wee hearts are free from the cynicism and doubt that cloud older hearts.

BBC's clay-mation film *The Miracle Maker* shows a scene with Jesus carrying wood for a fire while his disciples are bickering over their illusionary superiority. They have the gall to ask, "Who will be the greatest in the Kingdom?" Jesus brings their focus back to him: the greatest is the one who serves others, who lives with the open heart of a child, and who trusts in the one true greatness of the Father. He tells them they need to be like little children to even enter the Kingdom (Luke 9:46-48). How humbling.

When prestige and material gain cloud the eyes of the heart, believers forget about putting others first. Children often forget, too; they are also affected by the brokenness of sin. There is so much in their innocence that Jesus wants his followers to learn from and adopt. Is there a child in my community God is drawing me to minister to and learn from?

Abba, humble me and give me the teaching spirit of a child.

*And they said to him, "Grant us to sit, one at your right hand
and one at your left, in your glory.' Jesus said to them,
'You do not know what you are asking.'"*
MARK 10:37–38 ESV

Though we can admire the freedom and closeness they felt with Jesus, James and John's request was too worldly to be wise. Jesus' ministry was focused on God's kingdom and plans, not an earthly concept of royalty.

Satan can distract us from the work God has called us to with grandiose ideas of temporary riches and accolades. Scripture teaches us to be obedient and surrendered and not worry about success. Everything we do is ministry—and our calling may be centered on one city block, family member, or neighborhood. If we're truly living for Christ and not ourselves, our greatest ministry often happens one-on-one.

Maybe we minister to the cashier at Wal-Mart, or we put a cool rag to our son's face when he's sick. Perhaps we forgive our spouse one more time for a quirk that used to charm us but now irks us. Instead of worrying about how many Facebook "friends" we have, we call a friend to share the hope we have found, so that she knows she's not alone. Even when we're homebound due to illness, we can write a card to someone who needs encouragement. . .and send it.

Let's pray for opportunities to witness, stay open to the Holy Spirit's nudges, and plant seeds of grace wherever we go.

*You've called me to obedience, Father, whether or not it brings success.
Give me grace to follow Your example.*

RELATIONSHIP RESTORATION DAY

With a loud cry, Jesus breathed his last.
MARK 15:37 NIV

Jesus was different. Yes, He was the Son of God, and He didn't sin. While that explains everything, very few recognized this fact, yet they still saw Him as different. With the woman at the well He spoke the truth in love, and it changed her life. The Pharisees insisted that outward appearance was all there was to consider, but Jesus expressed greater truth.

To some He was a good man, others saw Him as a great teacher, but who He really was wouldn't become clear until one Friday when rough wooden beams held metal nails forced through flesh. The good man/ teacher died in the midst of jeers and weeping.

Despite the horrific scene, a day soon arrived when that "good man" came out of the grave and erased all doubt as to who He was. Mankind was released from daily sacrifices at the temple. A simple, yet solemn belief in who Jesus is and what His death meant makes God approachable, and One who inspires wonder.

Jesus accepted His purpose on earth. It had always been to come to the cross to redeem mankind. It was a gift inspired by a choice to love.

In Your life You brought real love; in Your death You paid the price for the sin of mankind. When You rose from the dead, You cleared the way for humanity to access a fully restored relationship with God. Someday You will return for those who understood Your gift and have accepted the grace found in the choice of belief. Thanks for Your amazing love gift. Amen.

"As the Father has loved me, so have I loved you. Abide in my love."
JOHN 15:9 ESV

The Merriam-Webster dictionary defines *abide* as "to remain stable or fixed in a state." When Jesus told His disciples to abide in Him, He invited them (and us) to find our stability and safety in His powerful love. Throughout the Bible, Jesus is described with imagery that portrays Him as the source of abundant life. He is the Head that takes care of all the needs of His Body, the Church (1 Corinthians 12, Colossians 1:18). He is the Vine and we are the branches who are nourished by Him (John 15:5). He is the Bread that came down from heaven, and He is the Living Water (John 6:51, 7:37-38).

The Christian life can't be lived perfectly this side of heaven, but we thrive by drawing our strength from Christ. We aren't branches who have to do our best to cling onto the vine, instead the vine holds us fast, sustaining us so we can "bear much fruit" (John 15:5 ESV). Abiding in Jesus means we rest secure because our salvation never depended on our effort, but on His love—" God shows His love for us in that while we were still sinners, Christ died for us" (Romans 5:8 ESV).

Abide with Christ in the Word and prayer, and you'll find rest that's filled with the delight of knowing Him. Allow Jesus to nurture the places where you struggle to abide. He'll bring you new life!

Dear Jesus, help me abide in You in everything.
Thank You for holding onto me. Amen.

THE PEACE OF JESUS

"Peace I leave with you; my peace I give you. I do not give to you
as the world gives. Do not let your hearts be troubled and do not be afraid."
JOHN 14:27 NIV

Where does the world go for peace? We are led to believe that we can find peace in many places other than Christ. The world offers peace through alcohol, sex, and work, but we know that these things are temporary at best. Jesus offers a completely different kind of peace from that of the world. Worldly attempts at peace merely numb and distract us, like a little baby whose attention is captured momentarily by a shiny object.

On the other hand, Jesus offers HIS peace. His peace is different from the world because it is true, it is lasting, it is relevant, and it is always available to us through the power of the Holy Spirit. If you are having trouble receiving His peace, focus on the above words, memorize them, and repeat them as a prayer. Soon His peace will find its way into your troubled heart.

Jesus, I long for the gift of Your peace. The world offers such shabby comparisons to the true and lasting peace You give. My heart gets troubled, and I feel afraid. Instill within me Your peace, I pray that it would overwhelm and envelop my very soul. Amen.

PRUNING PRODUCES FRUIT

"I am the vine, you are the branches. He who abides in Me, and I in him, bears much fruit; for without Me you can do nothing."
JOHN 15:5 NKJV

What does it mean to abide or remain in Christ so that He can produce much fruit in us and through us? John 15 speaks about sanctification (living the Christian life), not salvation (becoming a Christian). When we remain in fellowship with Christ, the True Vine, His nourishment enables us to grow in holiness and be useful to Him. His process, however, includes painful pruning. He cuts away our willfulness, apathy, distractions, and sins that prevent holiness.

When grapevines are pruned, they weep, as sap drips from every wound. Pruning makes us weep as well, but tears teach lessons we could not learn any other way. Weeping sends us running to Christ for comfort, endurance, and wisdom. Thus, pruning hurts, but it helps our fellowship with Christ if we submit to the sanctification process. A branch cannot bear fruit on its own. It must stay attached to the vine for its nourishment. How do we remain in fellowship with Christ? By resisting sin, staying connected through prayer, and occupying our minds with God's Word and thoughts about Him. Because He abides in us, His life can provide the power we need to abide in fellowship with Him.

Lord Jesus, You are my Source. Forgive my self-reliance and independent spirit. When I forget You during my day's activities, I accomplish nothing for eternity. Please help me be faithful and fruitful for Your glory. Amen.

PRACTICING ENDURANCE

*Jesus, the author and finisher of our faith, who for the joy
that was set before Him endured the cross, despising the shame,
and has sat down at the right hand of the throne of God.*
HEBREWS 12:2 NKJV

It is hard to imagine that the very Son of God would have to practice endurance. It doesn't seem possible that God would subject Himself to anything that would bring Him to that emotion. But He did.

Jesus endured physical limitations, pain, and death. He was from eternity, where there is no time, no boundary of space, no dying. Yet, He accepted all of this to bring us salvation. He became subject to human birth, to dirt, to hunger, to thirst, to scrapes and bruises, to the need for rest and friendship, and to the desire to live. He endured the curse of fallen humanity in all of its expression. He became subject to the very life that He came to sacrifice.

He endured misunderstanding, mistreatment, abuse, ridicule and torture. Still, the most difficult, yet most splendorous, thing He endured was a Roman cross. He knew that there was joy on the other side; the joy of redeeming us. He endured it because of His love.

Every believer is called to endure. Like Jesus, we must look past the present and take hold of the joy set before us in God's time.

*Jesus, thank You for enduring the cross for me. Give me grace today
to endure whatever You know is best and help me hold to the joy
set before me. In Your name, amen.*

A crowd gathered, jamming the entrance so no one could get in or out.
[Jesus] was teaching the Word. They brought a paraplegic to him,
carried by four men. When they weren't able to get in because of the crowd,
they removed part of the roof and lowered the paraplegic on his stretcher.
Impressed by their bold belief, Jesus said to the paraplegic. . . . "Get up.
Pick up your stretcher and go home." And the man did it—got up,
grabbed his stretcher, and walked out.
MARK 2:2–5, 11–12 MSG

Jesus was impressed by the faith of this man and his friends. Why? They did something unusual, out of the ordinary, and unexpected. They were so solid in their foundation of faith that they didn't allow the circumstance they faced to block them from receiving Jesus' blessing. They went against the protocol of society, opened up someone else's roof, and pursued what they needed from Jesus.

What a great example they are to us today. When we are faced with insurmountable odds, what is our response? Do we find a way to reach Jesus? Do we get creative in the choices we make? Or do we sit back and let circumstances dictate our decisions?

These men could have easily stopped when they saw the crowded house, but they didn't. Next time you are faced with difficulty, remember: Jesus responds to bold belief.

Jesus, help me push beyond my limits today and do something extraordinary and unexpected. I want to impress You with my bold belief.

OUR FAITHFUL HIGH PRIEST

For this reason he had to be made like them, fully human in every way,
in order that he might become a merciful and faithful high priest in service
to God, and that he might make atonement for the sins of the people.
HEBREWS 2:17 NIV

Jesus was fully human, and yet also completely God. My mind can't grasp that, but I believe it. If He hadn't been human, He couldn't have impacted society as He did. Even hardened atheists admit that Jesus was a person who lived on earth at that point in history. People who haven't put their trust in Him only believe in Him the same way they believe in Napoleon or George Washington, but they don't doubt His existence.

Because of His humanity, He had the ability to sin. Don't kid yourself by thinking Jesus couldn't sin. If He hadn't had the potential to sin, He would not have the authority to save us through His death.

Coming as a person equipped Jesus with a unique understanding of what people go through. Even though, as God, He knew because of His omniscience, as a human he experienced the same things we do. High priests of Bible times made sacrifices to cover sin. Jesus, our faithful High Priest, made the ultimate sacrifice, giving His sinless life to erase our sin—forever. No other figure in history lived a sinless life, died as a criminal, and was resurrected. Beyond that, He still lives and changes lives.

Holy Jesus, how I love You! I am amazed to think about all
You've done for me. You are magnificent!

THE PROMISE

From Paul, an apostle of Jesus Christ. God himself chose me to be an apostle, and he gave me the promised life that Jesus Christ makes possible.
2 TIMOTHY 1:1 CEV

The apostle Paul realized from the moment Jesus Christ revealed Himself that the new life he was granted was not his own doing. Because of his total dependence on Jesus, Paul became a humble, outspoken ambassador for his Lord. When any of us have a revelation that we have nothing without the Lord, all we want to boast about is our dependence on Him.

Paul apparently was thrilled to be counted worthy of being an apostle. He knew God Himself chose him. What is an apostle? It's more than a disciple, which means a follower. An apostle is described as an advocate, a promoter, a supporter, or a proponent. Apostles went on from discipleship to tell the world about Jesus.

The Bible says we didn't choose God, He chose us. Whether we're chosen with a dramatic encounter like Paul on the road to Damascus, or in the quiet of our own home, we are His very own. Everything about our relationship is His doing, not our own. So when we think of it, there's great joy knowing He selected us to be in His family. All we can do is thank Him and tell others about the wonderful life He makes possible.

Lord Jesus, I am so privileged, knowing You chose me. I matter to You! Thank You, and show me how to be Your advocate and tell others the fabulous things You've done for me.

CHRIST AS ADVOCATE

And if anyone sins, we have an Advocate with the Father,
Jesus Christ the righteous.
1 JOHN 2:1 NASB

A n advocate is someone who speaks in support or favor of another person. This is what Christ does for you. There is no logical reason for Him to want or need to defend you. In comparison to what He has done, none of us have done anything in return for Him. This is unfathomable love that He would speak on your behalf to the Father when you sin. Those very sins caused Him such suffering. By earthly standards, one would think that He would want nothing to do with those who sent Him to His death. All you can do is wonder at the purity of His love and thank Him for the utter selflessness He displays on your behalf.

So when you sin, go to Christ. There is no one better to be your Advocate because there is no one more righteous. Ask Him to intercede for you to the Father. Don't hold back anything from Him.

Lord, I need You to intercede for me every day. I cannot stand before the holiness of the Father covered in my filthy sins. Take them from me and be my defense. Your righteousness is my covering. Thank You for loving me so perfectly even though I'm the reason You suffered so intensely. Help me begin to fathom this kind of love.

ESPECIALLY PETER

For I delivered to you as of first importance what I also received: that Christ died for our sins in accordance with the Scriptures, that he was buried, that he was raised on the third day in accordance with the Scriptures, and that he appeared to Cephas, then to the twelve.

1 CORINTHIANS 15:3-5 ESV

In a sermon series on Jesus' appearances after the resurrection, Romanian pastor Claudiu Valcu pointed to the important fact that Jesus appeared separately to Simon Peter (Cephas). "The Lord has risen indeed, and has appeared to Simon!" (Luke 24:34 ESV). Paul also writes of this in his letter to the church in Corinth. Why is this important? Peter adamantly denied knowing Jesus on the night of Jesus' arrest. Yet, Jesus' death and resurrection is all about forgiveness and restoration.

Jesus had chosen Peter. Through all of Peter's failings: his quick-temper, his weariness while Jesus was in anguished prayer, his unbelief (he took his eyes off of Jesus and almost drowned), and ultimately his denial (three times on the night of Jesus' arrest), Jesus loved Peter. He prayed faithfully for Peter's faith to not fail, as Satan sought to "sift him like wheat" (Luke 22:31 ESV). He did not give up on Peter and slowly built him up to boldly witness about Jesus to Jews and Gentiles. Looking to Jesus, Peter exchanged his guilt for love and obedience. Jesus has called me to something, and He will not give up on me. In the darkest of times, He will reveal Himself, as He did to Peter.

Great Rehabilitator, thank You for interceding and providing for your own.

RUN TO GET THE PRIZE

Do you not know that in a race all the runners run, but only one gets the prize? Run in such a way as to get the prize.
1 CORINTHIANS 9:24 NIV

Laura never thought she'd be a runner. As a child, she always felt awkward, and she still didn't have a typical runner's body. Her legs were thick, her shoulders broad. Yet in her forties, after bearing two children in three years, she took up running to lose some baby weight and get healthier.

Laura was surprised when she fell in love with the sport. Not only did she enjoy having time to think and pray—without interruption!—while she ran, but God taught her much about the spiritual life from running, as well. The scriptures came alive in new ways when she read verses such as 1 Corinthians 9:24.

What did it mean to run to get the prize? Laura had medaled in several 5K's, and she knew that winning had cost her time and money. Her faith cost her, too. . .but the rewards were heavenly. In running, when she was tired, she kept going until her goal was complete. When she felt weak, she mustered up strength she didn't know she had. In her spiritual life, when Laura felt overwhelmed, she prayed for courage and endurance. She found that the physical changes in her body corresponded to changes in her soul. Maybe running wasn't a spiritual discipline, but Laura was thankful for the ways it had changed her, nonetheless.

I want to run hard after You, Lord. Give me the will as I follow Your ways.

Then he returned to his disciples and found them sleeping. "Simon,"
he said to Peter, "are you asleep? Couldn't you keep watch for one hour?
Watch and pray so that you will not fall into temptation.
The spirit is willing, but the flesh is weak."
MARK 14:37–38 NIV

Peter, James, and John followed Jesus to a garden called Gethsemane. These disciples were close to Jesus, and likely felt honored to be invited. Like always, Jesus needed to pray. He had one request for His friends, "Watch and pray so that you will not fall into temptation."

They meant well, but as Jesus prayed, knowing He would soon face death, the disciples fell asleep. They'd heard Jesus say that His soul was overwhelmed with sorrow to the point of death, but even these weighty words weren't enough to keep their eyelids open.

While Jesus wrestled in prayer over what He would face, Judas was in the act of betrayal. After inviting His disciples to engage in prayer three separate times, He informs them He's about to be betrayed.

It's easy to believe the disciples needed more self-discipline, but how often have we started to pray only to find ourselves tempted to think of other things or perhaps sleep? Prayer is active and necessary, but it's also a place where distractions come easy. Jesus still asks us to pray.

I want to be intentional about my prayer life. Seeking You is vital in developing and maintaining my walk with You. Let me accept Your grace, but help me do my best to make conversation with You a regular part of my day. Amen.

WHO IS THE REAL WINNER?

"So the last will be first, and the first will be last."
MATTHEW 20:16 NIV

When trees leafed out as spring came to Brad's rural community, the teen began early morning training rides for the upcoming bike races.

In the past, he had always won first place.

"What do you like best about these races?" a local reporter had asked him.

Brad grinned. "Winning—and the good-looking girls!"

However, when the new season began, the judges handed the first place trophy to David, who topped 35 miles per hour in some parts of the route. A frowning Brad received second.

David's recumbent bike was not like Brad's road bike. Its pedals were out front instead of underneath the rider, making it faster. It should have been in a different racing class because no ordinary racer could compete.

At home, Brad cried with disappointment, "No fair!"

Similarly, in a parable told by Jesus, the workers of a field all started at different times of the day and all were paid the same wage at the end of the day. The eight-hour crowd protested loudest. Jesus ended his parable with "Don't I have the right to do what I want with my own money? Or are you envious because I am generous?" [Matthew 20:15 NIV].

Jesus is teaching us about grace. Some are faithful followers from the cradle. Others accept Him at death. Yet He offers all his gift of forgiveness and a winning ticket to heaven. Praise God for all of His latecomers.

Jesus, we thank You for giving us victory.

BLESSED ARE THE PERSECUTED

"Blessed are those who are persecuted because of righteousness, for theirs is the kingdom of heaven. Blessed are you when people insult you, persecute you and falsely say all kinds of evil against you because of me. Rejoice and be glad, because great is your reward in heaven, for in the same way they persecuted the prophets who were before you."
MATTHEW 5:10-12 NIV

Believers should expect persecution. Depending on where and how you live, the persecution you experience may be great or may be miniscule. In many parts of the world, brothers and sisters in Christ are being denied jobs, food, and justice because of their faith. They are in danger of losing their families, homes, and freedom for Jesus' sake. Still, they cling to the Savior and share the Good News of His salvation. They trust that He will accomplish the justice that they cannot (Romans 12:19).

If, in contrast, you possess power, money, or safety, don't feel guilty. God has given you exactly what you have so you can bless the worldwide Body of Christ. More importantly, no matter our situation, we can all go before the Father and plead for our brothers' and sisters' faith to be strong and also for their persecutors to know Jesus' salvation! Ask the Spirit to prompt your heart to pray and to share Christ's kindness with your precious fellow members of the Body of Jesus.

Jesus, I am thankful that You are near to me and my faraway brothers and sisters. Please move my heart to pray for those who persecute Your Church. Amen.

*Summoning two of his disciples, John sent them to the Lord, saying,
"Are You the Expected One, or do we look for someone else?"*
LUKE 7:19 NASB

C hristians are not exempt from becoming disillusioned with God or questioning their relationship to Him. We can learn how to handle those doubts by looking at John the Baptist. His life purpose was to point people to Christ, and his ministry was wildly successful (Matthew 3:5). However, in what must have been the most exciting time of John's life, he suddenly found himself in prison. How could he fulfill his mission there? As he continued to suffer, his expectations crashed. *If I'm the messenger sent to proclaim the Messiah, why am I locked up? If Jesus is really the promised one, why doesn't He rescue me?* He sent two of his followers to ask Jesus point-blank, "Are you the Messiah or not?"

Jesus hardly ever answered a question directly, so He did not say, "Tell John to remember when he baptized me and heard God's voice speak to him." Instead, Jesus sent them back with Isaiah 35:3–7. He wanted John to consider the evidence based on scripture not on his thrilling experiences. John needed to discover for himself that Jesus' miracles were fulfilling the Old Testament prophecies about the Messiah.

So it is with us. When we doubt, we need to look to scripture rather than emotional events. The evidence is in what God has said, no matter how we may feel.

*Lord Jesus, when suffering makes me doubt You, remind me to run
to Your Word and respond by believing it. Amen.*

FACING THE DARK

Then Judas, having received a detachment of troops, and officers from the chief priests and Pharisees, came there with lanterns, torches, and weapons. Jesus therefore, knowing all things that would come upon Him, went forward and said to them, "Whom are you seeking?" They answered Him, "Jesus of Nazareth." Jesus said to them, "I am He." And Judas, who betrayed Him, also stood with them.
JOHN 18:3-5 NKJV

He came into this world under a cloud of suspicion; the townspeople of Nazareth never did quite believe Mary's story of an angelic visit and a miraculous pregnancy. When He came into His hometown, they said, "Isn't this the carpenter's son?" (Matthew 13:55 NIV). His enemies taunted and threatened Him and tried to make Him look bad. They ultimately came after Him, using one of His followers to do the dirty work of betrayal.

On that black night in the Garden of Gethsemane, Jesus faced them all. He stepped out into the light of their torches and asked who they wanted (though He already knew). Then He faced the darkness and went forward. In a few hours, He would win the victory, wresting the keys of hell and the grave from Satan and completing our redemption.

You and I will never face what He did, but we will be called to step forward to meet terrifying challenges. In that moment, we can know that He will give us the courage to conquer in His name.

Dear Father, I want to face the darkness with courage. Please give me strength to step forward and conquer. In Jesus' name, amen.

Large crowds followed Jesus as he came down the mountainside.
Suddenly, a man with leprosy approached him and knelt before him.
"Lord," the man said, "if you are willing, you can heal me and make me
clean." Jesus reached out and touched him. "I am willing," he said.
"Be healed!" And instantly the leprosy disappeared.
MATTHEW 8:1-3 NLT

When Jesus looked at this man, He didn't shiver at the body ravaged by leprosy. He didn't stop to pray and ask God's will about the matter. He didn't shun the leper because he was an outcast of society. Instead, Jesus touched him.

Jesus' touch was an act of faith. He didn't worry about what people thought or the power of the disease. The beat of His heart was to push back darkness and bring the touch of heaven to this man.

John chapter 2 gives us another example of Jesus' faith in action. Jesus ordered servants at a wedding to fill pitchers to the brim with water and then bring those pitchers to the host of the wedding. That water miraculously changed as they walked, because when the host tasted the liquid, it was wine!

What if the water hadn't changed to wine? That fearful thought could have easily constrained this miracle, but Jesus ignored fear and chose faith. What a great lesson we can learn: let faith, not fear, dictate our actions.

Lord, let all my actions today come from a heart of faith.
In Jesus' name, amen.

*Let your conversation be always full of grace, seasoned with salt,
so that you may know how to answer everyone.*
COLOSSIANS 4:6 NIV

Christ was impressively tactful. He was delicate and diplomatic with others' feelings, so as not to crush their spirits or turn them away. Oh, He could be blunt when the occasion required it. Christ always placed people as His top priority. He didn't want to prove He was right at the expense of damaging a soul. If He'd made cruel words and harsh reproofs a habit, He certainly wouldn't have had crowds following Him. They would have run the other way!

Grace is sadly missing from many of our churches and Christian circles. Often, we seem to care more about right and wrong than we do about people's hearts. Oh, we may prove our points, but at the cost of the very souls God wants us to love.

We're not called to compromise our standards of right and wrong. However, we are called to season those standards with abundant grace, love, and compassion. When the people around us are introduced to that kind of love, they are often drawn to God's standards of right and wrong. The Holy Spirit is certainly capable of doing this without us having to verbally beat our listeners into submission. Grace and diplomacy is always more desirable than a scathing rebuke.

---

*Dear Father, teach me tact. Let my normal, everyday conversations
be seasoned with grace and love. Amen.*

HEIRS OF ETERNAL LIFE

He generously poured out the Spirit upon us through Jesus Christ our Savior.
Because of his grace he declared us righteous and gave us
confidence that we will inherit eternal life.
TITUS 3:6-7 NLT

That is awesome! Because of His grace, we can stand before God and be declared righteous. That means we're right, just, and clean in His eyes, not due to our efforts—which, at best, are pretty paltry—but because of Jesus Christ. Even if we've done horrible things, turned our backs on the Lord, and tried to push Him out of our lives, He won't turn away from us. We can be confident that we will inherit eternal life if we accept His generous gift.

Eternal life is beyond the scope of our imagination, but God goes even further and promises a rich, abundant life here on earth right now, for believers. That doesn't mean we'll never have problems, but through the hard times, He's there with peace and joy and strength.

The next verse reminds us this teaching is trustworthy, good, and beneficial. Oh, yes it is! Once we understand how impossible eternal life would be without Jesus' unimaginable grace and mercy, we can only praise Him from the core of our being. Thinking of all He has done and is doing and will do stirs us to find a way to properly thank Him. Praise is a wonderful release. Our hearts can soar when we sing of His glory.

Dear Lord, what You do for us is beyond my comprehension.
All I can do is praise You and tell others of Your wonders.

LION AND LAMB

*And one of the elders said to me, "Stop weeping; behold the Lion
that is from the tribe of Judah, the Root of David, has overcome so as
to open the book and its seven seals." And I saw between the throne. . .
a Lamb standing, as if slain.*
REVELATION 5:5-6 NASB

Overwhelmed with grief because no one can open the book, John is told to stop weeping because there is One that has overcome and is worthy to open the book. He is described as "the Lion." This is the One that was prophesied about for centuries—the great Conqueror, the Prince of peace, the One who would destroy all the enemies of God's people. Everyone who knew these prophecies was expecting a mighty warrior that would muster an army and usher in a new kingdom on earth.

Yet, what does this Lion look like in the vision? A slain Lamb. Could there be a more amazing change of imagery? Many of the Jews of Christ's time didn't believe that He was the Messiah because this humble Man was nothing like the Lion in the prophecies. Christ's work as a sacrificial Lamb was far more powerful than anyone could have imagined. The earthly kingdom that the Jews were hoping for would have been overthrown, as all kingdoms eventually are. Yet this slain Lamb has conquered the most powerful of enemies and has ushered in a Kingdom that will stand for eternity.

Lord, thank You that You are the slain Lamb, the conquering Lion.

"These people draw near to me with their mouth, and honor Me with their lips, but their heart is far from Me. And in vain they worship Me, teaching as doctrines the commandments of men."
MATTHEW 15:8-9 NKJV

Jesus called the religious people out on their hypocrisy using the words of the prophet Isaiah (29:13). They had before them the One fulfillment of the law, and they were charging Him with not being religious enough. Jesus wanted people to understand that God's commandments are meant to change the very heart of a person. The Pharisees made the outside of "their cup" clean but filled the inside with greed and wickedness. Jesus wants to take away all the pretention and all the fakeness to produce cleansed characters who can truly be light and salt in the world.

Singing, praying, tithing, daily devotional times, and weekly church attendance can easily become forms without substance. Millions of people attend church services. However, true followers of Jesus do not just go to church, they are the Church. They are the redeemed; their words match the contents of their heart through the strength that only Jesus can give. Their actions also come out of the overflow of their love for the Lord, whose words they obey and live out. Jesus is the Truth which exposes lies.

El Emet (God of Truth), let Your Word become alive in me so I can worship You with my whole heart. Protect me from empty traditions and infuse my prayer, song, and scripture reading with the Spirit. Cleanse me from the inside out.

FEELING OTHERS' PAIN

Therefore, when Jesus saw her weeping, and the Jews who came with her weeping, He groaned in the spirit and was troubled. And He said, "Where have you laid him?" They said to Him, "Lord, come and see." Jesus wept.
JOHN 11:33-35 NKJV

Do you want to be like Jesus? Then enter into the pain of others. Jesus was not aloof from those who were suffering. He came alongside them; He carried it with them.

As the Son of God, Jesus knew all things. He knew the reasons why people were blind, deaf, and disabled. He understood the reasons for their poverty, dysfunction, depression, and fears. He knew that He would touch many of them, healing their diseases and calming their anxieties. Yet, He had compassion. He took the time to enter their pain.

We see this demonstrated here in the narrative of Lazarus' death and resurrection by Jesus. Although He knew that in a few moments Lazarus was going to walk out of the tomb, Jesus wept as He stood in front of His grave. No doubt He wept for the sisters and the crushing pain they had endured. He didn't rush to the miracle; first, He shared the grief.

In our times of disappointment and loss, we can know that He stands beside us, feeling our hurt and bearing our pain. Like Him, we can come alongside others who suffer, crying with them, praying with them, and lifting them up to His care.

Jesus, thank You for being the Friend who shares my deepest hurts. Help me bear the pain of others in Your name. Amen.

THE GIVING PERSPECTIVE

Calling his disciples to him, Jesus said, "Truly I tell you, this poor widow has put more into the treasury than all the others. They all gave out of their wealth; but she, out of her poverty, put in everything—all she had to live on."
MARK 12:43–44 NIV

Jesus had a radically different perspective on giving. We may look at our giving based only on a formula of percentages, but Jesus seems more interested in the motive and heart behind the act. Where we may view giving as something to mark off a checklist, Jesus wants giving to be more intentional and cheerful (see 2 Corinthians 9:7).

Like some who sit in a mall and observe the crowd, Jesus went to the temple and watched men make a production out of how much they were giving. Then Jesus spotted a widow who quietly placed two coins into the temple treasury, and He got excited.

From His vantage point, Jesus noticed a significant difference and wanted to make sure His disciples understood the reason He considered her gift more worthy. What gave it a greater value? Faith and obedience. She would wrestle with where her next meal would come from, but she would rest knowing she'd given to a God who provides. She received more benefit from her gift than all the money collected from men who made giving a stage production rather than an act of worship.

Help me never withhold what can be used by You to minister to others. I want to give cheerfully and with complete faith in what You provide today and for all my tomorrows. Amen.

*"Come to me, all who are weary and burdened, and I will give you rest.
Take my yoke upon you and learn from me, for I am gentle
and humble in hearts, and you will find rest for your souls."*
MATTHEW 11:28–29 NIV

"Who ever heard of ill-fated lasagna?" Cindy wondered. By the end of the day, she was convinced her potluck dinner dish was doomed. While she was loading the car, the family dog launched herself into the lasagna on her way to the seat. Four paw prints left dents the size of meteorite craters in the top of the foil-covered dish. Cindy smoothed them out with a fork. Later on the way home, she braked hard when a driver screeched to a stop. The leftover lasagna wallpapered the seat and the carpet.

Seeking peace, Cindy took the dog for an evening walk. Outside, neighbors were watering their flowers, moving watering wands back and forth over the blooms. The gardeners exhibited calmness while reflecting on beauty and blessings. Cindy needed to, also.

Jesus recognized we all feel burdened at times with many more serious issues than ill-fated lasagna. Guilt, mistakes, wrongdoing, illness, and responsibilities may leave us feeling overwhelmed. Yet know this: Jesus is a friend who always stands before us holding a casserole dish baked perfectly with peace, love, forgiveness, and healing. He shoulders our burdens in times of need.

---

*Thank You, Jesus, for helping with my burdens—no matter
how small or big they are.*

JESUS' WORK ETHIC

*Work willingly at whatever you do, as though you were working
for the Lord rather than for people.*
COLOSSIANS 3:23 NLT

While the Bible doesn't give specifics about Jesus' daily work schedule, it is clear He worked hard. As a young Jewish boy, He was educated, and by age twelve was amazing the leaders in the temple. He learned the trade of a carpenter from his earthly father Joseph. The Gospels indicate that Jesus often rose up early, while it was still dark, so He could spend time with His Father in prayer before the start of a busy day.

Jesus modeled a strong work ethic and commitment to His Father's will. He represented His Father in all He did, and others were drawn to Him as a man of integrity. Jesus was obedient to His Father until death. We are called, like Jesus, to work willingly. Our work ethic is not only a reflection of who we are, but who He is as well.

*Father, thank You for equipping me to work. Help me do my earthly
work with You in mind, and help me reflect Your work ethic
and Your character in my daily life. Amen.*

JUSTICE AND MERCY

Jesus entered the temple courts and drove out all who were buying and selling there. He overturned the tables of the money changers and the benches of those selling doves. "It is written," he said to them, "'My house will be called a house of prayer,' but you are making it 'a den of robbers.'"
MATTHEW 21:12-13 NIV

In *The Jesus I Never Knew*, Philip Yancey writes that Jesus had infinite patience with individuals but no patience for unjust institutions. The Messiah overturned the tables of the money changers and the sellers of doves, angry at the exploitation of the poor taking place in God's temple.

Following in Jesus' footsteps, believers are to seek justice, love mercy, and walk humbly with Him (Micah 6:8). "Walking humbly" is especially important. Filled with zeal for justice, we may rush headlong into a community to "help" without carefully researching the interconnected problems of the issue. We may also be tempted to abandon our work after it begins demanding too much of our time or resources. In all our service, we must move forward in prayer, our hearts drenched in the Word of God, fully relying on the Spirit's guidance and wisdom.

As much strength and ingenuity as we possess, it is God's power through the Gospel that transforms hearts, communities, and our world. Keeping the Savior's glory first in your mind, how can you seek justice and mercy?

Jesus, You were not content to leave us in our sorry state. Please give me compassion for my community and my world. I need wisdom to know how to follow You in pursuing justice and mercy. Amen.

And behold, a woman in the city who was a sinner, when she knew that Jesus sat at the table in the Pharisee's house, brought an alabaster flask of fragrant oil, and stood at His feet behind Him weeping; and she began to wash His feet with her tears, and wiped them with the hair of her head; and she kissed His feet and anointed them with the fragrant oil.
LUKE 7:37-38 NKJV

Although the crowds would later turn against Him, Jesus enjoyed some popularity during His ministry. He was sought after as a Healer and Rabbi and was invited to homes and gatherings.

However, the religious leaders were not happy with the common people who continually approached Christ. In their eyes, it was scandalous for a holy man to interact with the crowds and especially with "sinners."

Yet Jesus was approachable. He was available. His very manner invited people to come to Him; they could sense that they were welcome in His presence. Perhaps nowhere was this more evident than when a sinful woman entered the house of a Pharisee where Jesus was a guest and anointed Him with precious perfume. The "righteous" folks were incensed; Jesus was not. He came to show us that the Father wants to have a relationship with us.

As we live out our Christian witness, may you and I be approachable. May we let the love of Christ shine through us and draw others to His light and love.

Dear God, thank You for being approachable. Thank You for wanting me to come close to You. Let me show that love to others. In Christ's name, amen.

Being confident of this, that he who began a good work in you will carry it on to completion until the day of Christ Jesus.
PHILIPPIANS 1:6 NIV

It was love at first sight. I could picture my two-year-old climbing onto the seat of the child-sized wooden rocker sitting at the curb. The "free" sign next to it gave me the okay to claim it for my own.

My husband and I examined it closer. It was sturdy enough to keep it, but it desperately needed to be stripped down to its base coat of paint.

Fast-forward two hours, the kids were in bed and my husband and I were outside, taking the paint off the chair. The paint stripper wasn't working as easily as we thought it would, so we had a long way until it was finished. I remember thinking: *Is it worth it?*

At that moment, I pictured the end result: my son in his new chair with a big smile on his face, rocking back and forth. That made it worth it.

Jesus looks at us in this same way. When He looks at us, He sees the end result. He sees who we are and who we can become. The vision of our future with Him for eternity and the picture of us made righteous because of Him, propelled Him not only through His life on earth, but also a horrific death and tremendous resurrection.

Jesus' life is proof that you are valuable to God. Live from that understanding.

Lord, let the determination Jesus reflected propel me forward and remind me how valuable I am to You.

LISTEN CAREFULLY

So we must listen very carefully to the truth we have heard,
or we may drift away from it.
HEBREWS 2:1 NLT

L istening is a dying art. Especially "listening very carefully," as we're instructed to do in this verse. Modern society offers too many distractions, and we're fortunate if we can listen without interruption. Even when outside forces don't disturb us, our own thoughts take us in a thousand different directions.

Christ was attentive. When someone spoke to Him, He listened with His ears and with His spirit. He didn't just hear the words; He looked for the meaning behind those words so He could hear their hearts.

Our lives would be changed, our relationships revolutionized if we'd follow this one principal: be attentive. When we listen carefully to others, we send a message that they are valuable, that they're worth our time and consideration. When we pay full attention to what God's Word says, we gain wisdom and understanding.

Christ was alert and gave His full concentration to God and to other people. He didn't allow Himself to be distracted by things that, in the long run, wouldn't matter much. He valued His Father, and He valued the people His Father loved. By modeling our attentiveness after this aspect of Christ's character, we honor God and show His love to the people around us.

Dear Father, teach me to listen carefully, both to You
and to other people. When I get distracted, send me reminders
to give my full attention to people, not things. Amen.

I have been crucified with Christ; and it is no longer I who live, but Christ lives in me; and the life which I now live in the flesh I live by faith in the Son of God, who loved me and gave Himself up for me.
GALATIANS 2:20 NASB

This verse starts out with what may appear as an uncomfortably gruesome concept, but it is actually brimming with hope. Those who are in Christ have died with Him. He has taken over your life. You are no longer subject to the temptations and cravings of the world. You can say "no" to sin because Christ in all His power has taken residence in you. Because Christ lives in you, you have access to His strength, His joy, and His peace. Empty yourself of the thoughts, actions, and desires of your old self so that these things can fill you completely.

Paul lived his life on earth by faith in Christ. Inevitably, life will continue to be filled with struggles over sin. That is why you need to live in faith, looking forward to the day when Christ will perfect His work in you. Who better to have faith in than the One who loved you enough to give Himself up for you? If He was willing to go to those lengths, you can be confident that He will not fail you through this life.

Lord, help me recognize that it is no longer I who live, but You who lives in me.

HE FILLS THE HUNGRY

"The Powerful One has done great things for me. His name is holy."
LUKE 1:49 NCV

When Gabriel came to Mary and told her she was going to give birth to the Son of God, she had questions. After all, she was human. However, she was also humble, grateful, and quick to obey. Mary didn't say, "Now, wait a minute! I had plans! This isn't the way I had pictured things. I don't want a baby right now. I'm too young." Instead, she praised the Lord and surrendered her will to His. Her response is one of the most magnificent passages in the Bible.

Echoing passages in the Old Testament, Mary declared: "He has brought down rulers from their thrones and raised up the humble. He has filled the hungry with good things" (Luke 1:52–55 NCV).

God chose Mary because He anticipated her obedience. He knew that she had a heart of faith and that she longed for more than earthly things. When we seek Jesus, God chooses to bless us, as well. . .with spiritual gifts, ministry opportunities, and more.

What are you hungry for? Connection? Friendship? Understanding? Creative refreshment? Spiritual renewal? The Bible tells us that if you seek God, you will find Him. What a tremendous promise! He can provide you with connection, intimacy, refreshment, and renewal—much more than earthly friends.

Take heart: when you follow hard after Jesus, God will fill you with good things!

Heavenly Father, thank You for filling me with good things.
Thank You for the gift of Jesus. Help me be obedient to You
and surrender myself to You as Mary did.

FORGET YOUR AGE!

"Truly I tell you, anyone who will not receive the kingdom of God like a little child will never enter it." And he took the children in his arms, placed his hands on them and blessed them.
MARK 10:15–16 NIV

Marla dripped puddles while in line for the "Bonsai" at the water park. The mother of two didn't feel the least bit self-conscious about being the only one on the rides and in the water who wasn't a tween. When Marla reached the slide that shot swimmers into the pool as from a cannon, the lifeguard stopped her.

"I'm afraid you can't go on the Bonsai."

"What? I'm healthy and strong. Is this age prejudice?"

"No," the lifeguard answered. "More like swimsuit prejudice."

She glanced at her knee-length cut-off jeans. "What's wrong with these? Everybody swims in cut-offs during the summer."

"Jeans take the wax off the slide. Come back when you're wearing Spandex swimsuits like these kids."

Some would disapprove of Marla's youth-like zest. Yet Jesus does want us to come to Him like a child, openly trusting and taking chances. Christianity is not a spectator sport to be observed from the sidelines. Though he doesn't expect childish behavior from those who follow him, he does seek childlike trust and joy.

Look for it in your heart and spirit each day.

Jesus, I believe You are the Son of God. Keep my heart like a child's in trusting You and Your lifetime lessons for me.

*Let us therefore come boldly to the throne of grace, that we may obtain
mercy and find grace to help in time of need.*
HEBREWS 4:16 NKJV

W hy don't we take a lamb to church with us? When Jesus lived in Israel, being right with God required sacrificing unblemished lambs at the temple. Jesus' death as the perfect "Lamb of God, who takes away the sin of the world" ended the need for animal sacrifices and tore open the veil into the Holy of Holies (John 1:29 NIV). That room represented God's presence and could only be entered by the high priest once a year. Jesus changed everything. We now have boldness to enter God's presence, because Jesus is our "great High Priest" who continually intercedes for us (Hebrews 4:14 NKJV).

In light of this, Hebrews 10:22–25 lists three things we should pursue: Verse 22 – let us draw near in heart to God; Verse 23 – let us hold on to our hope without wavering; Verses 24–25 – Let us encourage each other to be loving and good and not neglect meeting together. The passage also gives reasons for these pursuits. (1) Because we are completely cleansed from sin. (2) Because God is faithful. Even if I do waver or become unfaithful, I will miss out on fellowship with Him but it will not cancel out His faithful relationship to me. (3) Because the end is drawing near.

*Jesus, my forever High Priest, the closer I get to the end of my life
and to the end times, the closer I want to draw near. Thank You
for providing the way. Amen.*

BLESSED IN HIS EMBRACE

"You're blessed when you're at the end of your rope. With less of you there is more of God and his rule. . . . You're blessed when you feel you've lost what is most dear to you. Only then can you be embraced by the One most dear to you."
MATTHEW 5:3, 5 MSG

When I was younger, nothing beat a bear hug from my brother. The older I got, the more I appreciated them. He was just under three years older and had wider shoulders than me, so I fit nicely inside his arms.

In 2009, he passed away from a rare form of cancer at the age of 30. Yeah. I know. It stinks—but in those months and years to follow, I can say the above verses have proven absolutely true. God has demonstrated His love, truth, faithfulness, and grace during a time of loss, heartache, and hurt. He has embraced me—mentally, emotionally, spiritually. . .and physically.

Around the time when my brother was diagnosed with the cancer, I met my future husband. One of the many things I love about him is that his shoulders are even wider than my brothers; I fit even better inside his arms. His hugs show me his love, but also remind me of my brother's hugs and of God's love.

The "end of your rope" will come at some point in your life. When it does, run to God. Stay in His arms. He will hold you, squeeze you, and provide you with the hugs and love you need.

Jesus, may I run into Your embrace in my darkest days and be fully surrounded by Your love.

And He did not answer him with regard to even a single charge,
so the governor was quite amazed.
MATTHEW 27:14 NASB

One of the most impressive traits of Christ, in the long list of impressive traits, is His ability to know when to keep His mouth shut. Here He was, standing in front of the governor with all sorts of accusations falling on Him. Most of us would have defended ourselves. Most of us would have done our best to tell our sides of the story. If we had the ability to zap our accusers into oblivion, most of us would have done that, too.

Not Jesus. He had sense enough to know He'd be wasting His breath. The people around Him had already made up their minds. To speak in His defense would have only created an even bigger riot. So He stood there and took it, without saying a word.

There are certainly times when it's prudent to speak up. Other times, it's best to just keep our mouths shut. When the listeners are hard-hearted, when they won't hear anyway and will only use our words against us, we need to follow Christ's example and remain silent. The God of justice will see it all, and in the end, those who follow Him faithfully will be rewarded.

Dear Father, It's so hard to control my tongue. It's hard to keep my mouth shut sometimes—especially when I know I'm right. Help me to follow Christ's example and remain silent when silence is the best course of action. Amen.

ONE HIGH PRIEST

Seeing then that we have a great High Priest, who has passed through the heavens, Jesus the Son of God, let us hold fast our confession. For we do not have a High Priest who cannot sympathize with our weaknesses but was in all points tempted as we are yet without sin. Let us therefore come boldly to the throne of grace that we may obtain mercy and find grace to help in time of need.
HEBREWS 4:14-16 NKJV

Faithful Christians may sometimes find themselves doubting their worthiness or overcome by their inability to appease a holy God. Jesus is the One who makes us worthy. He is our great High Priest who suffered through the same things as we do. God was giving Himself limitations to show us that He knows what it is like to live in this fallen world. Yet He kept Himself sinless through all the temptations, and there were many (one needs only count the times Jesus was confronted by cynical and threatening religious leaders).

Through His obedience, He became victorious over everything, and He calls believers to share in His victory. Unlike the earthly high priest who brought a yearly sacrifice for his own sin, Jesus offered Himself as the spotless sacrificial lamb once for eternity. Now He works in our hearts daily. We just need to boldly approach God's throne of grace on a daily basis and we will find the help we need.

Abba, let me hold tightly to my faith, no matter what trials and temptations may come. Thank You for Jesus, who always intercedes for us.

THE LOVE COMMANDS

One of the teachers of the law came and heard them debating. Noticing that Jesus had given them a good answer, he asked him, "Of all the commandments, which is the most important?"
MARK 12:28 NIV

Watch any debate and you'll identify with the one whose answers best fit your personal perspective. This individual may be warm, humorous, and eloquent or they might be cool, caustic, and unrefined, but they'll earn your respect for their willingness to stand for their beliefs.

Jesus met someone who'd heard Him debate. This observer (a teacher of the law) recognized good answers, and Jesus spoke clearly. Perhaps the teacher thought he'd trap Jesus, or maybe he was just curious, but he asked for Jesus' perspective on what was the most important of God's commands.

Jesus' answer had two parts and was relatively simple. Love God and love everybody else. These two summary statements reflected everything the teacher would have known to be true about scripture. Every law had something to do with either the way we love God or how we show love to others. For example, love doesn't lie or cheat. It isn't unfaithful or rude. Love believes, hopes, and cherishes (see 1 Corinthians 13).

To love God and others will always be more important than what you can give or sacrifice.

Love is something I share because it's something I receive. Because You love me, I can let that love spill over to others. Because You loved me first, You have shown me how to love You in return. While it's never easy, help me obey Your love commands. Amen.

And he said to them, "Well did Isaiah prophesy of you hypocrites, as it is written, "'This people honors me with their lips, but their heart is far from me; in vain do they worship me, teaching as doctrines the commandments of men.' You leave the commandment of God and hold to the tradition of men."
MARK 7:6-8 ESV

The way Jesus admonished the Pharisees would have surprised anyone in the Jewish community. These leaders were respected as the holiest and most Law-abiding men among the people. However, Jesus revealed the hypocrisy and legalism in their hearts. The Pharisees kept the Law to the letter but abandoned its heart, burdening the people with unnecessary rules for following the Law "correctly." Their obedience didn't spring from their love for God, but for the sake of their reputations. Holding tightly to their accomplishments, many Pharisees chose to reject Jesus' message rather than be proven wrong before the people.

If you are in Christ, you must stop practicing hypocrisy and legalism. God doesn't keep score on how well you do each day. He is interested in your heart—we obey out of gratitude for our salvation, not for man's approval. Instead of worrying about "how good you've been," humbly confess your sins and failures to Jesus. He is faithful and gracious to forgive and to strengthen our hearts so we can follow Him in joy.

Lord Jesus, thank You for forgiving all my sin. Open my eyes to see Your mercy and grace afresh. Holy Spirit, search my heart and show me any hypocrisy and legalism. Restore me to joy and freedom in Jesus. Amen.

Then, six days before the Passover, Jesus came to Bethany,
where Lazarus was who had been dead, whom He had raised
from the dead. There they made him a supper; and Martha served:
but Lazarus was one of those who sat at the table with Him.
JOHN 12:1-2 NKJV

D o you think Jesus had fun? Do you think He enjoyed "downtime" with friends?

We aren't told much about the social life of Jesus outside the realm of ministry, but these verses give a little insight. From this and other references in the Gospels, we are quite sure that this home in Bethany was one where Jesus was a frequent guest. This sibling trio of Martha, Mary, and Lazarus seems to be close to the Teacher.

Martha felt comfortable enough to ask Him to prod Mary to help her in the kitchen. Mary sat at His feet and poured precious ointment on His feet in an act of adoration. When Lazarus was sick and near death, the sisters sent a message to Jesus telling Him, "Lord, the one you love is sick" (John 11:3 NIV).

Jesus believed that friendships were important. It seems He took time to cultivate these relationships. If we are to follow His steps, we must not try to go through life alone. We must joyfully accept those God brings into our lives to encourage us, strengthen us, and gladden us. We must gather often with friends.

Lord, thank You for my good friends. Help me to be one as well. Amen.

*Therefore be imitators of God, as beloved children. And walk in love,
as Christ loved us and gave himself up for us,
a fragrant offering and sacrifice to God.*
EPHESIANS 5:1-2 ESV

It's been said that the highest form of flattery is imitation. When others want to be like us, it means they admire us. When we imitate God, we show Him we admire Him and long to be like Him.

A small, dearly loved child might share that she wants to be just like her mommy when she grows up. She dresses in high heels, puts on lipstick, and practices walking and talking like her mother. If given the opportunity to answer the phone, she might even mimic her mother's intonations when saying hello. She does this because she adores her mother, because she sees in her mother everything good and worthy and admirable.

The Bible tells us God is love. When we imitate Christ, we become living, breathing examples of that love. We begin to look more like Him, as we take off our own self-centered thoughts and dress up in His clothing, His way of thinking. Then, something miraculous happens. We begin to take on a family resemblance to God, and we more fully experience the other aspects of His character: joy, peace, patience, kindness, and goodness. When we imitate God, He transforms us into His image, and pours out His blessings on our lives.

*Dear Father, I want to be just like You. Help me to love the way
Christ loves. Amen*

Therefore He is able also to save to the uttermost (completely, perfectly, finally, and for all time and eternity) those who come to God through Him, since He is always living to make petition to God and intercede with Him and intervene for them.
HEBREWS 7:25 AMP

love the way the Amplified version of the Bible expands on the idea of people being saved to the "uttermost" (especially since that's not a word we use every day). The translators weren't adding words; it's just that the Greek means much more than the English, so they enhanced the word to encompass the fuller meaning. The New Living Translation uses the phrase, once and forever. Christians may toss around the word *salvation* without really thinking about what it means, but this gets our brains busy. Salvation is total redemption—perfect, final, eternal.

There is no other way to God except through Jesus. He said in the Gospel of John, "I am the way. . ." That was a bold claim when He was on earth. Lots of people already resented Him, and that didn't give them any warm feelings. Yet what assurance! It's all we need.

After Jesus ascended into Heaven, we're told He was seated at God's right hand, talking to the Father about us. He prays and intervenes for us. What an extraordinary privilege, to be in Jesus' mind and on His lips.

He went to the cross for you and me. How can we be ho-hum about Him?

*Precious Lord, Thank You for saving me perfectly and for all time.
I never have to worry about being unsaved.*

CHRIST'S ATTITUDE

Have this attitude in yourselves which was also in Christ Jesus, who, although He existed in the form of God, did not regard equality with God a thing to be grasped, but emptied Himself, taking the form of a bond-servant, and being made in the likeness of men. Being found in appearance as a man, He humbled Himself by becoming obedient to the point of death, even death on a cross.
PHILIPPIANS 2:5-8 NASB

You are to have the same attitude as Christ had. So what should you be emulating?

Christ did not feel that He was entitled to anything. He is God, and, therefore, has abundantly more reason to feel entitled than anyone on earth. Still, He did not consider Himself equal with God and became just like us.

Christ was willing to step into the experience of another. Instead of keeping His distance from those who could give Him nothing in return, He became human in order to fully understand and ultimately redeem us.

Christ emptied Himself for the good of others. He was not thinking at all about Himself and what He wanted. His only thought was to fulfill the will of God by loving humanity more than we could possibly deserve.

Christ was humble. With complete absence of pride, Christ silently endured unjust accusations and treatment and willingly died a shameful death on the cross.

Lord, help me be like You by being humble, unselfish, and concerned for the interests of others over my own desires.

LIFE OF THE PARTY

Then Levi gave Him a great feast in his own house. And there were a great number of tax collectors and others who sat down with them.
LUKE 5:29 NKJV

Jesus walked by the tax collector, Matthew (otherwise known as Levi), and beckoned him, "Follow me." Matthew immediately left all behind and followed Jesus. There was, however, one thing he did not abandon. His excitement at being called by Jesus was so great that Matthew decided to throw a party, and he invited his tax collector and other unpopular, sinful friends. Matthew still loved his friends. Now he loved Jesus more, and he wanted them to know Jesus as the Rescuer. Jesus loved them, too. He was willing to endure scorn from the Pharisees for sitting at a meal with sinners. These sinners were drawn to Jesus— the Doctor who came to heal their sin-infected hearts. Jesus extended to them the same love he showed to the former tax collector-turned-disciple.

Matthew did exactly what any believer should do: he heard Jesus calling him, he dropped everything, and obeyed; he let God's redeeming love inundate his heart, and then he spread the joy of saving grace to his lost friends. Jesus came to Matthew, and then Matthew brought his friends to Jesus. What better place to do so than at a feast! Do I invite people to my house to encounter Jesus?

Friend of Sinners, forgive me for not showing the same joy and hospitality as Matthew. Give me greater courage and love to share Jesus with my friends who are far from God.

OVERFLOWING HOPE

May the God of hope fill you with all joy and peace as you trust in Him, so that you may overflow with hope by the power of the Holy Spirit.
ROMANS 15:13 NIV

How do we find hope when life overwhelms us? Each day, the news is filled with reports of terrorist attacks, plane crashes, economic crises, and more. All the chaos swirling around the planet can make us want to crawl back in bed, pull the covers over our heads, and never come out.

Instead of burrowing our heads in our beds, let's hit our knees right after our feet hit the ground in the morning. There, we can ask God for His perspective. He knows the future, because He is already there. We don't have to worry about what will happen; we just need to trust that He will be with us, no matter what.

On our knees, we can also listen to His voice and determine to obey what He calls us to do. Perhaps He wants to use us to minister to those who have been hurt by the sinful choices of broken people. Perhaps we've made those choices and we need to ask forgiveness; or we need to forgive someone who hurt us.

If we live with ears tuned to the Spirit's voice, and eyes open to see His workings in the world, our lives become a living, dynamic portrait of God's presence, promises, and power.

Lord, You hold me close when the world seems out of control. You have the power to heal our broken world. Use me, Lord, to bring light to the darkness.

"GOOD SHEPHERD" SALVATION

*[Jesus said,] "I am the good shepherd. The good shepherd
lays down his life for the sheep."*
JOHN 10:11 NIV

Sheep are not smart animals. They require the care of a
compassionate shepherd who leads, refreshes, guides, prepares,
anoints, and loves (see Psalm 23). It would be strange if we naturally
thought that being compared to sheep made us look good. We are called
sheep because we need protection, guidance, and love.

We are described as sheep because we need a picture of the
vulnerability we experience due to our greatest adversary, the devil, who
is described as a thief who comes to steal, kill, and destroy (see John
10:10).

Jesus paints a picture of a place of protection for His sheep. He
describes himself as the gate through which we enter. He came to give us
abundant life. This life is available through the protection He offers, and
He demonstrated that love all the way to the cross.

Sheep recognize the voice of their shepherd, they express trust in
His goodness, and they know that He loves them without condition. The
Good Shepherd would die before He'd ever allow the adversary to take
His sheep, but *this* Shepherd can—and did—take up His life again (John
10:18).

Sheep need a shepherd. Humanity needs a Savior. Jesus *is* the Good
Shepherd Savior.

*I need Jesus. While I may not be thrilled with the idea of being compared to a
sheep, I also know that I look to You for protection, guidance, and love.
Keep me in Your care, and keep my feet from stumbling. Amen.*

ONE COUPLE, ONE FAMILY, ONE GOD

*Jesus was indignant. He reached out his hand and touched the man.
"I am willing," he said. "Be clean!" Immediately the leprosy
left him and he was cleansed.*
MARK 1:41–42 NIV

The people of Jesus' time feared leprosy. Today, it is easily cured with medicines. They saw it as a terrifying contagious disease. Aside from it being incurable at the time, it was a deal breaker in families, marriages, and communities.

Scaly sores which identified leprosy in Jesus' time were only the beginning. Lepers became shunned outcasts. No longer allowed to worship in the synagogue, to mingle with family, friends, and community members, they lost the ability to work and live in their own homes. If married, they could no longer have intimate relations. Aside from not feeling pain due to damage to the nervous system, many lost fingers, toes, and noses. Their eyes became deformed. Victims' only destiny was a leper colony—and death.

Yet God celebrates the whole person. When Jesus healed the leper, he also sent the man to a priest, where the victim would be pronounced clean. Then the former leper could return to his family, work, community, and place of worship.

Jesus gave him more than the gift of health. He gave him back his life. The head of household and his wife again became one couple, one family, worshipping one God. There is no better endorsement of God's love of the family.

---

*Thank you, Jesus, for valuing family and giving the strength of healing
to all in difficult family roles and responsibilities.*

WHAT DO YOU BELIEVE?

For since we believe that Jesus died and was raised to life again,
we also believe that when Jesus returns, God will bring back
with him the believers who have died.
1 THESSALONIANS 4:14 NLT

Since we live in a sinful world, we have the opportunity, when we are young, to develop negative belief systems about ourselves and others. For example, a young child who is abandoned by a parent may feel that everyone will abandon him. A child whose physical needs were neglected may come to believe that he is not worthy of receiving care. In psychology, these are called *schema*, and they have a profound effect on our ability to function well. We typically are not consciously aware of schema, but our behavior is greatly impacted.

We can develop spiritual schema as well. We may develop faulty beliefs, such as God loves others, but he doesn't love me, or I'm not worthy of forgiveness. Take a moment to examine your beliefs about Jesus. Do they match scripture? If you believe that Jesus died and was raised to life again, you will live in a way that is expectant and eager for His return.

Jesus, thank You for Your death on the cross. Examine my heart and see if there are any faulty beliefs in me. Use scripture to correct my faulty thinking, and allow my behavior to reflect what I know to be true about You. Amen.

Do not think of yourself more highly than you ought.
ROMANS 12:3 NIV

Jesus told a story that shatters the notion that what we do is more important than what we are (Luke 18:9–14). He said that two men went to the temple to pray. The Pharisee told God how good he was compared to other people, especially tax collectors. The tax collector, on the other hand, felt no worth before God, not even looking up. He beat his breast saying, "God, be merciful to me, a sinner." Jesus said the tax collector, not the Pharisee, went home justified (right with God). Why? Pharisees were the most respected members of society in first-century Judea, while tax collectors were despised. However, God's economy is opposite from ours. He despises the proud attitude of those who try to impress others with their religious rituals or spiritual experiences. The Pharisee used the wrong standard of comparison—other people, while the tax collector saw God's standard and realized his unworthiness. Jesus said the Pharisee was confident of his own righteousness and looked down on everyone else. In contrast, the tax collector humbled himself and received the mercy he requested.

Jesus commends those who view themselves as undeserving sinners, dependent on God, not those who concentrate on their own performance. I mistakenly crave human praise for my accomplishments, but God wants to develop my character until my driving motive becomes knowing and loving Him.

Lord Jesus, please forgive my selfish ambition, conceit, and superior attitude. Help me consider others above myself and value pleasing You above all. Be merciful to me, a sinner. Amen.

COURTEOUSNESS COUNTS

Now when they drew near Jerusalem, to Bethphage and Bethany, at the Mount of Olives, He sent two of His disciples; and He said to them, "Go into the village opposite you; and as soon as you have entered it you will find a colt tied, on which no one has sat. Loose it and bring it. "And if anyone says to you, 'Why are you doing this?' say, 'The Lord has need of it,' and immediately he will send it here."

MARK 11:1-3 NKJV

If ever there was a human who had the right to command and demand, it was Jesus. He was, after all, God in the flesh. He made everything, according to John 1:3, and for His glory, it is all sustained. Yet, Jesus was not rude; He didn't assert His divine authority over others in His everyday dealings unless it was part of the Father's plan. He was kind, humble, and polite.

Don't you wonder if Mary taught Jesus the common practices of etiquette followed then? It's amazing to imagine that He allowed Himself to be educated and trained. Yet, as God, He knew full well how to interact with others. He treated them with common courtesy. In this narrative, He instructs His disciples to explain to the owners of the colt why they are taking it.

Being a Christian doesn't negate the necessity of courteousness; rather, it heightens it. Of all people, Jesus' followers should be known for their consideration and respect for others. After all, that's the way He was.

Lord, remind me to be courteous in my dealings with others so that they may see You in me. Amen.

THE SAME FOREVER

Jesus Christ is the same yesterday and today and forever.
Do not be led away by diverse and strange teachings, for it is good
for the heart to be strengthened by grace, not by foods,
which have not benefited those devoted to them.
HEBREWS 13:8-9 ESV

Even if you watched every news channel on the planet, it would be impossible to keep up with all the changes the world experiences in a single day. Thankfully, we put our confidence in the One who never changes, even as the world goes whirling by. We know His love will never diminish nor will His promises fade; His love and truth are everlasting.

The author of Hebrews warns his readers to be wary of "diverse and strange teachings." From the context, the author was referencing teachings about ceremonial foods and practices, but the warning stands true for teachings about Jesus as well. If Jesus never changes, we ought to listen carefully to what is taught about Him. Does it match with what He declares about Himself in scripture? We should study deeply, examining the Word afresh. The Spirit will guide us into understanding the truth about our Savior (John 16:13).

Although He is unchanging, our Lord contains all the riches of wisdom and knowledge (Colossians 2:3). Though we study our whole lives, we will always have something more to learn about Him. In the surety of His love, keep seeking to know your Savior more and more deeply.

Dear Jesus, I thank You that You are an unshakeable foundation. Give me a heart that seeks after wisdom...that seeks after knowing You deeply. Amen.

BE PERFECT

"You therefore must be perfect, as your heavenly Father is perfect."
MATTHEW 5:48 ESV

What is this, some kind of setup? How can we be perfect? God's Word clearly tells us that all have sinned, and that no one is without fault. Yet, here is a command to be perfect, like God is perfect.

Many scholars translate the word as "blameless and pure." While we'll never attain sinless perfection here on earth, we can walk blamelessly before God. We can stand before Him with clean hands and a pure heart.

Sure, we'll mess up. Just as we bathe regularly to keep our bodies clean, a strong prayer life will help keep our hearts clean. Just as we avoid stomping in the mud or playing in trashcans, we can avoid romping in the sin and mire that will contaminate our spirits.

Avoid the dirty places. Bathe regularly in prayer. Perfume ourselves by loving the way God loves. When we're careful to do these things, we will keep ourselves clean, pure, and blameless before God.

Dear Father, I want to be pure and blameless before You. Amen.

LOVE AS HE LOVED US

"This is My commandment, that you love others as I have loved you."
JOHN 15:12 NKJV

What does loving others as Christ has loved us look like? Jesus was a servant, so loving others as He did means sacrificing our time, talents, and treasures. Jesus was compassionate, so loving the way He did also means having empathy and sharing someone's burdens. We don't stay at an arm's distance, but we wrap our arms around the person who is hurting and give them comfort and help.

Jesus often reached out to those who were different and ostracized. Loving as He loved might mean inviting someone—perhaps a coworker who is annoying and immature—to lunch. It might mean taking someone's side when they are being made fun of or defending a weak person against a bully.

Jesus also spent His time following God's commands and desires for Him, not the world's desires. If your friends are going down the wrong path and making sinful choices, you can be "Jesus" to them by warning them and holding them accountable (in love, not judging them but prayerfully and carefully talking to them about the decisions they're making). Maybe your spouse is feeling called to give a bigger portion of your income or to go to a specific mission field. Love them like Jesus by listening to them and seeking God's best for your family. . .whatever it might cost you. Loving others like Jesus loves them isn't easy, but He will bless us when we obey this commandment.

Jesus, thank You for the way You love me. Give me courage to love others the same way.

WITNESS THE BEAUTIFUL IRONY

Then the [blind] man said, "Lord, I believe," and he worshiped him.
JOHN 9:38 NIV

The church service was underway. The young man in the back seemed uncomfortable. While others connected with the song lyrics and the idea of assigning worth to God, the man seemed as if any place was preferable to a church pew.

There's a simple and compelling reason why some who attend a church service feel awkward. They don't understand why worship is important.

In today's verse, Jesus interacted with a man to whom He'd restored sight. That interaction explains why worship can seem difficult. When we struggle with belief, we'll also struggle with worship. The other side of the story is that when we believe, worship comes naturally.

How can we honor the God who saves when we aren't convinced He can? How can we worship the One who loves us when we haven't accepted His love?

The fact that this truth comes from the experience of a blind man is a beautiful irony. Before Jesus, there is much we can't see or understand about God. Salvation is God's way of opening our eyes to things we couldn't comprehend on our own.

Before belief in Jesus, understanding the need to worship God seemed more like a chore than an honor. By believing Jesus is God's Son, I see that He's the only One capable of paying for my sin and offering me new and everlasting life. What I've been saved from is one thing, but what I gained in becoming His child is worthy of worship. May I never lose the joy of praising You. Amen.

BETTER THAN ANY LED FLASHLIGHT

When Jesus spoke again to the people, he said, "I am the light of the world. Whoever follows me will never walk in darkness, but will have the light of life."
JOHN 8:12 NIV

A s the family got their dome tent staked down, with the wind snapping at it like a shopping bag, Dad shouted over the storm to his teen sons, "It'll rain soon. Let's hunker down inside!"

In time, their LED flashlights faded to a glow while the storm went on and on. With a furious gust, the wind lifted the rainfly off, took it up as high as a kite, and it was gone. As the four squinted at the mesh skylight overhead, their faces became wet with rain.

Dad sprinted for the truck and turned on the headlights. He spotted the rainfly pinned tight against a tree across the meadow. He retrieved it. The four wrestled it back on and stayed inside until dark melted into dawn.

Just as any outdoor family needs light for successful fishing, hiking, camping, canoeing, so we need Jesus to see our way. Just as an LED flashlight shines through small troubles, Jesus brightens our biggest challenges. However, unlike the LED, whose parts wear out, Jesus, the Son of God, gives us light that lasts forever. There is no darkness in him. There never will be. When we follow him, we're on the right trail.

Help us live our lives to reflect Your light and path, Jesus.

THE PASSWORD

For there is one God and one Mediator between God and men,
the Man Christ Jesus.
1 TIMOTHY 2:5 NKJV

God's people in Old Testament times had no access to God on their own. A priest had to mediate. We probably don't realize how good we have it today. Thanks to Jesus' death and resurrection, no one takes an unblemished animal to church as an offering, and we have direct access to God any time, any place. Three verses talk about access to God through Jesus. First, Romans 5:1–2 (NKJV) assures us that we have peace with God through our Lord Jesus Christ, and "access by faith into this grace in which we stand." Second, not only does Jesus give us peace with God, but He also provides peace with each other (Ephesians 2:14–19). Jesus demolished the age-old barrier between Jews and Gentiles (and any other ethnic group) so we all "have access by one Spirit to the Father." Finally, through faith in Jesus, we "have boldness and access with confidence" (Ephesians 3:12 NKJV).

If God required a password, it would be "Jesus." Through Him, we stand before God in Grace and boldly enjoy His company. We have undeserved peace and harmony with Almighty God, as well as equal footing with all other Christians. Jesus has removed the veil between us and God and broken down the wall between us and other Christians. Amazing Grace.

Lord Jesus, accept my humble praise for all You have done for me
and what You mean to me. I cannot comprehend even a fraction
of these privileges, but I am grateful. Amen.

BEWARE THE HYPOCRITE

Those who exalt themselves will be humbled, and those who humble themselves will be exalted.
MATTHEW 23:12 NIV

Have you ever met someone who can point out flaws, give a five-step plan to fix any issue, and portray themselves as faultless? It's possible to leave an encounter with someone like this and think: 1) I can never be as good as they are and 2) they can't really be as good as they seem.

Jesus viewed the teachers of the law and Pharisees of His day as individuals who weren't worth following. Jesus said, "They tie up heavy, cumbersome loads and put them on other people's shoulders, but they themselves are not willing to lift a finger to move them" (Matthew 23:4 NIV). Pharisees gave information that was technically correct, but they didn't follow their own instructions. They required others to follow, but they seemed to have acquired immunity from personal responsibility.

In contrast, we're told to be humble. Even when we do something good, we can bypass the desire for receiving public credit. God knows what we've done, and if He's the One we serve, then His approval is enough. Jesus was very vocal about our need to demonstrate a commitment that didn't just follow commands, but sought to graciously do that which honors a risen Savior.

If I'm honest, it's nice to be noticed for doing something right. It can be easy to ask questions that might allow me to determine whether others think I've done something good. Let me always remember that whatever I do is for Your honor. Let me serve humbly, walk carefully, and follow cheerfully. Amen.

FAMILY RESPONSIBILITY

When Jesus therefore saw His mother, and the disciple whom He loved standing by, He said to His mother, "Woman, behold your son!" Then He said to the disciple, "Behold your mother!" And from that hour that disciple took her to his own home.
JOHN 19:26–27 NKJV

Little is known about the home life of Jesus when He lived on earth. Before He began His public ministry, the record is sparse, and God must have a reason for that. We can surmise He grew up as many children did in His little town. His family wasn't well-to-do; His earthly father was a carpenter, and we know He had half-brothers and sisters. He was respectful of His earthly parents and obedient to their wishes as shown in the account of them finding Him in the temple talking to the teachers.

Some scholars feel that Joseph had died before Jesus went to Calvary. If so, as the oldest son, Jesus had been responsible for the family since that time. This may be the reason why He speaks to John from the cross, committing His mother to his care. Jesus was concerned for His mother, knowing the trauma she was experiencing and feeling the responsibility of His earthly duty to her. He was careful to assure that she would be safe and well.

Likewise, we must embrace the roles given us as husbands, wives, parents, or children and all the responsibilities entailed. In this way, we follow His great example.

Heavenly Father, thank You for creating the home and the family in it. Help me accept and embrace my place and my responsibilities. In Jesus' name, amen.

When Jesus rose early on the first day of the week, he appeared first to Mary Magdalene, out of whom he had driven seven demons. She went and told those who had been with him and who were mourning and weeping.
MARK 16:9-10 NIV

After Jesus was raised from the dead, the angels—and Jesus—appeared to Mary of Magdala first. When she saw Jesus, He simply said her name, and she recognized him. She must have embraced Him, because He told her, "Do not hold onto me" (John 20:17 NIV). He does ask her to do something—to go and tell the others what she's seen. She immediately obeyed her master and teacher. (Anne Graham Lotz says Mary Magdalene was the first evangelist.)

The fact that she mistook him for a gardener is significant. In the Garden of Gethsemane, Jesus asked his disciples to wait while he prayed. Remember what happened? They fell asleep, more than once. Here in the garden near the tomb, the disciples left. Yet Mary stayed—just as she did at the cross. Her reward? Angels—and Jesus—revealed to her in glorious life.

What does a gardener do? He plants, tills, pulls weeds, and waits. Such a glorious thought: *Jesus waits for us!* He waits for us to obey, trust, serve Him wholeheartedly. . .to go and tell!

Friends, Jesus' coming to earth was not just about swaddling clothes. It's about the empty grave clothes. Hallelujah!

Jesus, thank You for Your birth, life, death, and resurrection. I clothe myself in the promise of Your eternal life, so I can show an empty world His healing.

ONE MEANING

By this we know that we abide in Him, and He in us, because He has given us of His Spirit. And we have seen and testify that the Father has sent the Son as Savior of the world. Whoever confesses that Jesus is the Son of God, God abides in him, and he in God.
1 John 4:13-15 NKJV

God was always about revealing Himself to men and women. Though as Creator there are some things that will always be hidden from His creation, He wants humans to know Him and understand how He works. This is best seen when God took on bodily form through Jesus. After Jesus ascended, the Spirit continued His presence on earth by guiding the hearts of believers.

Christians today have God's Word, which God uses to give a deeper understanding and draw people back to Him. The Hungarian playwright András Visky said, "The Bible has one meaning. This meaning is a person. What does this meaning require? A relationship with the person. A relationship with the tri-unity of the person." The beautiful dance of the Trinity will illuminate thoughts and actions once a person grasps this meaning and continually builds up a relationship with Jesus through earnest prayer, Bible reading, and by spreading the Gospel. Not only do we witness the intricate working of the Trinity in and around us, but we live in God and God in us. We are brought into the dance.

Elohim, You give meaning and purpose to everything. Help me live out my faith as a relationship with You.

REDEEMED BY CHRIST

Who gave Himself for us to redeem us from every lawless deed, and to purify for Himself a people for His own possession, zealous for good deeds.
TITUS 2:14 NASB

What does it mean that Christ has redeemed you? He has bought you back. He has paid the price with His own life. This means that you are His. When you buy something, it becomes your possession. You paid for it so you have ownership and rights over it. Christ has paid for you. You belong to Him. Don't feel restricted by this thought. Instead, remember that before Christ redeemed you, sin owned you and was master over you. Belonging to Christ is exponentially better. There is immense freedom and grace in being in Christ's possession.

He redeemed you from every lawless deed. This means that every sin in your past no longer has ownership over you. You have been purified by Christ. Now that you are His, you are to be "zealous for good deeds." Look for ways to do good works throughout the day. Be zealous and passionate about showing Christ to others through your actions. In a world that is still enslaved to sin, doing good deeds is one way to show the world to whom you belong.

Lord, You have redeemed me from a life of being enslaved to sin. I am thankful that I belong to You now. Help me show the world this through my words and actions.

ONLY BELIEVE

Anyone who believes me and is baptized will be saved.
But anyone who refuses to believe me will be condemned.
MARK 16:16 CEV

Many people have a hard time with the concept that belief in Jesus is all it takes to be saved. Some think they have to do something profound. Or be exceptionally virtuous—they hope their good works will outweigh the bad when judgment day comes.

Maybe part of the problem stems from not understanding what *believe* means when it's used in the Bible. We might say, "I believe it's going to rain," or "Can you believe that game?" Yet the word we're talking about here is much more powerful. It means "adhere to, trust in, and rely on." The object of our reliance must be Jesus. It does no good to depend on a church or our own good works or any person except Jesus Christ.

Jesus came as a human being because of profound love. He took our place, suffered excruciating agony, and died because He wanted you and me to have a rich, abundant life and spend eternity with Him. All He asks in return is that we trust Him. Such love demands a response. The only acceptable response is for us to believe that what Jesus did is enough.

He loves for us to pray and sing praises and study the Bible, but those things don't make us any more worthy. It's all about Jesus and what He did.

Dear Lord, I believe You've done it all. I long to worship you forever
and give myself to You, totally, to glorify You in every way.

FLESH AND SPIRIT

The Word became flesh and made his dwelling among us.
We have seen his glory, the glory of the one and only Son,
who came from the Father, full of grace and truth.
JOHN 1:14 NIV

In all the frustration we may feel about our bodies' quirks, illnesses, or aging, we may forget that our bodies were "fearfully and wonderfully made" (Psalm 139:14 NIV). Though these bodies are temporary, our spirits don't just float around inside us. Our hearts and bodies are intimately connected.

Proverbs attests that if our hearts are hurting, then the body feels those effects, too—"a crushed spirit dries up the bones" (17:22 NIV). Studies have also shown that in chronic pain sufferers, anxiety triggers the brain to escalate pain in an attempt to protect the body part in question. If we suffer in any way, it touches all of us—mind, soul, and body.

Jesus profoundly humbled Himself when He came to earth in human flesh. Yet He can sympathize with all our experiences—our physical and emotional pain, and our joys, too—a delicious meal, a cooling breeze, a loved one's embrace. Scripture shows us how His body was connected to His spirit, too—He needed physical rest through times of prayer with the Father, and His great distress showed through Him sweating drops of blood in Gethsemane.

Jesus can empathize with what we feel, and He can comfort us in exactly the way we need. Lean on Him, and He will give you wisdom to take care of yourself well, body and spirit.

Jesus, help me take care of my whole self with wisdom and grace. Amen.

HEAVEN

"Do not let your hearts be troubled. You believe in God; believe also in me.
My Father's house has many rooms; if that were not so,
would I have told you that I am going there to prepare a place for you?"
JOHN 14:1–2 NIV

Isn't it wonderful waiting for guests to arrive? We launder the sheets and tidy the living room. We prepare favorite recipes for a meal joined together, and wait expectantly for our loved ones to appear. Even the wait is exciting. When they arrive, we take their bags, invite them to sit, and serve them with our best silver and china.

As dim as our world can be, we sometimes forget that Jesus is in heaven, at this very moment, preparing a place for us. Our journey is so long and we are tired, but the trials and tribulations we face here will be but a distant memory in the light of heaven. No matter how weary we are, we can hold true to the promise that Jesus has gone before us and is busy preparing the way.

Can you see your mansion? It's there, just over the hilltop.

Oh Jesus, how I long for the promise of heaven. Thank You for working so diligently to prepare a place for me. I cannot wait to share it with You. Amen.

He was despised and rejected by mankind, a man of suffering, and familiar with pain. . . . Surely he took up our pain and bore our suffering.
Isaiah 53:3–4 NIV

D o you sometimes feel like, "Nobody knows the trouble I've seen. Nobody knows but Jesus." Yes, Jesus knew great sorrow and suffering. This does not mean He could not be jovial or upbeat, but He knows the havoc that sin causes on earth and in our lives, and it grieves Him. When we make wrong choices, go astray like an ignorant sheep, or damage a relationship by our selfishness, it hurts Him. He took upon Himself our pain and sufferings. God laid on Him our sins and sorrows when He died in our place on the cross. Therefore, we can have spiritual peace and healing, "The punishment that brought us peace was on him, and by his wounds we are healed" (Isaiah 53:5 NIV).

That's not all. Philippians 3:10 (NASB) speaks about "the fellowship of His sufferings." Because Jesus experienced the gamut of human suffering and emotions, we can run to Him with all our pains and problems. Our sympathetic High Priest not only intercedes for us (Hebrews 4:15, 7:25), but abundantly comforts us in all our afflictions (2 Corinthians 1:5).

Lord Jesus, You suffered and died in my place so I can have spiritual healing. I run to You when I am grieving and lay all my burdens at Your feet. Thank You for taking my sins and sorrows, my afflictions and losses. Help me fellowship with You so I will know Your comfort and be at peace. Amen.

"Therefore everyone who hears these words of mine and puts them into practice is like a wise man who built his house on the rock."
MATTHEW 7:24 NIV

Many professions offer their staff members continuing education opportunities. These are usually in the form of training conferences or webinars. Many will have the opportunity to share new information about their industry with other staff members. These events offer great growth potential by encouraging the application of what you've learned to what you do.

What would happen if you filled notebooks with great information and then tossed them in the closet? Would your boss feel as though a good investment was made in providing the training?

Jesus used the visual image of home builders to bring this point to life for those who followed Him. The wise builder applied what he had learned and built a home on a rock foundation. The foolish builder heard, but never applied, the home building message; he placed his construction on sandy soil. When the rain fell, the wisdom of *application* was visibly evident.

We're responsible for internalizing the good news of the Bible and applying what we learn to the life we lead. When we do, we shouldn't be surprised when others notice the spiritual foundation on which our lives are built.

Teach me to honor You in what I say, what I do, and where I go. More than following You, I want to be one who finds ways to apply Your Word to how I live. May Your commands inform my decision, and may my decisions show wisdom in honoring Your sacrifice. Amen.

"Ask and it will be given to you, seek and you will find; knock and the door will be opened to you. For everyone who asks receives; he who seeks finds; and to him who knocks, the door will be opened."
LUKE 11:9–10 NIV

Mom, I have to go to the bathroom!" Christopher whispered from inside the dark tent. Sandy felt his small feet pressing on her sleeping bag.

She sat up blinking in the dark. "Can't you hold it?"

"No, Mom. I gotta go now!"

So she stood up and lifted the boy to the tent entrance. When she unzipped the door, the sound resounded like a chain saw. The dog woke and wanted a potty break, too. With all the traffic over the sleeping bags, Sandy's husband, Jim, and their other two sons glared at her crossly.

"What's going on? It's the middle of the night!" Jim groused.

Christopher's persistence paid off. He went back to catching Z's. Everyone else dozed until dawn.

Jesus told a parable of a friend who showed up at another's door at midnight asking for loaves of bread. In his time, families slept on mats or low cots close together, much like a family in a small tent. To get up to answer the door meant that the host had to climb over the family members, unlock the door, and see what the neighbor wanted. Yet, because of the visitor's persistence, Jesus said that the host would respond positively—just as God does when we keep asking.

Thank You, Lord, for answering persistent prayers.

THE MINISTRY OF MOTHERHOOD

*"Truly I tell you, whatever you did for one
of the least of these. . .you did for me."*
MATTHEW 25:40 NIV

Janice sighed as she took the laundry out of the dryer. Her mind raced ahead to the tasks that lay before her: fold towels, remove crib sheets, wash sheets, dry sheets, make dinner—not to mention waking the baby, Henry, from his nap, feeding and changing him, and keeping him somewhat happy until bedtime.

She'd been on her feet and in her PJ's all day and only caught a small break to have coffee and a cookie when Henry surrendered to sleep thirty minutes ago. While she loved her boy, the endless tasks mothering required often felt overwhelming and mind-numbingly repetitive. She held a graduate degree in theology from seminary and had given up her full-time job as a women's minister at a large church to stay home with Henry. She loved studying scripture, but in the last few months she barely had enough brainpower to read a short devotional. Beth Moore she wasn't.

Yet when she got really discouraged, the Holy Spirit reminded her—as did her mother, a godly mentor and prayer warrior—that her ministry hadn't ended. She'd just taken a new position. After all, Jesus urged his disciples to care for the "least of these," and babies surely qualified. "Lord, help me find contentment in this season," she prayed. "Give me ears to hear You and eyes to see You in the midst of dishes and diapers."

*Jesus, You Parent us so well. Grant us the strength we need to be godly
mothers to our children.*

This is my comfort in my affliction: Your promise has given me life.
PSALM 119:50 HCSB

In the months preceding her son's birth, Felicity endured a horrendous pregnancy with every symptom you can imagine. She hoped to find relief when Josiah was born. However, right away, she felt panicky. Josiah cried incessantly and slept little (which meant Felicity slept even less).

Depression and anxiety crept into her heart, clawing at the corners of her faith and courage. During the day, as Felicity juggled motherhood and tried to let her body heal from the rigors of childbirth, tears came frequently and her chest felt tight all the time. It felt hard to breathe. When a suicidal thought popped into her mind, Felicity knew it was from Satan. She called her husband, sobbing, and told him she needed to get help. He agreed—and they set up a doctor's and counseling appointment as quickly as possible.

Over time, a godly counselor, stellar support system, exercise, and medication gave Felicity her equilibrium. Her journey back to wholeness was not without its setbacks, but today she blogs as a ministry and often gives her testimony to moms' groups, telling them they are not alone. . . and they're not crazy. She encourages them to ask for help when they need it. "Jesus is my best friend," she tells them. "He gives me peace in the midst of life's chaos."

Jesus, thank You for the ways You help me cope with challenges. I thank You for Your comfort when I'm afflicted. Help me share that peace with others.

GOD LOVES US IN EMBARRASSING MOMENTS

*"Before I formed you in the womb I knew you, before you were born
I set you apart; I appointed you as a prophet to the nations."*
JEREMIAH 1:5 NIV

As Jana wrapped up her speech by pulling on a bathrobe, she noticed one couple following something with their eyes as it headed to the floor near her.

Jana looked down. It was a pair of her lacy underwear!

The red-faced speaker was grateful that she was often introduced as a humorist. Then she smiled. Jana remembered that God loves us through all our worst and most embarrassing moments.

Jesus, the Son of God was sent by his Father. God appointed Him to be Messiah, or "God With Us," as in his name *Immanuel*. [Isaiah 7:14]. His life on earth was full of surprises. Was He a political king riding to victory on a horse? Jesus didn't even have a donkey. Was He an itinerate Rabbi passing a funeral profession? He raised the dead boy to life. Was He an exhausted speaker sleeping in a fishing boat? He stopped the storm.

Jesus demonstrated love and compassion in healing the sick. He raised three from the dead. He fed crowds of thousands after multiplying a few fish and rolls.

He was doing his Father's work, and the Father filled in the blanks: "I knew you before I formed you. Before you were born, I appointed you as. . . the Messiah, the Savior of the World."

*I praise You, God, for the person you have appointed me to be.
Though I am still a work in progress, You love me always.*

Then Jesus came to them and said, "All authority in heaven and on earth has been given to me. Therefore go and make disciples of all nations, baptizing them in the name of the Father and of the Son and of the Holy Spirit, and teaching them to obey everything I have commanded you."
MATTHEW 28:18-20 NIV

Military officers receive commissions. Artists receive commissions. *You* also have received a commission.

A simple way to understand the term 'commission' is as an authorization to produce or deploy. An officer would deploy while an artist would produce. The idea of commission is found in the above words Jesus spoke.

As Christians, we "go" being strengthened by God for a specific purpose. We are both deployed for a mission and authorized to produce disciples. This combination of duties keeps us active, alert, and authentic.

Discipleship is a key directive in being commissioned. While we can never personally save anyone, we can point them in the right direction, and invite them to learn more by following Jesus.

If the commission seems lonely, we need to remember that Jesus doesn't leave us and never lets us down. Accept the commission and deploy good news to neighborhoods, towns, states, nations, and the entire world. Don't panic—just start where you are.

Knowing You have a plan for me is a reminder that You care, but You've also given me a purpose, and that purpose comes with instructions. Whenever I feel as if I am never good enough, let me remember Your commission, seek out Your Word, and find ways to make Your name known. Amen.

Deeply moved, Jesus put out his hand, touched him, and said, "I want to. Be clean." Then and there the leprosy was gone, his skin smooth and healthy. Jesus dismissed him with strict orders: "Say nothing to anyone. Take the offering for cleansing that Moses prescribed and present yourself to the priest. This will validate your healing to the people." But as soon as the man was out of earshot, he told everyone he met what had happened, spreading the news all over town. So Jesus kept to out-of-the-way places, no longer able to move freely in and out of the city. But people found him, and came from all over.

MARK 1:41–45 MSG

Jesus had a specific request for this man. "Say nothing to anyone [about your healing]." What a strange request. Isn't glorifying God one of the reasons He heals?

Continue reading the story, and you'll see Jesus had a reason for asking the man to keep quiet. Jesus' ministry became limited, and He was "no longer able to move freely in and out of the city" because of that man's disobedience.

When Jesus asks us to do something, we may have a logical reason why we shouldn't listen or obey. *It won't hurt anything. I'll just bend the rules slightly. It isn't that big of a deal.* The truth is, when God asks you to do something, He always has a reason. You may not know the reason and may never know the reason. The important thing is that you listen and obey.

Lord, help me obey Your direction, even when I don't understand. In Jesus' name, amen.

A GENEROUS SPIRIT

*"Give, and it will be given to you. A good measure, pressed down,
shaken together and running over, will be poured into your lap.
For with the measure you use, it will be measured to you."*
LUKE 6:38 NIV

It's impossible to out-give God. This verse wipes away any concern we may have about giving too much. When we give to God with wisdom, the right motives, and pure hearts, He gives it back.

Oh, we can't use this promise for our own personal gain; God doesn't always give back the way we expect. Though He sometimes does bless us financially when we give faithfully, He often blesses us with lower bills or a better job or sending a friend to fix our car so we don't have to pay a mechanic.

What we give comes back to us, even with other people. When we show kindness, people tend to be kind to us. When we go the extra mile, others want to go out of their ways for us. If fallen, sinful human beings give back when we give to them, how much more will our heavenly Father show generosity to us when we've held back nothing from Him?

Christ was generous to the point of laying down His life for us. I want to understand that kind of generosity of spirit. I want to give all I have to God and wait with expectancy to see the blessings that follow.

*Dear Father, teach me to have a generous spirit.
Everything I have belongs to You; I give it freely. Amen.*

CONFIDENCE BEFORE THE KING

*So whenever we are in need, we should come bravely
before the throne of our merciful God. There we will be treated
with undeserved kindness, and we will find help.*
HEBREWS 4:16 CEV

O f all the beautiful young women of Susa, King Xerxes made Esther his queen. He put a crown on her head, held a banquet in her honor, and declared a national holiday in her name. Even then, the law was the same for Queen Esther as it was for everyone else. If anyone approached the king without being summoned, they would be put to death, spared only if the king extended the scepter of gold. Esther risked her life to approach the king.

Not so with our King. We have been invited, as His sons and daughters, to come bravely before His throne, whenever we are in need. We will find our God to be merciful and to shower us with undeserved kindness and help from His hands. His gold scepter is forever extended, and we may approach Him at any time.

*Merciful Father in heaven, I thank You for allowing me
to approach You whenever I am in need. You are kind and helpful;
You show Your love to a thousand generations. Thank You
for extending Your golden scepter to me, Your child. Amen.*

A FAIRY-TALE ENDING

He who was seated on the throne said, "I am making everything new!"
Then he said, "Write this down, for these words are trustworthy and true."
REVELATION 21:5 NIV

In his essay "On Fairy-Stories," J.R.R. Tolkien coined the word *eucatastrophe*—"a sudden and miraculous grace" that turns the story from potential doom into a happy ending for the main character. Whether it's a fairy tale or a news story, our hearts are wired to hope for a good ending: that villains will receive their just due and the heroes will live to fight another day.

We wait expectantly for "a happy ending" because our hearts long for restoration. We especially want the world's story to have a happy ending, since often it looks like the bad guys are winning. The Good News is the *eucatastrophe* for the world's story that has already happened! The "sudden and miraculous grace" of Jesus rising triumphant from the grave marked the beginning of the world's restoration. The Book of Revelation makes the end of the story clear. Jesus is making all things new. All evil will be eliminated, and all pain and tears will vanish. Peace will reign forever in the new heaven and the new earth.

As we await our Savior's return, we're still living through the middle of the story. In the midst of a troubled plot, we take hope in His resurrection—the beautiful promise of a happy ending.

Lord Jesus, I know You are bringing Your kingdom in this world and in my life, too. Help me wait patiently for You and Your restoration! Amen.

LET ME SERVE

Jesus, knowing that the Father had given all things into His hands, and that He had come from God and was going to God, rose from supper and laid aside His garments, took a towel and girded Himself. After that, He poured water into a basin and began to wash the disciples' feet, and to wipe them with the towel with which He was girded.

JOHN 13:3-5 NKJV

Serving God sounds like a grand occupation. Yet what if it means serving Him by serving others? What if it means washing dirty feet?

Jesus taught us that greatness in God's eyes is doing what no one else will do. He assured His disciples that the greatest among them would be "the servant of all." Then He gave them a visual by tying a towel around his waist and kneeling before them, washing the dust from their feet as a servant would. The God of the universe stooped to cleanse the skin He had made. We know He wasn't doing it with a vengeful spirit. He was sinless in His motivation, as well as His actions. He did this because He was a servant; He wanted them to embrace that attitude as well.

Throughout Christian history, those who have been great have been quick to serve. That is the secret power of Christ in us, this ability to stoop and serve and do so with a glad heart.

Jesus, show me the towel that You want me to pick up. Give me the grace to serve with a glad heart. In Your name, amen.

THE VALUE OF LIFE: GOD SETS THE STANDARD

[Jesus asked,] "Why all this commotion and wailing?
The child is not dead but asleep". . . . "Little girl, I say to you, get up!"
Immediately the girl stood up and walked around.
MARK 5:39, 41–42 NIV

Jesus valued life. In His days on earth, he honored women and children when most considered them property. Usually, though daughters were counted in a census, only sons were named in genealogies. Jesus raised to life a dead twelve-year-old girl. It was a gift of love for her parents.

FREE REGNANCY TESTS the sign read in front of the family assistance center. In addition to pregnancy tests, the staff provided Christian counseling, diapers, parenting classes, Bible studies, and housing.

High school senior Julie went inside, knowing she was pregnant. She had thought about aborting the fetus. "It isn't a baby, after all," she rationalized. Julie just wanted more information.

"We have a new sonogram machine," nurse/technician Patty told the teen. "Let's see how far along you are." As the nurse moved the instrument over her belly, Julie saw the baby moving. Then she saw it sucking its thumb. The teen was astonished. A tear tracked down her face.

"That's your baby, Julie."

Julie changed her mind. She chose life for her child.

That's just what God does.

Jesus, I thank You for valuing and loving all of us, Your creations.
Teach us to show the same love and care for people that You do.

For the grace of God has appeared, bringing salvation for all people.
TITUS 2:11 NLT

After more than twenty-five years of living life less-than-honestly, Cari suffered depression, anxiety, and panic attacks. However, with Christian counseling, she realized that she was holding onto anger and grief. She was also listening to Satan's lies, believing that she had to be perfect for God (and people to love) her.

By immersing herself in the truth of God's word and rehearsing those truths (meditating on them whenever she felt scared or down), Cari became much freer to grieve whatever needed to be grieved—her sin, others' failures, loss, etc—and then *move on.*

If you think you're depressed, get help! It's not a sin. It can lead to sin, but being depressed is a normal human emotion. Elijah, a prophet of God from the Old Testament, got depressed. So did David and Job, Jonah and Jeremiah.

Oh, precious friend, you're not alone—and you don't have to "suck it up" and "pull yourself up by your bootstraps." (You've probably tried those things—they don't work!) If you are struggling in this area, find a godly Christian counselor to talk to. Read books and do Bible studies like *Search for Significance* or *Breaking Free* by Beth Moore. Find a good doctor who will run tests to determine whether or not your depression is chemically-based. If you need to, take medication.

Just don't let Satan keep you in bondage! Salvation through Jesus is for YOU. He is with you. He loves you more than you can imagine.

Lord, thank You for Your salvation. . .thank you that it is for ME.

OUR BLESSED HOPE

While we wait for the blessed hope and appearing of the glory
of our great God and Savior, Jesus Christ.
TITUS 2:13 HCSB

Three times in the last chapter of the Bible, Jesus says, "I am coming quickly." That truth puts everything we go through in perspective. When Jesus returns, He will take us to Himself so that we will be with Him where He is. Looking forward to His coming gives us hope (confident expectation) that our losses will be reversed and redeemed. Hardships are temporary, and afflictions are light and momentary compared to the "absolutely incomparable eternal weight of glory" to which we look forward (2 Corinthians 4:17 HCSB).

In this life we have no explanation for dilemmas, such as why did my loved one die so soon? Yet Jesus is coming. We struggle against temptation and often fail. We hurt others and cause permanent consequences. Still Jesus is coming. We have chronic illnesses, physical disabilities, emotional scars, and disturbing memories. Yet Jesus is coming. Living with Jesus' return in view makes everything worthwhile. Suffering is temporary. Death is defeated. Eternal life is a promised gift that we could never deserve. All of our tears will be wiped away. We don't need explanations. We only need Jesus. He knows what He's doing in our lives, and that means we don't have to. Someday when we see Him in person, He will make everything right. "Amen! Come, Lord Jesus!" (Revelation 22:20 HCSB).

Lord Jesus, when I consider the painful aspects of earth-life,
I long for eternity. In Your presence there is fullness of joy
and peace forevermore. Amen.

ABUNDANT LIFE

The thief comes only to steal and kill and destroy;
I came that they may have life, and have it abundantly.
JOHN 10:10 NASB

Who or what are you serving on this earth? Are you serving something that desires only to steal, kill, and destroy you? It may be that you have given your devotion to something that seems good now, but later will prove worthless or even destructive. Don't allow the thieves of this world to steal your life, passions, and peace from you. Instead, be devoted to the One who offers you abundant life.

In this verse, Christ cites that one of the major reasons for His coming is to give you abundant life. He has accomplished this by dying. You can have abundant life because you live free of your condemning sins. You can have abundant life because Christ offers you His joy, peace, power, and intercession to the Father. You can have abundant life because you have confidence that life does not end with death, but only becomes more beautiful. You can have abundant life because you know that no matter what happens here, you are placed securely in the watchful care of your Savior. So take hold of that life now. Live and rejoice in the freedom that Christ has earned for you.

Lord, thank You that you offer me abundant life, both on this earth and for eternity. May I live in this abundance now. Protect me from giving my devotion to anything other than You.

ONE TREASURE

"For where your treasure is, there your heart will be also. . . .
But seek first the Kingdom of God and His righteousness,
and all these things shall be added to you."
MATTHEW 6:21, 33 NKJV

Jesus' greatest treasure is his relationship with the Father and bringing creation back into fellowship with Him. He is consumed with this treasure, as seen through His sacrifice on the cross. Humans were also created to have this, but in their rebellion, they look to other forms of treasure: materially, relationally, and spiritually. People fill their time, and thus their hearts, with various things: fashion, sports, movies, careers, friends, etc. While not bad in themselves, these things can easily replace the growing relationship with God in our hearts. Jesus taught people to look for obedience to God and fellowship with Him and His people as the most important thing. God then provides all necessary things; hobbies and passions will be brought under God's sovereignty so a person can still enjoy things without letting them dominate thoughts and actions. Partaking in God-honoring hobbies with the mind of Christ also turns those actions into Kingdom-work.

Jesus includes over five parables in Matthew 13 which describe the Kingdom of God, showing how difficult it is to "dig" for the Kingdom. Satan sends so many things to get in our way. Being with God is worth the difficulty. We find that unexplained peace. Our hearts are made more like Jesus, and His heart is the very heart of God.

El Shaddai, I thank You that creation is a treasure worth dying
and living for. You are the treasure that I seek.

LET YOUR LIGHT SHINE

"Let your light shine before men, so that they may see your good works and give glory to your Father in heaven."
MATTHEW 5:16 HCSB

Francine felt frustrated. Her friends had asked her to come on a summer mission trip with them, but she needed to save her vacation days in order to visit her ailing mother, who lived several states away.

Francine had always imagined serving God would be fulfilling, but it seemed that lately she had spent more time in a cubicle than anywhere else. Why had God given her this job? What did He want her to learn?

She thought back to a worship service several months ago when she had rededicated her life to Jesus. "I'll serve you anywhere, Lord," she prayed. She expected He might change her work title, but it seemed that He was more concerned with changing her heart.

Maybe I need to look around me for opportunities to share Jesus, Francine thought. I know Jim is an atheist, and Jamar is a Muslim. I could stop avoiding them and instead engage them in conversation during breaks and after work. Her agnostic mother was lonely—she could call more, and send letters weekly.

Where has God put you? How could you witness to those around you by meeting their needs, serving them unselfishly and listening to their hearts? Perhaps God wants you to see the places you live, work, and play as the most important mission fields of all.

Jesus, just as You shine Your light into the hearts of men, give me the courage to shine brightly where I live and work.

When the woman realized that she couldn't remain hidden, she knelt trembling before [Jesus]. In front of all the people, she blurted out her story—why she touched him and how at that same moment she was healed. Jesus said, "Daughter, you took a risk trusting me, and now you're healed and whole. Live well, live blessed!"

LUKE 8:47-49 MSG

This particular lady had spent twelve years afflicted with hemorrhaging. When she decided to go out in public to search for Jesus, she took a risk because her bleeding made her an outcast from society. Making her way through the hustle and bustle of crowds was another risk, given that anyone she touched would become unclean according to the law. She pushed through all the risks, knowing that if she could only touch Jesus, she would be made whole.

Trusting Jesus doesn't always seem to be the safest option. It will take you beyond your comfort zone, outside of society's standard, and above what your mind can handle. Still, taking a God-spoken risk will be the safest option every time because you'll find yourself right in the middle of God's will.

Next time you have an idea that intimidates you as you pursue God, remember that God rewards risks of faith.

Lord, show me what I can do that stretches my faith, increases my trust, and takes me beyond my comfort zone. I want to jump first into Your arms, no matter the risk, because I know You will catch me every time.

HOW GRATEFUL ARE YOU?

"Two men were in debt to a banker. One owed five hundred silver pieces, the other fifty. Neither of them could pay up, and so the banker canceled both debts. Which of the two would be more grateful?" Simon answered, "I suppose the one who was forgiven the most." "That's right," said Jesus. Then turning to the woman, but speaking to Simon, he said, "Do you see this woman? I came to your home; you provided no water for my feet, but she rained tears on my feet and dried them with her hair. You gave me no greeting, but from the time I arrived she hasn't quit kissing my feet. You provided nothing for freshening up, but she has soothed my feet with perfume. Impressive, isn't it? She was forgiven many, many sins, and so she is very, very grateful. If the forgiveness is minimal, the gratitude is minimal."
LUKE 7:41–47 MSG

A harlot came to Simon's home while Jesus was visiting. She sat at Jesus' feet, washed them with perfume and tears, and then dried them with her hair. Simon watched, appalled that Jesus let the harlot interact with Him. Jesus replied with the above story.

It stirred a question in me: How grateful am I that Jesus has forgiven my sins? My thankfulness for God's forgiveness should be no less than this harlot's. As Romans 6:23 (NIV)says, "The wages of sin is death, but the gift of God is eternal life in Christ Jesus our Lord."

Jesus, You have forgiven me of both past and future sins.
May my life reflect my gratefulness.

Jesus answered, "My kingdom is not of this world. If My kingdom were of this world, My servants would fight so that I might not be delivered to the Jews. But now My kingdom is not from here."
JOHN 18:36 NKJV

It would have been a truly catastrophic day in Pilate's court if Jesus' mission had been for the present time. That's what His followers thought all along. They had been oppressed and abused by the Roman invaders for more years than they cared to count. They were a proud people, a called people, and a people with a mandate chosen by God Himself in a covenant with Abraham. They hated the Romans and looked constantly for a deliverer, a Messiah.

When Jesus was born, few recognized His divine importance. When He rode into Jerusalem on a donkey as prophesied, many joined the fray, sure that He had come to put down the Romans and establish a Jewish nation.

Then came Gethsemane and Golgotha, condemnation to a cross, humiliation, ignominy, and death. There would be no earthly kingdom. Jesus had tried to tell them all along that everything He did was in view of what was to come.

He challenges us to do the same. He invites us to ignore the crush of Hollywood, the pull of fashion, the siren call of wealth. He beckons us to live for the kingdom to come, not for today.

Dear God, put within me recognition of the importance of eternity. Help me choose this day to live with it in view. In Jesus' name, amen.

COMPASSIONATE ONE

But when He saw the multitudes, He was moved with compassion for them,
because they were weary and scattered, like sheep having no shepherd.
MATTHEW 9:36 NKJV

The hustle and bustle of every day brings people into contact with multitudes. However, people seldom stop to *see* the individuals they pass. We hide behind our fear of misrepresenting the Gospel, our unpreparedness, or our busyness. We forget that He who is in us is greater than the dangers of the world. Jesus saw the multitudes. He saw their weariness and their lostness. Though he also must have felt tired, his life-giving compassion moved Him to action. He equipped his disciples to be part of His redemption work—to also go out teaching and healing in order to reach as many as possible.

It was the spiritual brokenness in the crowd that most affected Jesus, who came to be their much-needed Shepherd. Spiritual brokenness results in physical, material, and emotional brokenness. Jesus came to fix the root of the problem—separation from God. He had time to feed the people around him both spiritually and physically, and He calls his followers to do the same today. If we are like Jesus, we will see with His compassionate eyes and speak with yearning hearts to every person we pass of reconciliation with God through Jesus.

Great Shepherd, give me boldness and great wisdom to be moved to love
and to act compassionately toward the people with whom
You bring me into contact.

And his mother and his brothers came, and standing outside they sent to him and called him. And a crowd was sitting around him, and they said to him, "Your mother and your brothers are outside, seeking you." And he answered them, "Who are my mother and my brothers?" And looking about at those who sat around him, he said, "Here are my mother and my brothers!"
MARK 3:31-34 ESV

When Jesus' ministry started, the people of Israel were surprised. "A prophet came out of Nazareth? Nothing good comes out of Nazareth!" (see John 1:46). The people He'd grown up with were the most surprised. To them, He was Joseph and Mary's son, not a prophet. They'd seen Him celebrating during feast days and weddings and mourning at funerals. Finally, it was unbelievable when Jesus seemed to deny His relationship to His mother and brothers before the crowd. As the firstborn son, He was expected to lead the family after Joseph died.

However, Jesus said what He did to illustrate a truth that transcends earthly family ties—those who believe in Him for salvation are a part of God's family. The priorities and allegiances of a believer change when Christ enters her life. She no longer only cares for her biological family's welfare, but also for that of her spiritual family, her brothers and sisters in Christ.

May the Church practice being a family where believers can depend on each other for prayer, help, and encouragement in Christ!

Lord Jesus, I'm so grateful I'm in Your family! Please give me grace to love others well and grow Your Church. Amen.

HE DISPELS THE DARKNESS

*We're squinting in a fog, peering through a mist. But it won't be long
before the weather clears and the sun shines bright! We'll see it all then,
see it all as clearly as God sees us, knowing him directly just as he knows
us! But for right now, until that completeness, we have three things
to do to lead us toward that consummation: Trust steadily in God,
hope unswervingly, love extravagantly.*
1 CORINTHIANS 13:12–13 MSG

Scripture gives us a clear picture of faith in the trenches. Maybe right now you feel abandoned and afraid. However, no matter what you're going through, know that God is for you, not against you. He aches with you. He offers us a choice: be chained in fear or changed by grace. Jesus stepped off the throne of heaven and took on the limitations of humanity to free us from our bondage. . .to free you and me from the limits of our broken, sinful frames. Without Him, we have no hope. Yet with Him, we have glorious completeness.

So the question is: which will we choose? Fear or faith? Will we choose to reach out—to reach up, from the depths of our pain—and grasp His nail-scarred hand? When we do, a pinprick of light pierces our darkness, and as we spend time with Him and follow His healing nudges, we find more and more light, until it floods our entire soul.

Beautiful Savior, help me trust You even when I'm afraid. Thank You for Your light. I can't wait to see You face to face, when You will dispel all darkness.

You can tell for sure that you are now fully adopted as his own children because God sent the Spirit of his Son into our lives crying out, "Papa! Father!" Doesn't that privilege of intimate conversation with God make it plain that you are not a slave, but a child? And if you are a child, you're also an heir, with complete access to the inheritance.

GALATIANS 4:7 MSG

The Lord assures us over and over of His magnificent love, and this is one of those scriptures. When we let that promise sink in, we surely bubble over with joy and excitement and contentment.

Picture yourself as an orphan who longs to be rescued from life in a drab institution. Then Someone comes to take you home. You've been adopted into His family. He's full of love, has wonderful plans for your future, and for the first time, you feel totally accepted. You know you weren't chosen because of your beauty or talent. In fact, you're dirty, you've been neglected and abused, but He sees beyond that.

He sees what you will become. He provides everything you need and shows you, by His own example, what He wants. Sometimes you fall flat, but He doesn't toss you aside. When you're discouraged and cry out, "Papa!" He draws you to Himself—into His tenderness, assuring you again of His amazing love that is beyond comprehension. He whispers, "You belong to Me. You're my child."

Dear heavenly Father, I can never find the words to thank You for all You do for me. I can only praise You all my days.

RUN IN STEP WITH JESUS

If you are tired from carrying heavy burdens, come to me and I will give you rest. Take the yoke I give you. Put it on your shoulders and learn from me. I am gentle and humble, and you will find rest.
MATTHEW 11:28-29 CEV

Anyone who has run a three-legged race knows that cooperation is the key. When we are out of step with our partner, we become tangled up and weary. Being bound to the other person feels more like a burden than a benefit. However, when we fall in step with our partner, it makes all the difference in the world. Imagine being tied to Jesus in this way. When we are tired, we can yield to Him, and he will carry the burden. Jesus invites us to come to Him, to yoke ourselves to Him, and to fall in step with Him. We will be transformed by His gentleness and humility. It will bring us rest. We can stop fighting and stumbling and making the race difficult. Lean on Him; He longs to give you rest.

Jesus, You are my companion on this journey. I don't know why I try to go my own way, getting out of step and fighting You. Please help me fall into step with You, to join You, to lean on You, and to allow You to provide me rest for my weary soul. Amen.

"Where did this man get these things?" they asked. "What's this wisdom that has been given him? What are these remarkable miracles he is performing? Isn't this the carpenter?"
MARK 6:2–3 NIV

I can't believe that Rachel has done all the things she said she has done," the resident of a small town commented about a classmate who just moved back to her hometown after many years.

"Yeah, right. I don't think it's a bit true, either!" responded her friend.

In those two comments, Rachel's neighbors had judged and sentenced her. The women would not change their minds. They would let others know what they thought of Rachel. Respect and honor would not follow, no matter what.

Jesus faced the same type of doubts and criticisms in his hometown of Nazareth. He summed up their attitudes in these words: "A prophet is not without honor except in his own town, among his relatives and in his own home" [Mark 6:4 NIV].

Discouraging? It could have been. Yet it didn't stop Jesus from His Father's work. Remembered in His home town only as a carpenter, He continued to teach, work miracles, mentor disciples, and infuse the whole world—then and now—with hope.

Jesus' persistence proves that whatever we do for and about Him is not dependent on appreciation, honor, and respect. Jesus calls everyone.

For us, the messengers, the response that matters is Christ's.

Jesus, thank You for showing me the way that passes discouragement on its way to a great destination.

Jesus said, "It is finished." With that, he bowed his head
and gave up his spirit.
JOHN 19:30 NIV

Sometimes finishing a job may only happen with sheer determination and commitment when a person thoroughly dislikes or dreads what is ahead.

Leslie loved to cook but hated to wash dishes. As she stopped by the grocery store on her way home from a cooking demonstration, she was eager to try the new recipes from the professional chef who taught the class.

The foodie lost track of time as she put together two Beef Wellingtons created from filet mignon and puff pastry. Leslie was so pleased, she took pictures. As she studied the countertop of dirty dishes and prep pans, Leslie cringed.

The dishwasher only took care of about one-third of the pans. The rest of the mess and the floor? She had to do it herself—and fast. Otherwise, she wouldn't be able to truly enjoy the beautiful meal she had prepared.

Jesus modeled finishing the job that he started. Though He had only a few years of earthly ministry, Jesus knew God sent Him to teach, heal, mentor, and to be a flesh and blood sacrifice. His death honored God's will and gave those who believe a clean slate.

Reflecting on Jesus' gift, the dirty dishes don't seem so bad after all!

Jesus, thank You for modeling finishing the job we are given. We thank You for your love for us shown in forgiveness and a second chance.

ACTIVATE HIS PEACE

Peace I leave with you, my peace I give unto you: not as the world giveth, give I unto you. Let not your heart be troubled, neither let it be afraid.
JOHN 14:27 KJV

left you our phone number, so if you need anything, just give us a call." I heard that a lot as a babysitter. Better yet was the phrase, "I'll leave you with twenty dollars for dinner, just in case you need it."

Any time someone leaves you with something, you have the option to use it.

Jesus left us with His peace. That means we have the option to use it. We can let our heart be troubled and afraid, or we can activate His peace in our lives.

In a world that can overwhelm us with worry, how can we activate this peace? Philippians 4:6-7 (KJV) has an answer: "Be careful for nothing; but in every thing by prayer and supplication with thanksgiving let your requests be made known unto God. And the peace of God, which passeth all understanding, shall keep your hearts and minds through Christ Jesus."

If you want God's peace in your life, start by praying and end by thanking. When thoughts of worry come after you pray, "let not your heart be troubled, neither let it be afraid." Know that you have Jesus' peace and heaven's answers on your side.

Thank You, Jesus, for leaving me with Your peace. I intend not to worry and instead use Your peace as an anchor for my soul.

SACRED JOY

These things have I spoken unto you, that my joy might remain in you,
and that your joy might be full.
JOHN 15:11 KJV

Jesus calls us to joy.

In this chapter in the Gospel of John, He was teaching His disciples, giving them instruction and promises. He speaks of being the true Vine—the Source of all life and growth. He speaks of having love for one another and of keeping His commandments and of being hated by an ungodly culture. He speaks of the coming Helper, the Holy Spirit. He tells them they are chosen and that they are His friends. He tells them these things so they may have joy.

Jesus' personal joy came from doing His Father's will. It was not the result of good luck or the weather or money or health. It was not based on this world, but on eternity. It was a real and present joy because He was in constant relationship with the Father and was committed to His plan.

You and I can have the joy of Jesus right now. Regardless of present circumstances, we can have the certainty that we are in relationship with the Father and we can follow His plan for us. Jesus wants us to have joy, and He has shown us how to have it. It is ours for the embracing.

Jesus, I want to have the joy You wish for me. Please help me live in a
relationship with You and follow the plan You have for me.
I ask this in Your name, amen.

LIFE IN THE LIGHT

How priceless is your unfailing love, O God! People take refuge
in the shadow of your wings. They feast on the abundance of your house;
you give them drink from your river of delights.
For with you is the fountain of life; in your light we see light.
PSALM 36:7-9 NIV

David packs so many beautiful metaphors in the verses above that reveal to readers important aspects of God's character.

His love is unfailing and no price could ever be put on this love.

People find comfort and protection when they turn to God's love and when they seek to do everything according to God's will- this is what it means to be in the shadow of His presence.

It is in the presence of God that people have a veritable feast for the soul which is evidenced materially or physically. God fills the spiritual thirst of people by giving them of Himself- knowledge of Himself, instilling in them His love, and giving them His characteristics.

Just as Jesus preached in the Sermon on the Mount in Matthew, chapter five (where he also provided physical bread): God will bless and fill those who hunger for and thirst after the goodness and purity of God. The Creator God is the source of all life and it is only through Him that humans can understand the meaning and purpose of existence. It is His Light- Christ- that gives us life.

Great Refuge, illuminate the minds and hearts of your daughters to see the light that is Christ and to be beacons from which this light shines on to others who are in darkness.

UNENDING MERCY

*"So which of these three do you think was neighbor to him?..." And he said,
"He who showed mercy on him." Then Jesus said to him,
"Go and do likewise."*
LUKE 10:36-37 NKJV

We all know that Jesus is merciful. He offers forgiveness for all the sins we've committed—that takes a lot of mercy. His mercy is all encompassing. It goes beyond the big stuff. It's for small things, too. That's where it is more challenging to imitate Him.

It is difficult to forgive blatant wrongs, make no mistake, but there is nobility to it. Yet in the everydayness of our lives, it is much harder to be merciful in the trivial, "piddly" things. You know what I mean—the shopper who takes the newly opened checkout lane in front of you, the driver who doesn't yield and then makes a face at you, the coworker who never returns your greeting. . .you get the idea. These small things grind away at your inner reserve of mercy. They can deplete your well if you don't have a source of renewal.

Jesus, of course, is that Source. His mercy is never-ending. As we let Him be Lord in every area of our lives, He will lend us His mercy. We can reflect His life in us to our "neighbors"—after all, by God's definition, most everyone fits in that category.

"O God, show Your mercy through me to those who make my life difficult—in big and small ways. In Jesus' name, amen.

"Are you tired? Worn out? Burned out on religion? Come to me. Get away with me and you'll recover your life. I'll show you how to take a real rest. Walk with me and work with me—watch how I do it. Learn the unforced rhythms of grace. I won't lay anything heavy or ill-fitting on you. Keep company with me and you'll learn to live freely and lightly."
MATTHEW 11:28-30 MSG

Religion is exhausting: it compiles a list of things to do and a specific method to get there, both of which wind up being impossible to uphold. A relationship with Jesus, on the other hand, is restful and refreshing and propelled by "unforced rhythms of grace."

What should a grace-filled relationship look like? Jesus gives us the answer in Matthew chapter 11: we are to walk with Him and work with Him. To me, that means we walk with Jesus as we spend time alone with Him in His presence and read His Word. We work with Him as we take the things He teaches us individually and we bring them to the world throughout the rest of our day.

Jesus said in Matthew 12:7 (MSG), "I prefer a flexible heart to an inflexible ritual." Next time you feel overwhelmed by all you have to "do" as a Christian, stop. Remember Christianity is simply about developing a relationship with Jesus, our Savior.

Lord, I don't want to get stuck in the rut of religion. I want to be free in following my heart and investing in my relationship with You. Teach me how to both walk with You and work with You on a daily basis.

MAN-MADE RELIGIONS

And if by grace, then it cannot be based on works; if it were,
grace would no longer be grace.
ROMANS 11:6 NIV

Why are there so many religions in the world? It is because it is fairly easy to invent a false belief system by either discounting the Bible or adding to it by writing your own sacred book, or assuming that people are basically good and can earn their way to a happy afterlife. Most non-biblical religions teach adherents to DO certain things in order to become worthy of heaven. However, the Bible teaches us how to have an eternal relationship with God, not what religion to practice. The way to God is by His grace, not our works. Adding our own efforts to what God has provided compares to God inviting us to a banquet with every possible delicacy laid out in golden dishes. He says, "Come, eat freely what I have prepared for you" (see Revelation 22:17; Isaiah 55:1; John 6:35). We might say, "Oh, I'd like that, but I need to bring something, too." Then we offer Him everything we have—a saltine cracker crumb! That's how ridiculous it is to add our good works to the work Christ finished on the cross. God's grace and our works are mutually exclusive. We cannot make ourselves worthy to live in heaven with God, but He makes us worthy by forgiving us.

Lord Jesus, I am not depending on what I can do for You, but on what You
have done for me. To receive Your grace and forgiveness as a free gift,
I accept it by faith. Thank You, Amen.

The woman came and knelt before him. "Lord, help me!" she said.
He replied, "It is not right to take the children's bread and toss it to the dogs."
"Yes it is, Lord," she said. "Even the dogs eat the crumbs that fall from their
master's table." Then Jesus said to her, "Woman, you have great faith!
Your request is granted." And her daughter was healed at that moment.
MATTHEW 15:25-28 NIV

The most remarkable trait of this Canaanite woman was her "chutzpah"—the Hebrew word for audacity, which can be a good or bad trait. As a Gentile woman, she deserved no attention from a Jewish rabbi, but she continued to follow after Him, boldly begging for His help. Even the disciples were getting irritated by her constant cry for healing for her demon-possessed daughter.

Driven by desperation, the Canaanite woman's answer to Jesus showed her fervent belief that the mercy of God overflows national or religious boundaries. Jesus, marveling at her, answered her faith-filled petitions by healing her daughter. Scripture doesn't record her name, but her conversation with Jesus is known all over the world.

As children of God, how much more boldly can we bring our requests to our Savior? We should practice *chutzpah* ourselves, entering His presence again and again, in full confidence that He answers those who call on Him for help. There is no limit to His mercy!

Lord Jesus, strengthen my faith so I can pray with chutzpah.
I may have big requests, but I know and believe You are strong enough
for anything I bring before You. Amen.

"The Son of Man must suffer many things, and be rejected by the elders and chief priests and scribes, and be killed, and be raised the third day." Then He said to them all, "If any one desires to come after Me, let him deny himself, and take up his cross daily, and follow Me."
LUKE 9:22–23 NKJV

Peter boldly declared Jesus to be the Messiah sent by God. Living truth from the mouth of Peter! However, Jesus had to clarify some things. Yes, He was the Messiah, but this Rescuer sent from heaven would have to suffer and even die. He will have the final victory, but only after the greatest of sacrifices. The disciples' concept of the Messiah was still incomplete. They needed to understand the sacrifice that would be required of them as well.

The followers of Jesus today must, through the power that comes from God, reject the things that build up "self" as god; they must let go of their pride, self-righteousness, and other sins. This is a constant and daily battle, and this is the cross that believers must carry as they follow Jesus. Some days the cross may seem too heavy and the worries or delights of this world overwhelming. However, if Jesus' followers look at His example and remember His promises, they will be infused with the renewed strength of the Messiah to carry their cross to the end and then share in His victory.

Elohay Mauzi (God of my strength), give this follower of Jesus the strength to daily say "no" to the things that pull me away from You, no matter how innocent they seem.

And this is what God has testified: He has given us eternal life,
and this life is in his Son. Whoever has the Son has life;
whoever does not have God's Son does not have life.
1 JOHN 5:11-12 NLT

Just before this scripture, we read a powerful message in verses 9-10 (NLT): "Since we believe human testimony, surely we can believe the greater testimony that comes from God. And God has testified about his Son. All who believe in the Son of God know in their hearts that this testimony is true. Those who don't believe this are actually calling God a liar because they don't believe what God has testified about his Son."

That's about as straightforward as we can get. What it all boils down to is whether we believe God or not. If we don't, we're calling Him a liar. That should be a terrifying pronouncement for any unbeliever, but for those who love God and trust in Jesus, there's nothing to fear. In fact, it's reassuring.

Believing isn't difficult. We don't need to strain and struggle. For some, that's a problem. They believe the adage: God helps those who help themselves. That's simply not true. The fact is: God rescues us when we realize we can't do it on our own. We can never make ourselves holy; we can only rely on the work Jesus already did for us. He's there, right now, welcoming every sinner who has gotten to the end of himself.

Dear heavenly Father, thank You for showing us the perfect way.
Thank You for bringing us to Yourself, through Jesus.

OUR ACCESS TO THE FATHER

For through Him we have access in one Spirit to the Father.
EPHESIANS 2:18 NASB

Christ is the reason we can come before the Father. Stop and think about this: you have access to the Creator of the universe. Before Christ's sacrifice, God's people had to perform daily rituals and sacrifices in order to make themselves right before God. His holiness was so unapproachable by sinful humans that only an appointed priest could come trembling into His presence. God has not changed. Because of what Christ accomplished, the way you can approach him has completely changed. The Father no longer sees a sinful people in need of redemption when He looks at us. He sees Christ. Christ has washed you clean with His blood. There is not a single spot of sin on you. So go before the Father with boldness. Take your fears, hopes, thanksgivings, and desires to Him, knowing that you stand in His presence as a redeemed child. Go humbly, knowing that apart from Christ you would still be separated from your Creator. Most of all, be thankful for what Christ has done for you.

Lord, thank You for Your immense sacrifice that allows me to come before my Father with boldness. Thank You that I am washed with Your blood so that I am spotless before the holy eyes of God. May I never take for granted this access You have purchased for me.

SIMPLICITY

"For where your treasure is, there your heart will be also."
MATTHEW 6:21 NIV

He who dies with the most toys wins. . .

Although we come into this world with nothing and we leave with nothing, many people make it their life's ambition to accumulate as many earthly treasures as they possibly can. They work hard to stay current with the latest cars, clothing, and electronics. Even though it's impossible to *always* have the latest and greatest of everything, they continue to try.

Jesus has a radical view on our stuff. He says, "Your heart will always be where your treasure is." If you're having trouble finding yourself, start looking around at what you treasure. Jesus says you will find your heart there. Storing up treasures in heaven, like Jesus, is counter-cultural. When you make a conscious decision to live this way, you will feel that you are a fish swimming upstream, going against the tide. However, there are great rewards for choosing this path. Ask the Lord to give you a heart for *His* treasures.

Heavenly Father, it is so easy to get consumed by stuff. As if accumulating massive treasures here on earth will make a difference in the end. Please help me put my things in the right perspective—that they are only necessary to sustain my life here and aid me in doing Your work. Keep my heart and my treasure close to You. Amen.

I can do all things through Christ which strengtheneth me.
PHILIPPIANS 4:13 KJV

Have you ever had that pickle jar that just won't open? You do everything you can, but finally have to surrender the jar to someone else in hopes that their extra strength will finish the job.

I've always considered Philippians 4:13 in this way, but I never understood how that would work. How could Jesus, who isn't physically with me, provide me with strength?

Then, one night my four-month-old wouldn't go to sleep, even though I had been rocking him for 45 minutes. My arms were exhausted from holding his 19-pound body, and I needed literal strength to rescue me.

I prayed a quick prayer: "Help me, Lord! I can't do this on my own." Philippians 4:13 came to mind, followed by the melody to a song from long ago. I started singing, "There's no mountain too high, no valley too low; I can do all things in the name of the Lord."

I started bouncing up and down, smiling inside and out. The rejuvenated perspective Jesus gave me was exactly what I needed to finish rocking my baby to sleep. Moments later, my little one had relaxed. Even though my arms ached, I kept singing, smiling, and thinking of Jesus. Within five minutes, I had a sleeping baby.

Lord Jesus, let Your perspective invade mine so I can truly do all things not in my own strength or perspective, but in Yours.

ASK, SEEK, KNOCK

"Ask, and it will be given to you; seek, and you will find; knock,
and it will be opened to you."
MATTHEW 7:7 NKJV

Hearts often plead with the Father for someone or something. Too often behind such petitions there is little more than wishful thinking or a demand as of a genie. God does not limit Himself within such boundaries. In order for petitioners to benefit from this time of talking with God, they need to dig deep into the character of God and into His promises. Then they can come to understand His seemingly cryptic responses. The Father always answers prayer. The recipients need to be keener to observe and accept.

Jesus teaches His followers to ask boldly. Our Daddy listens and will give that which was asked in all sincerity and wisdom! Jesus showed great persistence in prayer, spending whole nights talking to God. He teaches his followers that they must search out God's plan with a humble heart and God will reveal it. When they knock, desiring to enter into a beautiful time of fellowship, God will not only open the door, but He will reveal to them that He was the one who beckoned them to knock. Prayer is the heartbeat of a life with Jesus. As we ask, seek, and knock, we will see Him give, reveal, and open a bounty of contentment no matter the answer or the circumstance.

Holy Spirit, teach me to pray. Let my asking, seeking, and knocking be as a
beautiful offering before God. When necessary, let me graciously accept an
answer of "no." May our times of communion be sweet.

LIFE OR DEATH

Jesus told her, "I am the resurrection and the life.
Anyone who believes in me will live, even after dying."
JOHN 11:25 NLT

Jesus said these things to Martha, the sister of Lazarus, who died and was buried before Jesus arrived on the scene. Then Martha said, "Lord, if You had been here, my brother would not have died."

Martha, Mary, their brother Lazarus, and Jesus were good friends. It's thrilling to imagine spending time with the Creator. Maybe He came to their house for dinner or even overnight visits. They were so comfortable with Jesus; Martha didn't hesitate to chastise Him a bit about not coming earlier. After all, they sent a messenger to tell Jesus that Lazarus was sick. If He hadn't dawdled along the way, maybe He could have kept her brother alive.

Martha and Mary obviously knew about Jesus' authority over sickness, but by the time He arrived, it was too late. Their brother was already dead. He'd been buried days ago. Martha's heart was broken, and it never occurred to her that Jesus could still intervene. We know He called to Lazarus from outside the tomb—simply said, "Lazarus, come forth," and he did (John 11:43 NKJV). Their brother was alive and well. Still, Jesus grieved over their lack of faith.

He understands that physical death isn't the end. In fact, for those of us who trust Him as Lord and Savior, it's just the beginning of real life.

Lord Jesus, You are amazing! I don't ever want to doubt Your love or power.
Pour Your Spirit into my heart to teach me Your ways.

ONLY TRUTH MATTERS

"How can I account for the people of this generation? They're like spoiled children complaining to their parents, 'We wanted to skip rope and you were always too tired; we wanted to talk but you were always too busy.' John the Baptizer came fasting and you called him crazy. The Son of Man came feasting and you called him a lush. Opinion polls don't count for much, do they? The proof of the pudding is in the eating."
LUKE 7:31-35 MSG

H ave you ever found yourself stuck in a circle of opinions? *My family says that I'm too talkative; my boss says I don't talk enough; my friends say I talk about nothing; my spouse wished I talked about everything.*

It's easy to get caught up in the opinions of others and, as a result, base our actions on what others think. Jesus realized, though, that the opinions of men and women are fickle. They will praise you one moment and disapprove of you the next. The most important thing for you to do is follow God. His is the only "opinion" that matters—for His opinion is always true, and as John 8:32 (NIV) says, "You will know the truth, and the truth will set you free."

Jesus, as I walk with You, remind me that it is Your truth alone that will keep me on the right path. May I not be swayed by man's opinion and only be led by You.

So that at the name of Jesus EVERY KNEE WILL BOW, of those who are in heaven and on earth and under the earth, and that every tongue will confess that Jesus Christ is Lord, to the glory of God the Father.

PHILIPPIANS 2:10–11 NASB

These verses are incredibly awe-inspiring. Take a moment to imagine this scene. Everything and everyone doing what they were intended and created to do—worshipping the one true Lord and Savior. This same Jesus who bowed His head in death at the hands of men has been glorified so that when He is revealed, all will bow to Him. Don't let other people or earthly things take away your devotion to Jesus. Come reverently before Him confessing that He is Lord over your life. Worship Him now and look forward to the time when all will join with you.

In light of His Lordship, be bold in proclaiming the Gospel. Don't be afraid to tell others what Christ has done for you. Even those who ridicule Him now will be awestruck and will have nothing to say but, "Jesus Christ is Lord," when they see Him in His glory.

Lord, I confess even now that You are Lord and Ruler over everything. Forgive me when I give my devotion to something else and when I let anything other than You rule my life. I look forward to the day when all will worship You together.

EQUAL BUT SUBMISSIVE

But I want you to understand that the head of every man is Christ, the head of a wife is her husband, and the head of Christ is God.
1 CORINTHIANS 11:3 ESV

Most people struggle with being submissive. We feel it demeans us as inferior or stifles our true self. Perhaps we need a closer look at Jesus' example in Philippians 2:6–8. Jesus did not consider equality with God something to be grasped. The passage says that He emptied Himself and humbled Himself. Note the participial phrases: taking the form of a servant, being born in the likeness of men, being found in human form. . . becoming obedient even to death on the cross. Although Jesus was God—equal in relationship and attributes and purpose to Father God, yet He willingly submitted to His role, playing His part in the sovereign plan of redemption.

Relating this to gender, men and women are equal in their relationship with God and position in Christ, but they have different roles to play in God's Church, roles that are equally important and necessary. In God's plan we complete and balance each other, so we need the mindset of Jesus (Philippians 2:5). Marsha Thyren says that submission was not "a result of the fall—part of the curse. Actually lack of respect and [lack of] submission resulted from the fall." So even if submission goes against our personality types, it is part of the process of becoming more like Christ.

Lord Jesus, I cannot please You when I'm seeking my own agenda or rebelling against authority. Help me to accept my role and submit like You did. Amen.

GROWING LIKE HIM

*Jesus grew in wisdom and in stature and in favor
with God and all the people.*
LUKE 2:52 NLT

A s parents, we delight in seeing our children grow. We mark their milestones in baby books and record their height on the wall. Jesus' parents no doubt delighted in His growth as well. He not only grew physically, but He grew in wisdom and in God's favor and the favor of others.

No matter how long we've been God's child, the Christian life is never done. As Jesus grew, we must grow, too. He grew physically and spiritually, as well as in His personal relationships. As He grew closer to God, His favor with others grew as well. This shows His integrity and authenticity, which drew people to Him. God was pleased with His conduct; others were drawn by His heart of love. Ask God to continue to grow you to be more like Him.

Father, help me never stop growing in wisdom and in favor with You. I am amazed at all You have to teach me; help me to be an eager pupil. Amen.

RESTORATION

That evening they brought to him [Jesus] many who were oppressed
by demons, and he cast out the spirits with a word and healed
all who were sick. This was to fulfill what was spoken
by the prophet Isaiah: "He took our illnesses and bore our diseases."
MATTHEW 8:16-17 ESV

Jesus' miraculous healings did more than just heal broken bodies—
they restored community. The once-shunned leper could now walk
freely among the people and worship at the temple. The formerly blind and
lame didn't have to beg for a living anymore. Those freed from demons had
peace in their hearts, and their neighbors no longer feared them.

Jesus' healing also extends to the heart, restoring the connection
between us and God. As He lifted the paralyzed man to his feet, Jesus
forgave his sins in the same breath (Mark 2:5). The Messiah opened
the eyes of the blind—both the physically and spiritually blind—to see
themselves and Him in a clear light.

We all need restoration, reconnection with our communities and with
God. Our Savior knows what you or your loved ones are going through,
physically or spiritually. He's heard your prayers. The One who can raise
the dead to life again can strengthen your heart to trust in Him to redeem
and bring blessing from even the worst situations. There is nothing we
can suffer where He won't draw near to comfort us.

Jesus, thank You that You have power over all things. Please give me the
strength to comfort and pray for the people in my life who are suffering.
Through all things, help me keep my eyes on You. Amen.

THE OBEDIENCE OF GIVING

Each of you should give what you have decided in your heart to give,
not reluctantly or under compulsion, for God loves a cheerful giver.
2 CORINTHIANS 9:7 NIV

Chonda squirmed in her seat. The preacher's sermon series on "Giving Back to the Lord" made her uncomfortable. She made very little money as a teacher's aide and felt that God was asking too much of her to give 10 percent back to Him as a tithe.

Yet week after week, she had sat in the congregation and heard testimonies of how God had miraculously provided for people when they gave sacrificially. Some of them were downright exuberant as they exclaimed phrases like, "You can't out-give God!" "Watch and see what He will do!"

Maybe this week, since she had just gotten paid, she could experiment and see what difference it would make to tithe. "Lord, I am scared. . .will you please help me?" She prayed as she reached for her purse.

Before the offering basket came to her row, she grabbed a pen and checkbook and wrote out a check. She took a deep breath as the usher handed her the basket with a smile. She felt peace as she passed the basket on. "I know You'll take care of me, and You've given me my job and everything I have," she prayed silently. "Give me joy as I give, and forgive me for not trusting You before."

You have graciously granted me everything I need, and much of what I want.
Thank You for the opportunity to give. Help me be a joyful giver.

When Jesus saw her weeping and saw the other people wailing with her,
a deep anger welled up within him, and he was deeply troubled.
"Where have you put him?" he asked them. They told him,
"Lord, come and see." Then Jesus wept.
JOHN 11:33-35 NLT

Most of us don't like to cry. We often think of anger as bad, and are uncomfortable at public displays of emotion. Our emotions can embarrass and even cause us to feel ashamed. However, emotions are completely natural and, when appropriately expressed, provide a powerful way of communicating our needs. The Bible portrays Jesus as having a wide range of emotions, which He always expressed appropriately. Jesus wept; He got angry. He raised His voice and spoke with tender compassion. Jesus showed that emotions can be expressed without sin. It is important for us to identify and name our emotions. When we repress them, they are more likely to leak out in sinful ways. If you are sad, allow yourself to shed a tear. If you are angry, explore the reasons for your rage. Trust Him with your emotions, and He will give you an appropriate outlet.

Jesus, thank You for the example You shared of the perfect balance and
blend of emotions. We tend to think of emotions as weak or unnecessary,
yet it's clear You created us to experience a wide range of feelings.
Help me avoid fearing my emotions and share them with You. Amen.

BURDEN TO REST

*"Take my yoke upon you and learn from Me, for I am gentle
and lowly in heart, and you will find rest for your souls.
For My yoke is easy and My burden is light."*
MATTHEW 11:29-30 NKJV

The rabbis during Jesus' time commonly referred to their teachings as a yoke, a burden that their students and disciples had to carry. In examining Jesus' teachings from the Sermon on the Mount, people are confronted with what seem to be the strictest of all teachings. Coveting is equated with theft, lust with adultery, and anger with murder. This is an easy yoke and a light burden? Jesus knows that human ambition and strength only lead to death and that on our own we could never achieve the holiness required to be in perfect fellowship with our perfect Creator. That is why Jesus said, "Come to me. . .and I will give you rest" (Matthew 11:28 NKJV).

Unlike the other rabbis, who expected their pupils to follow the Law, Jesus pointed to Himself as the only One who could follow it completely. He is the One able and willing to lift the burdens of sin when His followers trust in His strength. Jesus' teaching sets believers free from self-righteousness. We see our weaknesses as they truly are. We see His grace in using them for God's greater glory. His yoke takes away anger and makes us gentle; His burden exchanges the pride in our hearts with humility.

*Greatest Teacher, let me look for no other teaching but that of Christ.
I am wear, and I come to You for rest.*

*Let the peace of Christ rule in your hearts, to which indeed
you were called in one body; and be thankful.*
COLOSSIANS 3:15 NASB

You are to let the peace of Christ rule your heart. That little word, *let*, implies a sense of surrender. Don't hold on to the anxiety of trying to rule and control your life and the circumstances around you. Instead, let the peace of Christ fill your heart and life. Decide to rely on Him and not your own strength.

You are to let this peace rule your heart. To rule is to govern and control. There is no space for two things or people to be ruling at once. The position of rule is absolute and all-encompassing. With Christ's peace ruling in your heart, there will be no room for anxiety or fear. His peace will guide and govern all your thoughts and decisions.

This peace is available to you because of Christ. There is no true peace apart from His redeeming work. True peace comes from knowing that you stand blameless before the Father and that no matter what happens here, you are placed securely in the palm of His hand and will spend eternal life in His glory. So, just as this verse says, be thankful!

---

*Lord, bring this peace to rule in my heart even now.
Let all my thoughts and perspectives be governed by Your peace.
Thank You for earning this peace for me.*

FOLLOW THE LEADER

Jesus is the faithful witness, the first among those raised from the dead.
He is the ruler of the kings of the earth. He is the One who loves us,
who made us free from our sins with the blood of his death.
REVELATION 1:5 NCV

What an awesome Savior. Jesus rules over kings, and yet He loves us. Most people never have an opportunity to chat with a king or president, but we're able to come to the One who rules all of those important people. We can talk to Him, listen to Him, and spend time with Him whenever we choose. We never have to go through His secretary, asking if He has a spare moment to spend with us. No, He's waiting for us every minute of every day. That is beyond amazing.

Some world leaders choose to ignore Him, but ultimately Jesus can lift them up or put them down. Each of us is in the same place. We can follow Him or not—He doesn't force our allegiance—but He shows us in so many ways how He will care for those who love and trust Him.

Jesus was the first to be raised from the dead for eternity, and each of us can experience the same resurrected life, just by following Him. He shed His blood to free us from being tangled in sin. We are offered incredible freedom that can't be earned. All we can do is accept the salvation He provides.

Praise You, King Jesus! You are magnificent in every way,
and I'm so blessed by Your love and forgiveness.

CONTRIBUTOR INDEX

JoAnna Bloss

JoAnna Bloss is a personal trainer, writer, and student living in the Midwest. She is a coauthor of *Grit for the Oyster: 250 Pearls of Wisdom for Aspiring Authors.*

JoAnna's readings can be found on pages:

17, 21, 29, 47, 58, 69, 84, 92, 103, 115, 124, 135, 136, 149, 158, 166, 181, 192, 205, 214, 235, 259, 281, 303, 319, 329, 345, 358, 365, 368

Renae Brumbaugh

Renae Brumbaugh lives in Texas with her two noisy children and two dogs. She's authored four books in Barbour's Camp Club Girls series, *Morning Coffee with James* (Chalice Press), and has contributed to several anthologies. Her humor column and articles have appeared in publications across the country.

Renae's readings can be found on pages:

15, 23, 33, 40, 51, 62, 73, 86, 96, 107, 108, 117, 128, 139, 151, 163, 168, 185, 196, 207, 218, 224, 239, 250, 252, 274, 285, 291, 296, 307, 328

Dena Dyer

Dena Dyer is a writer who resides in the Texas Hill Country. She has contributed to more than a dozen anthologies and has authored or coauthored three humor books.

Dena's readings can be found on pages:

12, 25, 36, 37, 44, 55, 75, 82, 100, 121, 132, 143, 155, 171, 178, 189, 211, 226, 243, 256, 267, 287, 300, 308, 314, 323, 324, 333, 337, 343, 367

Glenn Hascall

Glenn A. Hascall is an accomplished writer with credits in more than fifty books, including titles from Thomas Nelson, Bethany House, and Regal. His articles have appeared in numerous publications including the *Wall Street Journal.* He's also an award-winning broadcaster, lending his voice to national radio and television networks.

Glenn's readings can be found on pages:

13, 20, 38, 45, 56, 67, 83, 87, 101, 133, 145, 156, 160, 165, 179, 190, 204, 212, 227, 233, 244, 257, 268, 279, 293, 301, 309, 312, 321, 326

Marcia Hornok

Marcia Hornok, managing editor of *CHERA* magazine for widows/ers, raised six children in Salt Lake City, where her husband pastors Midvalley Bible Church. She has numerous publishing credits in periodicals, devotional books, and online.

Marcia's readings can be found on pages:

7, 27, 48, 59, 70, 77, 93, 104, 110, 122, 125, 148, 159, 173, 182, 193, 200, 215, 228, 236, 247, 260, 271, 289, 304, 311, 320, 334, 353, 364

Ardythe Kolb

Ardythe Kolb writes articles and devotions for various publications and is currently working on her third book. She serves on the advisory board of a writers' network and edits their newsletter.

Ardythe's readings can be found on pages:

9, 31, 34, 41, 52, 63, 79, 97, 112, 118, 129, 142, 152, 169, 175, 202, 208, 225, 230, 240, 253, 263, 264, 275, 297, 317, 344, 356, 361, 371

Emily Marsh

Emily Marsh lives in Virginia with her husband, Seth. She works at a downtown real estate firm and part-time on a local food truck.

Emily's readings can be found on pages:

10, 24, 35, 53, 64, 74, 88, 98, 119, 130, 140, 153, 170, 176, 187, 197, 219, 231, 241, 249, 254, 265, 276, 286, 298, 316, 335, 357, 363, 370

Iemima Ploscariu

Iemima Ploscariu is a history researcher who spends most of her time in Sacramento, California. She holds an MLitt in Central and Eastern European history and is pursuing further studies. Along with her freelance writing she also serves in the children and women's ministries of her local Romanian church.

Iemima's readings can be found on pages:

11, 19, 43, 81, 89, 99, 113, 120, 131, 141, 154, 164, 177, 188, 203, 209, 220, 232, 242, 255, 266, 277, 292, 299, 315, 336, 341, 350, 355, 360, 369

Valorie Quesenberry

Valorie Quesenberry is a pastor's wife, mother, musician, editor of a Christian ladies' magazine, and a writer. She periodically contributes devotionals to a Christian literature provider. Her first book was released with Wesleyan Publishing House in April 2010.

Valorie's readings can be found on pages:

8, 22, 49, 60, 71, 85, 94, 105, 116, 137, 147, 161, 167, 183, 194, 206, 216, 229, 237, 248, 261, 272, 278, 283, 295, 305, 313, 331, 340, 349, 351

Jo Russell

Jo Russell is an author from Arizona.

Jo's readings can be found on pages:

16, 26, 39, 46, 57, 68, 76, 80, 91, 109, 123, 134, 146, 157, 172, 180, 191, 199, 213, 221, 245, 269, 280, 288, 302, 310, 322, 325, 332, 346, 347

Karin Dahl Silver

Karin Dahl Silver is a former Air Force kid, voracious reader, and rock climbing novice (getting braver!). She and her husband, Scott, live in Colorado Springs, Colorado.

Karin's readings can be found on pages:

18, 30, 42, 54, 66, 78, 90, 102, 114, 126, 138, 150, 162, 174, 186, 198, 210, 222, 234, 246, 258, 270, 282, 294, 306, 318, 330, 342, 354, 366

Laura Wegner

Laura Wegener resides in Minnesota, and loves being a wife and mom of two boys, cooking for her family, and encouraging others through her writing. You can follow her story at laurawegener.blogspot.com.

Laura's readings can be found on pages:

14, 28, 32, 50, 61, 65, 72, 95, 106, 111, 127, 144, 184, 195, 201, 217, 223, 238, 251, 262, 273, 284, 290, 327, 338, 339, 348, 352, 359, 362

SCRIPTURE INDEX